DIRTY
DEEDS

JUSTICE PREVAILS

About the Author

Paul Anderson spent fourteen years as a police reporter with the *Herald Sun* before becoming the newspaper's chief court reporter in 2009. He has won team Walkley and Quill awards for crime coverage, and most recently won a joint Quill for Best Feature in Print. Paul is the author of five true-crime books: *Shocking Australian True Crime Stories*; *Melbourne's Gangland Killings*; *Bodies, Bullets and Betrayal*; *Reloaded*; and *Done and Dusted*. His first work of fiction, *The Robbers*, a gritty crime saga following the trials and tribulations of Melbourne's most fearsome police squad, was published by Hardie Grant in 2012.

DIRTY DEEDS

JUSTICE PREVAILS
True crime stories that gripped Australia

PAUL ANDERSON

hardie grant books
MELBOURNE · LONDON

Published in 2013 by Hardie Grant Books

Hardie Grant Books (Australia)
Ground Floor, Building 1
658 Church Street
Richmond, Victoria 3121
www.hardiegrant.com.au

Hardie Grant Books (UK)
Dudley House, North Suite
34–35 Southampton Street
London WC2E 7HF
www.hardiegrant.co.uk

A Cataloguing-in-Publication entry is available from the catalogue of the
National Library of Australia at www.nla.gov.au

Dirty Deeds: Justice Prevails
ISBN: 978 1 74270 032 8

Cover design by Nada Backovic
Cover photo Newspix/Aaron Francis
Typesetting by Kirby Jones
Typeset in ITC New Baskerville
Colour reproduction by Splitting Image Colour Studio
Printed and bound in Australia by Griffin Press

Acknowledgements

Once more, for the sixth time now, thanks to those on all sides of the law for their ongoing help and advice. Special thanks, again, go to Supreme Court media guru Anne Stanford and her County Court counterpart Anna Bolger for their swift responses to all requests and queries. Thanks also to High Court registrar Rosemary Musolino and Victorian Office of Public Prosecutions media chief Lisa Walker. And then there's the Hardie Grant crew—Rose Michael and my handler this time 'round, Rihana Ries— for their unwavering professionalism and commitment. Also thanks to my editor Susan Keogh, and all the crew at the Victorian Government Reporting Service.

Contents

The King is Dead, Long Live the King   1
How Matthew Charles Johnson was able to kill Carl Williams
in Barwon Prison

Hen-pecked?   41
Mild-mannered account manager Anthony Sherna kills his
wife after years of mental torment

The Facebook Killer   76
Ramazan Acar stabs his daughter to death and taunts the
mother on social media

Slaughter House   103
Double murderer John Leslie Coombes strangles and
dismembers his third victim in a bathtub

A Heart of Darkness   136
Who is Arthur Freeman, the man who threw his own daughter
off the West Gate Bridge?

Death Struggle   179
The murder of an everyman in cold blood is a terrible thing
to witness

Lust's Fatal Bondage   201
Eileen Creamer kills her sex-crazed husband

The Stepfather   234
A young woman pushed to the brink by years of abuse kills
her stepfather with his own gun

A Tale of Passion   265
Lovelorn lad Leon Borthwick mows down his perceived
love rival

Murder Call   295
Victorian detectives foil a Gold Coast man's plot to kill his
wife, thanks to a randomly bugged public telephone

1

The King is Dead, Long Live the King

*'He was very high profile but at the end
of the day he had no prison sense ...
He appointed his own assassin.'*

CARL WILLIAMS WAS A CHATTY BLOKE. WATCH CCTV
footage of him in Barwon Prison's high-security Acacia
Unit 1 and there he is nattering away to either or both of
his two fellow inmates: career criminal Matthew Charles
Johnson and a convicted killer we shall call Mr Red, for
legal reasons. On another occasion he sits at the unit's
dayroom table, his hands gesticulating as fast as his mouth
can move. In the concrete recreation yard he jabbers
away while 'cutting' laps with his two criminal pals. And
there he is, still humbugging away only minutes before
Johnson crowns and kills him with the steel stem of an
exercise bike. While Williams may have been an annoying
cellmate because of all his chit-chat, what really got under
Johnson's skin—according to Crown prosecutor Mark
Rochford, SC—was the fact that Carl Anthony Williams

was assisting police with an investigation. In Johnson's eyes Williams had turned into what criminals colloquially term a 'dog'. And Johnson, quite possibly the most fearsome and influential prisoner in the Victorian jail system at that point in time, hates 'dogs'—make no bones about it. Much to Matty Johnson's surprise, he was able to smash Williams eight times in the head with his heavy makeshift weapon without any immediate reaction from prison guards.

'In my mind I thought the officers would have got there before I finished hitting him,' Johnson would say in court.

A convicted drug trafficker, Williams was serving life in jail with a minimum term of thirty-five years for organising the gangland murders of mortal enemies Jason and Lewis Moran and perceived foes Michael Marshall and Mark Mallia, as well as conspiring to murder a man, when Johnson walked up behind him and bashed his head in like it was a watermelon. While Williams may have built a reputation as an unlikely crime boss on the outside, he was a naïve sitting duck in jail. As one prison Intelligence Unit supervisor would explain to Ombudsman George Brouwer:

He was very high profile but at the end of the day he had no prison sense … And then all of a sudden Johnson comes out of nowhere. And Johnson wasn't part of the gangland set up; he was a prison thug … How they [Corrections Victoria] ever let it happen [Johnson and Williams being housed together in the same unit] I will not know. Because basically as soon as Johnson found out that Williams was cooperating with police to either get years off his own sentence or help his father out, he was doomed. 'He appointed his own assassin' are the words that I've used, and I stick by it.

George Williams knew his son Carl was fond of a chat. 'He was a talker, yes,' George would say in court.

Apparently Williams was also a prolific letter writer.

'Yeah, Carl wrote a lot of letters,' Matt Johnson would confirm while giving evidence at his own murder trial. 'He was always running out of stamps.'

When George was jailed mid November 2007 for drug trafficking, he immediately began to ask to be housed with his son, the gangster who called himself 'The Premier' and who was considered by his dad to be a 'big time' drug dealer.

'[Carl] said he made the hard decisions,' George would say during Johnson's trial in the Victorian Supreme Court. 'I think he liked the notoriety a lot.'

Carl Williams's former wife Roberta also gave some rare insights during Johnson's trial. She painted Williams as a 'caring' and 'generous' man despite the fact he once fired a gun at her while she was pregnant with their daughter. Under cross-examination by one of Johnson's two defence barristers, David Drake, Roberta told how Williams often lavished her with gifts and expensive jewellery. The couple lived a high life obviously well beyond any lawful means—and they milked it hard.

> **DRAKE**: You had a fairly extravagant lifestyle, would you say?
> **ROBERTA**: To some extent, yep.
> **DRAKE**: There was plenty of money floating around?
> **ROBERTA**: Yes.
> **DRAKE**: Holidays—did you take holidays together?
> **ROBERTA**: Yes.
> **DRAKE**: Stay at the best places?
> **ROBERTA**: Not necessarily the best places. Whatever we liked at the time we chose and stayed there.

DRAKE: Regularly go out and wine and dine?
ROBERTA: Yeah.

Drake asked Roberta if it ever crossed her mind to wonder what her husband did for a living.

'Of course it crossed my mind,' she replied, 'but I just pushed it to the back of it.'

DRAKE: Well, there's a lot of money that was flowing through that house, wasn't there?
ROBERTA: There was, yes.
DRAKE: And you believed that it was just from buying and selling jewellery?
ROBERTA: No I didn't but, like I said, I didn't really think about it.
DRAKE: Was there any mention ever of selling drugs?
ROBERTA: Any mention? We were arrested for selling drugs.

In court, George Williams spoke of the hatred his son bore toward half-brothers Mark and Jason Moran. The Moran boys shot Williams in a park over a drug debt in October 1999. The Morans were into Williams for $1 million, according to Roberta, and it was Jason who pulled the trigger. Jason's decision to shoot and wound Williams in the guts instead of acing him in the head sparked Melbourne's gangland war, a war Roberta denied any knowledge of.

'It wasn't apparent to me that some drug war was happening, no,' she told the Supreme Court. 'I don't believe everything I read in the newspapers.'

The Moran boys created a paranoid and vengeful monster when they shot Williams, who would go on to develop a knack of befriending ultra-violent criminals and convincing them to do his deadly dirty work. (While it is believed Williams may have organised seven or more gangland murders, police suspect he pulled the trigger on one man—Mark Moran in June 2000).

'Many times he said that he'd like to kill Jason Moran,' George told Justice Lex Lasry. 'He had a passion to kill Jason Moran. He had a hatred for the man.'

Nearly three years to the day after Mark Moran was shot dead, a hitman working for Williams blasted Jason— and his mate Pasquale Barbaro—at a Saturday morning kids' footy clinic. George Williams said of that shooting: 'I don't condone the killing of someone in front of kids but I didn't say it was a horrible thing to happen.'

Roberta told Johnson's trial that Williams never told her of any of his kill plots.

'Carl was the most placid, quiet person you could ever come across,' she said with a straight face. 'Even with my ranting and raving and yelling and screaming that I often did, Carl would sit there quietly and not even answer me back. That's how quiet he was.'

In December 2008, well into his prison sentence, George Williams was moved to Acacia Unit 4 at Barwon Prison. He spent one night there before being taken to a location outside jail where his son was meeting with detectives. Williams Junior and Senior spent eight nights at that location with the cops. Johnson told the Supreme Court he believed Williams was allowed to see his girlfriend and have sex with her during the organised outing. In an investigative report compiled by George Brouwer about Carl Williams's murder, Brouwer wrote: '[The lead detective with whom Carl Williams was dealing] denied that prostitutes visited Mr Williams, however confirmed that Mr Williams' then girlfriend and his father's partner had a supervised visit at the permit location.' Upon their return to Barwon, Williams and his dad were placed in the Melaleuca Unit. Johnson formally requested that he be housed with Williams as, according to Ombudsman Brouwer's report, 'they had formed a friendship'. Williams, meanwhile, wrote to Corrections Victoria requesting he be accommodated with Johnson. The placement of prisoners is the responsibility of the Sentence Management Unit. A range of factors is considered before certain prisoners are housed together.

Peter Hutchinson, the manager of the prison Security and Emergency Services Group (the prison system's version of the Victoria Police Special Operations Group), agreed at Johnson's trial that prison gossip, media reports in relation to prisoners, outgoing prison phone calls, prisoners' letters and general correspondence were all reviewed by staff when considering the initial and continuing placement of prisoners.

In January 2009, the Sentence Management Panel approved the move of Johnson to the Melaleuca Unit after Rod Wise, the acting commissioner of Corrections Victoria, sent an email to Penny Armytage, Secretary of the Department of Justice, warning of the move. Brouwer's report stated 'Mr Wise identified significant risks to Mr Williams' safety should Mr Williams and Mr Johnson be placed together.'

'There is little doubt that Johnson is capable of causing Williams harm if he were to find out the true nature of Williams' co-operation with police,' Wise wrote in part. He cited three reasons why Johnson might want to harm Williams: financial incentives; an opportunity to enhance his jailhouse reputation; and the fact he was already facing a murder charge, so any subsequent sentence for another serious offence would run concurrently.

According to Brouwer's report, senior police dealing with Williams supported the proposed move to house Williams with Johnson. 'Victoria Police considered Mr Johnson's criminal history and noted that he was not aligned with any key members involved in Melbourne's then long-running gangland violence,' Brouwer wrote.

> They formed the view that Mr Johnson did not pose a threat to Mr Williams arising from any gangland allegiances and supported the proposed co-placement … [But] Mr Johnson was known to Corrections Victoria to have participated in two serious assaults on fellow prisoners in the past, with one assault in retribution for a prisoner's co-operation with police.
>
> In my view, the placement decision relied too much on: police advice; Mr Williams' perception of his own safety; and his wish to be accommodated with Mr Johnson. It gave too little weight to knowledge Corrections Victoria had about Mr Johnson that mitigated against the co-placement request … Despite [the three reasons why Johnson might want to harm Williams], Mr Wise recommended to Ms Armytage that the placement be allowed unless Ms Armytage had any 'major concerns'. He also suggested that the placement be monitored 'very closely' and reviewed if Mr Williams was to be taken out of prison in the future to assist Victoria Police.

In a response email, Armytage had written to Wise:

> I feel reasonably comfortable with your proposal and note the fact that you have consulted the police and they

have no concerns about it. Balancing all considerations it appears appropriate to accede to Carl Williams' request on the basis that we will monitor the situation and review it as soon as any new factors emerge …

Armytage would later tell Brouwer: 'I was mindful that no placement involving Mr Williams was risk free, other than a placement in total solitary confinement.'

Less than four months later (on 13 May), Carl and George Williams and Matt Johnson were moved from Melaleuca to Acacia Unit 1. According to George, his son had kept Johnson up to date about his police dealings.

'He said Mr Johnson was okay with that,' George said at Johnson's trial.

Mr Johnson was saying that Carl should get everything down. There was a bit of a disagreement about what benefits Carl was getting off [the police], and Mr Johnson said he should get it down pat. And then Mr Johnson said, 'Can you get me on board?'

In evidence, Johnson denied ever saying that. He claimed Williams told him he was only going to talk to police and 'spin 'em a yarn' to get his father moved in with him. 'He said that they [the police] … would gobble it up,' Johnson claimed in court.

As was widely reported in the media, and detailed in court, Williams had received several benefits from police. Those benefits included having his daughter's $8000 school fees paid.

'Roberta found herself in a position where she couldn't pay the fees so she was using Carl and his relationship with us to seek some relief with those fees,' the detective directly dealing with Williams said in court. 'In other words, "Carl, if you don't get them to pay these fees"—and I am paraphrasing—"then I want you to withdraw your cooperation with them."'

Williams also demanded police pay his dad's $750,000 tax bill. (That deal would later fall through due to a higher court decision interstate.)

'Carl was very up-front about that,' the detective dealing with Williams told the court. 'He insisted that that be paid because he felt that he didn't want George to be effectively homeless or turfed out on to the street if the houses were seized in lieu of the debt at any stage.'

Williams was also chasing a police reward and hoping to have up to ten years lopped off his minimum term.

'I found Carl to not be a stupid person,' the lead detective said.

George Williams was released from jail on 20 June 2009. His replacement in Acacia Unit 1 was a bloke called Mr Red, who was moved there on 29 July. Mr Red was doing a minimum fifteen-year stretch for a road rage murder. He and Williams were close, from their days on the outside.

Carl Williams stayed in daily contact with his dad after the old man's release. During the phone calls between father and son, George spoke to Johnson on the phone every now and then, and each month put $200 into the big bald prisoner's jail 'spend account'.

'While I was in there Mr Johnson and I got on quite well, and he didn't have much in the way of income or family to look after him,' George explained.

In February 2010 police wanted to take Carl out of jail to talk to him again. According to George, his son was reluctant. 'Carl spoke to me on the phone and I think on a visit, and he said that he didn't want to go out, that he wanted it held in the prison,' George said in evidence.

'I spoke to [the lead detective] about it and he said, "No, it's too dangerous to be held in the prison … it would be better if he went out."'

High-security offenders like Williams, Johnson and Red are interviewed by the Major Offenders Review Panel on a regular basis to gauge any underlying or brewing animosity. There was no sign of any trouble between the trio in Acacia Unit 1, according to all relevant prison staff who gave evidence at Johnson's trial. But, according to Brouwer, some intelligence suggested that 'the dynamic between Mr Williams and Mr Johnson was changing'. On 14 February 2010, Red had a telephone conversation with an associate that should have rung alarm bells. Brouwer wrote:

> The associate referred to a 'lot of people being unhappy' with Mr Williams … He described Mr Williams as a 'dog'. The associate urged Mr [Red] to separate himself from Mr Williams. While this telephone call was entered onto the prison's PROTEL (intelligence) system on 15 February, no further action was taken. It was not reported to the panel monitoring Mr Williams' placement.

Barwon's then–acting general manager Nicholas Selisky held a meeting with Williams, Johnson and Red in the week before Williams was killed.

'I attended the unit and spoke to the prisoners, had a general conversation with all of them and there was nothing [in terms of personal issues] brought to my attention,' Selisky told the Supreme Court.

A hulk of a man at around 188 cm tall, and weighing a muscle-bound 100 kilograms, Johnson has a frightening aura. By the time he was a raw and ready twenty-one-year-old with a growing list of criminal convictions, he was serving his third stretch in Pentridge Prison.

'This young man has been in the system for many years now,' his barrister, Duncan Allen, told a County Court plea hearing back in September 1994.

While the Dickensian jail and its tough-nut population no doubt proved daunting to most young inmates, Matt Johnson used his time in Pentridge wisely—as good grounding for his eventual position as 'The General' of Barwon Prison. For a bloke a Supreme Court judge described as 'intelligent and articulate', Johnson squandered any potential he may have had. The man is an enigma: disciplined in the ways of personal fitness and prison regimes yet unbridled when it comes to matters of violence. His eyes peer from dark recesses hollowed into his gaunt, bald head. In a black hooded cloak with sickle in hand, Johnson would make a formidable Grim Reaper. In prison he is top dog and self-contained. He walks with the strut and talks with the guttural slang of an institutionalised criminal. He refers to jail as his 'paradise'. At the time he so clinically and brutally murdered Williams, his cell resembled the living quarters of an army drill sergeant: shoes lined up in straight pairs, clothes and towels squarely folded, his desk in neat order. If it wasn't for the fact that his toilet was positioned in his cell, he would be a man to certainly never shit in his own backyard. For the most part, Johnson's history—and with it any possible reasons for his criminal behaviour—has proved a closed book. One has to delve back to the September 1994 County Court plea hearing for any detail of his past. Born on 9 August 1973, Johnson was four when his father died. His mother, Carol Hogg, remarried and had another son: a boy with cerebral palsy.

'I spent that whole pregnancy in hospital … and Matt was put into, like, a type of foster care because Wayne had to work,' Carol Hogg told the County Court in 1994.

Johnson's stepfather was said to be a harsh taskmaster who liked a drink. He ended up walking out on the family, leaving them to fend for themselves. Johnson was about nine at the time.

'Since those early years it seems that he has been a child initially, adolescent and now a young man with his unresolved anger and hurt,' Allen said in '94.

Ms Hogg said:

> [Matt] missed Wayne in one sense because the only time that Wayne really paid any attention was when he was playing football, because Matthew has always loved his sport. He used to instil into Matt, you know, you have got to be tough, you have got to be strong … He was just very cruel in the words and the way he would speak to him.

Johnson grew up in the Dandenong area, living in a Housing Commission home. He went to Dandenong Technical School from Years 7 to 9, but was expelled as an undisciplined student. His mum explained:

> He was starting to muck up a lot at school and the teachers used to say that they would get frustrated with him because if he misbehaved in class they would put him outside the classroom and even if they brought him back in he would always pass whatever they had learned that day.

Duncan Allen added: '[He had] a general unruliness with great problems of relating to people and disciplining himself.'

Johnson was moved to the St Kilda Community High School, which specialised in dealing with problematic students. He passed Year 10 at age sixteen and never returned.

He was a chronic cannabis user. 'He could never get enough,' Allen told the court. Johnson also used amphetamines. Despite a couple of months' work as a concreter and in a bakery before that business shut down, Johnson—who wanted to be a chef—remained long-term unemployed.

'Like so many others it seems that he may have dropped the bundle in terms of any prospect or hope of finding employment,' Allen said.

Johnson's criminal career began in typical fashion with car theft and a weapon offence. Drug and more theft crimes followed. Despite his bleak outlook, he always respected his mum and tried to help care for his younger brother.

'I never had any problems with Matt at home,' his mum said in the County Court. 'Matt has never been rude to me. He has never sworn in front of me.'

And he liked to set the ground rules for his mates. 'Even to this day his friends sort of know that once you hit that front door there is a rule that they all treat me with the utmost respect,' Ms Hogg said.

It was said that Johnson had experienced an epiphany while in jail in 1994, and vowed to come out clean the other side of whatever sentence he was about to cop for intentionally causing injury and affray. Allen told the judge:

He tells me, Your Honour, not only does he never want to go to jail again once he has got all this behind him, but he never wants to see the inside of a police station again. He acknowledges that the police dislike him very deeply and he accepts that they have good reason for doing that. He just wants to keep out of their way in future.

It was a hollow hope. Johnson had no strong father-figure and was disillusioned with society. A psychologist would later deem him an institutionalised man 'living in jail by the law of the jungle in order to survive'. The prison system only helped channel Johnson's inner demons. In March 1999, County Court judge Michael Strong would sentence him to six years' jail with a minimum of four on five counts of armed robbery. Armed with a knife and a gun, Johnson and another man broke into an elderly couple's Safety Beach house thinking they were running through a drug dealer's den. They robbed the elderly pair anyway, before moving on to another home and robbing separate victims. Judge Strong described Johnson and his co-offender as 'lawless thugs'.

Four months later, in May 1999, Johnson was sentenced to twenty months' jail for an aggravated burglary committed against another prisoner whom he planned to assault. It seemed a common theme. In October 1998, Johnson and four other Barwon inmates had kicked and rammed their way into Acacia Unit 4 and bashed deadly career criminal Gregory John Brazel—because they believed Brazel was providing information to prison authorities. The gang's makeshift weapons included a sandwich maker and a vacuum cleaner extension. An exercise bike seat was also used by one of the prisoners. The assault led to what became known as 'the trial from hell', during which County Court Judge Warren Fagan was abused in an extraordinary fashion. Two of the five accused men flashed their buttocks from the dock,

Johnson farted into a microphone and a bag of excrement was thrown at the jury.

After being found guilty, Johnson told the judge: 'Been in the slot [maximum security] for three years and love it ... I don't want to plea. I want to get sentenced right now. I've got more dogs to bash.' In late 2000, Johnson and two of his co-defendants received cumulative sentences of eight years with minimums of six for the Brazel bashing. They successfully appealed and were granted a retrial, pleaded guilty to a lesser assault offence and received concurrent 12-month sentences on top of time for contempt of court.

After his eventual release, Johnson and criminal mate Mark Alan Morgan went on a robbery rampage. It started on 24 May 2007 when the pair terrorised a woman, her fifteen-year-old daughter and a male teenager in a car outside a McDonald's store in Doveton. Johnson held a semi-automatic handgun to the woman's head and Morgan punched the teenage girl before the duo commandeered the car. In Craigieburn, the two criminals forced their way inside a house where Johnson placed his gun to an innocent man's head. The duo robbed the place. Police arrested them that morning at Tooronga Railway station: Johnson's handgun was cocked and loaded.

Before Johnson answered to those crimes, he went before a Supreme Court jury (in 2009) for the murder of an eighteen-year-old by the name of Bryan Conyers. BJ, as the kid was known, was shot with a 9 mm Luger pistol in a Berwick garage on 22 May 2007 (two days before Johnson's arrest at the railway station). At a disused house in Pakenham, the youth was sliced open and his insides doused with petrol before his body was incinerated. Police alleged Johnson shot Conyers after giving the kid $50 cash to go and buy cannabis and cigarettes—an errand Conyers failed to complete. During the trial, a man named Timothy Prentice claimed in evidence that Johnson pulled the gun on BJ, asked about the missing money and then shot the kid. Conyers was stripped to his boxer shorts, wrapped in a tarpaulin, placed in the back of a ute with a jerry can of petrol and driven away, according to Prentice. He said a wooden pallet was propped up with bricks, the body was placed on the makeshift pyre and mutilated and doused in fuel. Prentice told the jury he lit his cigarette lighter to look at a bag of clothes. He told the court he was accused of being a 'a fucking idiot' and a 'scatterbrain' for causing the ensuing explosion.

Cop killer Peter Allen Reid also gave evidence for the prosecution during the Conyers murder trial. Reid claimed that, while in Barwon's Banksia Unit, he overheard a conversation between Johnson and another prisoner. 'He knew that [the other prisoner] Paul … was getting out very soon and he was rallying him, as we call it, to help him with the disposal of a witness and some evidence pertaining to this case,' Reid claimed.

Reid also told the jury that Johnson admitted to shooting Conyers. Reid said Johnson also talked of other things. 'He talked about things like that if Paul needed weapons or anything of that nature he could go to some people … That they were extremists and they were the type of people that didn't like Australians. Didn't like authority.'

In his own defence, Johnson said it was Prentice who had shot Conyers. Johnson told the jury that Prentice had shot Conyers because he said he was not going to give him any speed. 'I said to Tim, "You fucked up now cunt … you're a fucking idiot. What's wrong with you? You've just shot him."'

Johnson also denied confessing to the killing in jail, branding Reid a 'slimy little critter'. 'A dog is someone who gives somebody up,' Johnson said.

A lying dog is someone who makes up lies about someone when they give them up ... A lot of people know what Mr Reid's about. What he does. His trickery ... He's known to make things up about people to better his own situation.

In the end, the jury found Johnson not guilty of murdering Bryan Conyers.

Johnson did not fight the charges relating to the Doveton car-jacking and the Cranbourne armed robbery. In November 2010 (having already murdered Carl Williams while on remand), he pleaded guilty to armed robbery, aggravated burglary, theft and being a prohibited person in possession of an unregistered firearm. In sentencing him to a maximum term of sixteen years with a minimum of thirteen for the car-jacking and the hold-up, County Court Judge Geoff Chettle said:

Your extensive criminal history, together with your conduct on 24 May 2007, demonstrate you to be a career criminal who is a real menace to society. You have not been specifically deterred by prior jail sentences. Your prospects for rehabilitation must be seen as effectively nil. The community needs to be protected from you.

At the time he bashed Carl Williams to death, Johnson had a correctional history of seventy-six separate incidents including multiple assaults on inmates and prison staff, starting a fire, returning positive drug tests, making threats, possessing contraband and damaging property. He had established himself as the founder and leader of a group of inmates who called themselves the Prisoners of War. That group openly loathed anyone who sided with or assisted police. During the Williams murder trial in November 2011, Security Emergency Services Group general manager Bruce Polkinghorne was asked about the POW group and its mantra.

> **ROCHFORD**: In the system, for instance, do Vietnamese prisoners associate together, do Koori prisoners associate together and in this case in Barwon Prison was there a group of prisoners who colloquially were known as the Prisoners of War?
> **POLKINGHORNE**: That's correct.
> **ROCHFORD**: And Mr Johnson was the self-titled 'general' or one of the leaders of that group in the prison system?
> **POLKINGHORNE**: That's correct.
> **ROCHFORD**: Is one of the codes that that group adopt and tend to live by that they don't like informers— people who give information to authorities?
> **POLKINGHORNE**: That's correct.

Despite his obvious standing within prison ranks, Johnson claimed at his trial that Williams was able to intimidate him and even threaten him after Red moved into Acacia Unit 1. When asked how he would have fared in a fist fight with Williams, Johnson admitted that he would have won quite easily. That was an understatement. Johnson would have destroyed Williams in a punch-on at close quarters.

'He seemed to think that he had to show [Red] that he was the boss of me, sort of try and talk down a bit—get his own way,' Johnson claimed in evidence.

> As time went on it got a bit worse. Some days I'd come out of me cell and I'd make it a habit of saying good

morning to everyone. He'd just look at me, stare through me like, 'What are you talking to me for.' I'd just let it go … There was many times I would have liked to have punched him in the jaw but you've got to think of outside issues. He let it be known that he got Mario Condello killed while he was in jail. He let it be known that when he fell out with the Morans he went after their family. He was always boasting about things like that.

(Mario Condello was a reputed leader of the criminal group commonly referred to as the Carlton Crew. Condello was shot dead in his garage on 6 February 2006. At the time this book went to print, no-one had been charged.)

In court, Johnson claimed Williams boasted of personally killing three men: Mark Moran, a standover merchant named Richard Mladenich, and an unnamed bloke he supposedly hit with a hammer when he was in his twenties. According to Johnson, Williams also bragged that he had organised other gangland murders including that of Moran family ally Graham Kinniburgh.

'Like I'd be talking to someone about the footy, he could talk about having people murdered,' Johnson said during his trial. 'He claimed that there was fifteen people all up.'

> **BILL STUART [DEFENCE BARRISTER]:** What was his reputation in the prison?
> **JOHNSON:** We all watch TV—underworld kingpin. Serial killer … [he] lapped it up.

Mark Rochford challenged Johnson on the subject of Williams's alleged jailhouse confessions.

ROCHFORD: There's one golden rule in prison—you don't talk to other people about what you've done because someone might turn into a dog and bring up a jailhouse confession against you. Correct?

JOHNSON: Some people live by that rule. Yep.

ROCHFORD: I suggest to you … it's completely unbelievable for you to be saying that Carl would be telling people about murders he's committed—in the [unit] gym, in the exercise yard, so loud that you could overhear it … Because you wouldn't do that in jail because someone might turn around and actually use it against you.

JOHNSON: I wouldn't but, you know, Carl was different.

To prop up his desired image of Williams, Johnson told the court a tale of how Williams once threatened his life. He said Williams walked up behind him, ran his finger across his throat and told him that's how easy it would be to kill him.

'He thought it was funny,' Johnson said. 'Carl was silly for the way he would treat people—very silly—but [he was a] very dangerous man.'

For protection, Johnson told the jury, he placed makeshift weapons around the unit for the time if push ever came to shove. Johnson claimed if that did happen he would have had to kill Williams to ensure his family's safety on the outside. 'I had the bike out the front of me cell for easy access,' he told the jury. 'I had the sandwich maker up the other end of the unit if I ever needed that … Most people are armed up in jail to protect themselves.'

Prison letters tendered during the trial revealed great insight into Johnson, his true mindset and prison allegiances. It might not surprise many that when it comes to Australian Rules Football he is a Collingwood supporter. He is a fitness and training fanatic. Nicknames of some among his circle include the likes of Andre the Giant, Crazy Eyes, The Chook, Goldmember, and Drama and Turtle of *Entourage* fame. Camaraderie is strong, and the members try to use code. Enemies are referred to as 'dogs' and 'skunks'. More importantly, the letters— and prison visit conversations—revealed Johnson's true standing as the self-appointed general and the fact that he viewed Williams as nothing more than a 'fat sook' who 'bit off more than he could chew'.

A Johnson letter to Red, dated 1 January 2010, was written while Red was temporarily moved from Acacia 1. It read in part:

> I trust that this letter will find you, my friend, in the very best of health and fighting spirits. Don't let the dogs win, not ever. I can't believe that some mindless idiot somewhere actually thinks that your and mine friendship could be under any sort of strain let alone be breakable. Are these people for real?
>
> Mate, just let these idiots know that whatever bullshit intelligence they think they have picked up on is nothing at all but a misreading on their behalf and I'll be letting them know the same. People make mistakes and this is one. I miss ya big time already, buddy. This bloke here [Williams] now thinks that I have to train with him again in the gym now. Fuck, it took me long enough to sack him as my training partner and now I'm back to the start. He means well. Just reads too many of these bullshit books that all end the same way. Happy New Year mate. We are another year closer to being able to kick back outside one day

on a yacht laughing about these bullshit times of our past … See now the enemy even think that they know what is going on and they wouldn't even know if they had the rubber dick act themselves. I shouldn't laugh because you're over there freezing your big balls off while I'm still over here. I'm sure that the powers that be will see this is just a very bad mistake and you'll be back here cooking up a storm again very soon. I'm still not sold that you have your certificate but you can cook not too bad. But truth be known I do not truly think you've worked in any quality restaurants— not the sort that I dine at anyway. But you can cook a decent soup but who can't, true? I love ya buddy. I'm just stirring. You can also do decent toasted sangas.

Red replied on 4 January. His sense of humour was obvious. In this letter he talked about his new temporary fellow inmate.

Fuck he's funny this bloke. He's shorter than me and 145 kilograms and says he only eats salads. He has got ten containers of chips, chocolate, et cetera, et cetera … He got a mad laugh on him, too. He's got more chins than a Chinese phone directory. I also think they have to lay out speed humps when they seen him going for a smorgasboard. Anyway my friend, train hard and miss you buddy. Your friend always until the end.

Another inmate wrote to Johnson on 14 February 2010.

I'm really glad that the football has started again as I believe that the Pies are going to be a big chance this year. You should have heard [two other inmates] go off last night when Hawthorn was playing. They are already talking about Buddy [Franklin] kicking one hundred goals and Hawthorn winning the flag. I told them to pull up as they only beat Richmond, who in my opinion with their current list would be lucky to make the top eight of the Diamond Valley league. Ha ha. I bet you and Carl are going to give [Red] heaps over the Tigers this year.

I watched a really top Spanish movie on SBS last Thursday night called Amores Perros which was about dog fighting, rooting, armed robberies, hitmen and drugs. It was pretty trippy. Did you watch it? Apart from this brother, not much else going on so I'll sign off for this week and hope to hear from you soon. Your loyal brother from another mother.

Melbourne city gunman Christopher Wayne Hudson wrote to Johnson on 29 March 2010. Hudson addressed his mail to Matty 'Hot Pies' Johnson.

I hope this letter finds you in good spirits as it left here that way … Not much else to say other than Hot Pies. What a win and all the so-called experts had the Doggies as premiers already. I was rapt and let everybody here know it will be the year of the Magpie if we play like that week in, week out. Spewing I'm stuck here and not out there collecting, ha ha. Thanks for the paper clippings. Always find them interesting and good to keep up on the latest—even got a quick mention. Fuck I laughed at Bubbles having Viagra. Ha ha. The villains are killing it and heroes are self destructing. I'm loving it. My time here is good. I have to say I don't mind it one bit at all so I'll just cruise until cleared, whenever that may be … Train hard buddy and take the very best of care. Strong and constant. Love and respect. Huddo, Hells Angels MC.

In a letter dated 5 April, about two weeks before he killed Williams, Johnson warned a relative that there would be some upcoming publicity about him. It seems that, even at that point, Williams was a marked man.

Cuz, there will be some media attention soon. I just don't want you to worry so I'm giving you the heads up. You know what these idiots are like. I'll be sweet so don't stress about your big Cuz.

The faithful letters, in the meantime, continued. Another inmate wrote to Johnson on 12 April.

Dear Matty. Hello brother. How are you going? As always I hope that you are well. Thanks very much for the birthday card. It was greatly appreciated and put a big smile to my face … So what's been happening lately? Are you still training like a machine and if so, what routine are you doing? I had a really strange dream last night that it was your birthday and we were all gathered for drinks at your place. There were bitches everywhere. However we did not get to root any of them which was a shame. However, it looked as though you were enjoying the party which is the main thing. When I woke up I tried to will myself to go back to sleep and continue the dream in the hope that it would turn into one big orgy followed by a massive torture session involving 1) all the cunts we don't like, 2) sharks, 3) a blowtorch, 4) a nice boat. Unfortunately this did not occur. Ha ha ha ha.

In a letter dated 15 April, Johnson told how prison was a great leveller and returned to the subject of Williams—and how he was expendable. 'All these so-called underworld gangsters are full of themselves and get a huge shock when they realise they're all just another bare bum in the shower here. Nothing more.' Johnson would later say at trial: 'Jail is a great equaliser. We're all the same in prison.'

In letters sent the day before he murdered Williams, Johnson hinted through some ominous code about what lay ahead for Carl Williams. One stated, in part:

Adonis, what's doing buddy? I trust that you and Turtle are coping okay after such an awful loss to the mighty Magpies. Not to worry buddy, as there's always next time. By now you'd know that Charlie's [Williams's] team also lost. What can you do buddy—life goes on, and the vouchers must come to an end. No bad feelings I trust. Well brother, not a lot doing over this way. Same old shit. Just another day in paradise. My paradise.

Go the Pies for the flag this year. Biggest year ahead yet mate. What's the Turtle reckon? I hope he understands that it's more than just a game. The chocolate factory is no good through and through. Easter is over—there is no grey area on the footy field. Love you buddy, your loyal friend till they kill me— Matty the General.

In a separate letter he wrote: 'Not much doing here brother, just D2TE [death to the enemy], the way it should be … I love this shit. I'm the true general so I must keep things in good order true.'

Mark Rochford explained to the jury who Johnson was referring to as 'the enemy' in his 'D2TE' code.

'The enemy are the dogs ... the people who the Prisoners of War hate,' Rochford said. 'Johnson is the founder. He is the general. He feels so strongly about this that in fact, he has it tattooed down the left-hand side of his body.'

Ombudsman Brouwer's investigation found that, due to a staff shortage, prison collators were up to a week behind in listening to inmates' recorded phone calls and up to three days behind in reviewing prisoners' mail. Hutchinson told Brouwer:

> Prisoner mail is usually very cryptic and for this reason most gangland-related mail was read by a supervisor [of the Intelligence Unit] ... as he ... had the experience and the background knowledge to, in most cases, understand the meaning of the mail ... This could also lead to a delay in actioning mail if [the supervisor] ... was on days off. In the ideal world we would have a number of staff devoted to gangland management but our staffing levels prevent this.

Secretly recorded conversations in visit rooms further revealed Johnson's contempt for Williams.

'He's a fat fucking sook and he bit off more than he could chew,' Johnson told one visitor.

> Out there, the only reason he got away with so much is 'cos no-one suspected him 'cos he was a fucking idiot ... [He's] never done one in his life. Forget Mark Moran mate. He never shot Mark Moran. He never shot a man in his life mate. But [he's a] very evil thinker ... He will get something done if he's got someone to do it.

At trial, Johnson would claim he was talking shit to a mate when he said that.

'Just came up in conversation,' he told Rochford. 'Talking about the *Underbelly* movie and how much shit it was.' Johnson was also heard to describe Williams as a 'broken man'.

'He just couldn't handle the jail,' he muttered. 'He was like an evil dangerous cunt but just a weak person.'

The basis for Johnson's defence was that he killed Williams in self-defence.

'I had to kill him to keep myself safe and so there could be no repercussions on my family or friends outside,' he claimed during cross-examination.

The jury was told that Red stuck his head into Johnson's cell as the Acacia Unit 1 trio were being locked down at 3.30 pm on 18 April. The claim was that Red told Johnson that Williams was planning to kill him. Johnson claimed in court: '[Red] said, "Don't say anything but this one"—meaning Carl—"is planning to get you with pool balls."' Johnson's story was that he sat and stewed in his cell that night and decided to 'get in first'.

'I decided that I'd get the bike stem and get him in the morning when he's eating breakfast, when reading the paper,' he claimed. Johnson went on to say that Red filled him in with more information the following morning as they walked laps of the yard.

> He said he walked into Carl's cell a couple of days earlier, or the day earlier, and Carl was stretching a sock in his hands. He told [Red] he was going to put pool balls in it and get me with it when I'm eating.

Defence barrister Bill Stuart told the jury that Johnson was a marked man in a 'kill or be killed' situation.

According to police statements, Red had told prison staff of tension between Johnson and Williams in the days before April 19 2010. When told that Johnson better not direct any animosity towards officers, Red replied: 'Johnson told me that the war was not with the staff.'

Rumours that one of Johnson's mates on the outside had been bashed by Hell's Angels bikies may have added to Johnson's frustrations. In his report, Brouwer said that Johnson believed members of the Williams family may have been spreading that information.

'On 6, 8, 12 and 18 of April 2010, Mr Johnson made a series of telephone calls to a criminal associate concerning rumours of an assault involving his associate,' Brouwer stated.

> In these telephone calls, Mr Johnson sought to establish whether the associate had been physically assaulted by members of the motorcycle gang. Mr Johnson refers to Mr Williams's family members as being the source of these rumours. Mr Johnson states that he is very upset about the rumours and from the tone of his voice and the language used, appears keen to find the source of the rumours. Mr Johnson seems increasingly angry during each of these phone calls when the involvement of the Williams family is discussed.

A unit supervisor and seven staff were working in the Acacia Unit on the day Carl Williams was to die. Williams had ordered the *Herald Sun* newspaper for that morning. A story about taxpayers picking up his daughter's private school fees and his dad's tax bill happened to be on the front page. George Williams, in his evidence, said those payments were 'old news' to Johnson. Nicholas Selisky had read the article before allowing the copy of the paper into Acacia 1.

'I had no specific concern that Mr Johnson would take any particular view of it,' Selisky said of the article. 'It was just another day in Acacia.'

Prison officers Brendan Butler and Suzette Gajic unlocked the cell doors at 8.10 am as normal, releasing the three Unit 1 inmates for their seven-hour 'run out'. This was life in Acacia.

'They [the three prisoners] were the same to me as any other day,' Butler told the court. 'There was nothing that stood out to me.' Butler handed Williams his pre-ordered copy of the *Herald Sun*, and mentioned that he'd made the front page again. Butler clearly recalled Williams saying back to him: 'Front page today, fifth page tomorrow. It's just another day.'

Two cameras monitored the Acacia Unit 1 dayroom. The area contained a billiard table, table tennis table, treadmill, weight station with Swiss balls, an exercise bike and kitchenette. There was also a laundry off-camera. The open-air concrete recreation yard was also monitored by camera. The camera feed was relayed to a central post.

'In the centre [of the Acacia Unit block] is the officer's post and there's an area where an officer is rostered for the day to look at the monitors and the alarms that may go off around the whole unit,' Brendan Butler said at Johnson's trial. 'There are a lot of cameras.' Ombudsman Brouwer found that the CCTV system in the Acacia Unit was 'unfit for purpose'. 'There were five monitors, three of which displayed live vision from numerous cameras simultaneously, rotating through different source material. Each small split-screen image was displayed for four seconds only, before the image cut to another source.'

Unit 1 CCTV footage on the morning of 19 April 2010 shows Williams, Red and Johnson going about just another mundane day in jail. As Selisky suggested during his evidence, life in Acacia 'can get a bit like Groundhog Day'. Johnson does not seem hyper vigilant of Williams, who by that stage of his prison term had dropped about fifteen kilos and weighed in at 87 kilograms. The muscle-bound Johnson turns his back on Williams regularly. Mark Rochford suggested that was odd behaviour for a man who believed that Williams was going to bash his head in with billiard balls. During the morning, Williams rang his barrister, Shane Tyrrell. They spoke about the *Herald Sun* article.

According to Tyrrell, Williams never expressed any concerns about Johnson, or Red for that matter.

'He expressed to me that he was happy to be running out with those two people,' Tyrrell told Johnson's trial.

Williams also spoke to Roberta on the phone that morning. It was a rushed conversation, thanks to her. 'We had a small disagreement,' she said in a police statement. 'I had to go to a photo shoot for a magazine and Carl wanted to keep talking. Carl seemed a bit agitated about something, but he did not mention any problems.'

Prison officer Butler escorted Williams to the visits area for a meeting with dad George at 10.30 am. Afterwards, Williams said everything was good and Gajic returned him to the interior of Unit 1. In joking fashion she suggested it was his lucky day as she took him in through a different entrance from normal, an entry she referred to as the 'tradesman's entrance'. Williams didn't smile or smirk or crack a funny, as Gajic might have expected. She sensed he was unusually quiet and that something was awry. 'Carl was usually a pretty jovial type of person.'

Prison officer Stuart Drummond delivered the three inmates their lunch. 'It's basically a salad bowl and a roll. They assemble it,' he explained.

The CCTV footage shows the three inmates pottering around after lunch. Williams sits at the dayroom table and rereads the newspaper while chewing Johnson's ear off. Johnson stands and disappears into a cell. He reappears brandishing the bike-seat stem (which he had earlier unscrewed after placing his mattress against the bike for cover). He stands behind Williams for a second or two and then marches right up behind him. At 12.48 pm Johnson lands the first blow. It is a mighty whack, much like a baseballer at bat taking a swing. Williams does not know what hit him. He falls out of his chair: lights out. Johnson rains seven more blows down on his head. He openly admitted in court that he was trying to kill Williams when he hit him the first time. Bill Stuart asked him what he was intending when he hit Williams the other seven times.

'Make sure he was dead,' Johnson replied deadpan.

Even though the attack was cold-bloodedly quick, the prison officer with the duty of watching the monitors at central post presumably missed the bashing. Johnson said he was surprised guards did not immediately storm the unit when he started to pound Williams's head in. Johnson also had time to dump the murder weapon in the laundry before dragging Williams's limp body by the feet into his cell. Johnson placed a towel over the pool of blood and brain matter on the dayroom floor. Once Williams's body was in his cell, there would have been no reason to think anything untoward had occurred in Acacia Unit 1. Brouwer would determine that due to the cut feed system in the monitoring room, it was understandable how the console operator failed to witness the killing.

'It is difficult if not impossible to monitor these screens and take in all the information they transmit,' Brouwer wrote in his report.

> At interview … [the prison officer monitoring the screens] said that at the time of the incident she had directed the self-controlled monitor to view Acacia Unit staff taking a prisoner to another area of Barwon Prison … Prison staff raised concerns that the functionality of the CCTV system in place in the Acacia Unit at the time of Mr Williams' death was both 'inadequate' and 'faulty'. Prison staff used words such as 'antiquated', 'pathetic' and 'abysmal' to describe the CCTV system.

One guard told Brouwer: 'I'm not saying [a better system] would have saved Carl's life but it would have stopped the questions as to why it took us so long to find him.'

At 12.54 pm, about six minutes after the brutal murder, Red picked up the unit landline telephone and called his sister's number.

'I can't talk for long … something's happened here,' he said. 'I think he's … done something to him … he just went crazy … he's all right with me—we're good friends. I don't know what happened. He just went crazy.'

The sister asked what happened.

'Oh, he hit him,' Red replied. 'I don't know what happened. I wasn't looking. I don't know …'

At 12.58 pm, Red called an associate. 'I'm shocked, mate,' Red told him. 'Something just really terrible just happened. I think Carl's dead … I think Carl's dead, mate … Matty just went crazy.'

The associate asked what happened.

'I don't know, mate,' Red said. 'The screws haven't come yet or nothing ...'

No-one from the jail was monitoring the calls.

It was some twenty-seven minutes after the jailhouse murder when guards came across Johnson and Red marching laps in the recreation yard. The two moved like caged animals in a zoo: confined and annoyed with something playing on their minds. Johnson approached the prison officers and told Gajic to press her alarm buzzer.

'Carl's hit his head,' Johnson said. 'Don't send any females in there.' Gajic asked Johnson what the fuck he'd done. Johnson said that Williams was in his cell. Gajic announced an emergency. 'Carl's down! Carl's down!' Several guards ran into the unit and located Williams's body lying face down in a pool of blood in Cell 2. Looking down from the wall with a big blonde smile was a topless centrefold. It was her turn to leer.

'We've ran in, noticed on the ground a towel, an awful lot of blood on the floor and the cell door was pulled ajar,' Butler recalled of the gory find. 'I actually opened the cell door and ... we have seen Carl lying face down on the ground with an awful lot of blood around him. I could see a large open wound to the back of his head.'

Williams appeared not to be breathing. A 'Code Black' was called. Stuart Drummond felt for a pulse. There wasn't one, and Williams's pupils did not respond to stimuli. Johnson and Red shook hands before being separated. They stripped off their orange prison gear and were put into empty Cells 5 and 6. Prison staff swarmed the unit. Williams was dragged from his cell back out on to the dayroom floor where prison medicos commenced CPR. They worked for some time in an effort to get his heart beating again. It was like trying to pump petrol through a smashed engine. Williams's head just gushed red oil. With a battered face and gaping skull, Carl Williams had long departed. MICA paramedics arrived and pronounced him dead.

Johnson yelled at Red in the adjacent cell. 'I think he's gone.'

Later, Johnson asked senior prison officer Ashley Langsworth if he could have a shower to wash Williams's brains off. Langsworth replied: 'C'mon Matthew, there's no reason to say things like that.' An emotionless Johnson then said: 'Come on boss, people die every day. What's the big deal?' In a later recorded interview with Detective Senior Sergeant Peter Harrington, Johnson made a mostly 'no comment' interview. The only thing he did say: 'I acted alone.' Johnson wrote a short letter to Red nine days after Williams's death.

He wrote in part:

> How are ya doin' buddy? Stay strong my friend. I'm sure soon enough they will see you had nothing to do with what happened. As I said, just a short one so take care and keep training the body and the mind. Love ya […], you're a good man. Your loyal friend till the end. Matty.

Matthew Johnson's murder trial before Justice Lex Lasry kicked off on 6 September 2011. Before it began, Lasry issued a stern warning to the jury members about what would constitute evidence in the high-profile case.

'I tell you now that publicity about Carl Williams and any previous publicity that you may have seen about this case you must put out of your mind,' Lasry said. 'The publicity is irrelevant to the case. Also the fact that the accused man, Matthew Johnson, was a prisoner at

Barwon Prison and the circumstances which led to that are likewise irrelevant and should be put out of your mind.'

In his opening address, Crown Prosecutor Rochford told the jury that the killing was deliberate and intentional. While the Crown did not have to prove motive, Rochford suggested the slaying occurred because Williams had talked to police about an investigation. Before playing CCTV footage of the killing to the jury, Rochford warned of its graphic nature.

'It is real,' he said.

> It's not TV, it's not a movie. It is expected that you will have some sort of emotional reaction to it. Everyone in this courtroom, I expect, asks you to get that past you and then to concentrate on the intellectual task in which you are asked to engage … It's graphic but it's necessary.

While Rochford told the jury the Crown did not concede 'in any way, shape or form' that Johnson felt threatened by Carl Williams, he asked Nicholas Selisky about what other options Johnson may have had if he *had* felt threatened. Rochford wanted to show the jury that Johnson had other courses of action open to him if, in fact, his tale about being scared of Williams *was* true.

> **ROCHFORD**: If Mr Johnson on the morning of 19 April 2010 had wanted to be put into an isolation unit, even for a short period of time, could he have abused a staff officer—pushed or verbal abuse— something of that nature, and been moved into a loss of privileges unit as a matter of course? Would that have happened?

SELISKY: There's an intercom in the cell. You can just press the intercom and alert the staff and say, 'I need to get out of this unit.'
ROCHFORD: But if he, for instance, didn't want to inform authorities could he have chosen that other course?
SELISKY: Yes … It's what's termed as a professional bail-out in the prison system. The prisoner will do a disturbance to get moved.

Michelle Hosking, acting manager of the Major Offenders Unit, told the trial that Johnson never raised any concerns about Williams or requested a transfer. Johnson tackled that issue while being examined by his counsel.

STUART: Why not during this period speak to the prison officers when you were going to your monthly meeting or just a prison officer who happens to come in on a particular day. Why not tell them?
JOHNSON: Because we don't do that. That's informing.

In his opening, defence counsel Bill Stuart foreshadowed the defence case. It was a case of kill or be killed, he said. 'Mr Johnson was a marked man and, as such, he killed Carl Williams in self-defence,' Stuart offered up to the jury. 'There could be, as you will hear, no running from Carl Williams. There could be no hiding from Carl Williams.'

During the three-week trial, Detective Senior Sergeant Stuart Bailey, of the taskforce investigating the murder, said CCTV footage showed that Johnson read a *Herald Sun* article about defensive homicide a week before the killing. The headline on that story read: 'And he said it was self defence'.

Johnson told the jury: 'I don't read every article. I mainly read the sports or if there's things about people I know.'

In his closing address, Rochford said Johnson did *not* have a belief that it was necessary to kill Williams in order to defend himself. 'He has other options available to him if he believed he was being threatened by Carl Williams,' Rochford said.

> The fact that he chooses not to exercise those other options because of whatever code of behaviour he chooses to live by doesn't mean it was necessary to do what he did in order to defend himself. He, on the Crown case, preferred to kill Carl Williams rather than choose one of the other options, such as go to the authorities and ask to be moved … If someone is coming at you with a samurai sword trying to harm you, it becomes necessary to do something about that then and there, but this isn't that sort of situation.

Rochford repeated phrases from Johnson's letters written in the days before the prison murder. '"I am the true general so I must keep things in good order." That's got nothing whatsoever to do with a man believing he had to act out of self-defence,' Rochford said.

> That has got to do with the general applying the rules to the Prisoners of War. 'I must defend myself'—he doesn't write that.
> He is not scared. He is not worried about Carl Williams. Williams is just 'another bare bum in the shower'. He is not a big-time anything to Matt Johnson.

Rochford said the case was not about the history of Carl Williams.

'It doesn't matter what you think of Carl Williams,' he said.

It doesn't matter if someone in the community thinks Matt Johnson did the world a favour by killing Carl Williams. It is not about that. Carl Williams was a prisoner sentenced in a high-security unit sitting reading the newspaper, doing his sentence, when Johnson came up behind him and took him out deliberately. It doesn't matter what Carl Williams was or who he was. That's no excuse.

Bill Stuart wanted the jury to believe that Williams wanted the role of top dog in jail. 'Carl Williams was probably, and in fact I suggest, the most dangerous man to have walked the streets of Melbourne in our times,' Stuart proclaimed. 'He's a drug trafficker. He's a gangland boss. He was a murderer. He was a hirer of assassins. He was a liar. A perjurer. A master manipulator of people. And a "fugazi"; a fake.'

'With the death of Matthew Johnson, the general of the Prisoners of War would be gone,' Stuart continued.

You see, the bottom line for Carl Williams was that whilst he walked the streets of Melbourne he thought himself top dog; kingpin … Did Carl Williams no longer wish to be top dog; kingpin, simply because he was removed from the streets of Melbourne? Or did he then decide to become the most dangerous man to walk the corridors of Victoria's prisons?

Life inside as top dog was what he was looking to.

The jury found Johnson guilty of murder on 29 September 2011 after two days of deliberations. The big bald man, flanked by four prison guards as stout as rugby-union fullbacks, showed no emotion as the forewoman announced the verdict.

In December 2011, Justice Lasry sentenced Johnson to life with a minimum of thirty-two years, telling him his defence of self-defence was 'fanciful'. Lasry also said he was staggered as to why Johnson and Williams were allowed to remain together in the same unit, considering the dynamic between the two.

'How the prison authorities permitted that to happen is beyond me,' he said. 'It was a killing which appears to demonstrate your belief [Mr Johnson] that you have some special entitlement to kill when you think it appropriate or your ego demands it according to some meaningless underworld prison code.'

At the time this book was written, Johnson was living in Barwon Prison literally like a caged animal. Bill Stuart had told Johnson's pre-sentence plea hearing of the Spartan conditions Johnson would have to endure for many years to come.

'He is effectively in isolation and he expects to remain in isolation for the very, very distant future—and that's a certainty,' Stuart said. 'Since the murder of Mr Williams … he spends up to twenty hours a day locked in his cell.'

Johnson was allowed out of his cell for four hours each day, most of which was used for physical training. His yard contained a boxing bag, weights, a treadmill and … an exercise bike.

'He spends a couple of hours doing exercise and pacing in the yard but cuts short that period out of his cell because there's no-one to talk to,' Stuart said. 'No-one to interact with.'

Every third day, Johnson was allowed into a yard next to other inmates and could converse with them through a cage across a metre-wide walkway.

'There's two sets of bars between himself and [the other inmates] ... and that is the extent of his contact with any other prisoners face to face,' Stuart explained. 'Because of the general absence of interaction with other humans he chooses to return to his cell earlier than would be otherwise allowed.'

In his cell Johnson had a computer, television, radio and books. He was permitted thirty-two phone calls a week, and one contact visit and four box visits—where he is separated from the visitor— per month.

'It is patent from this that this man will, for the best part of his life, be isolated from other direct contact with people,' Bill Stuart said. 'It is a harsh regime ... and it is one that he expects will continue perhaps forever.'

In April 2012, Ombudsman George Brouwer presented to State Parliament his report outlining his investigation into Corrections Victoria and the extraordinary murder of Carl Williams. The report ran to 163 pages.

'As a result of my investigation, I consider that Corrections Victoria failed in its statutory duty to ensure Mr Williams' safety,' Mr Brouwer wrote.

This case also highlights several shortcomings which need to be addressed by Corrections Victoria in its administration of Victoria's correctional system ... During my investigation, several witnesses including experienced prison staff raised concerns about Correction Victoria's decision to allow Mr Johnson to be placed with Mr Williams. They said that they were 'never comfortable with the placement decision' and 'were not surprised' when they heard that Mr Williams had been killed by Mr Johnson.

2

Hen-pecked?

'It was a horrible damn life and I had to live it. I had to endure it every day.'

MILD-MANNERED ACCOUNT MANAGER ANTHONY SHERNA felt the only way to deal with the anguish after strangling his de facto wife in a fit of rage was to get out of the house—and head straight to the pub to play the pokies and then hire a prostitute for an hour. Sherna was a victim of abuse, according to his account of married life: a man said to be suffering the psychological effects of 'battered woman syndrome'. Yet Sherna was a killer who told police it took him three minutes to strangle the life out of a woman who pleaded, 'Tony, no. Don't do it.' In evidence he gave during his Victorian Supreme Court murder trial, a timid-looking Sherna swore that his de facto wife Susanne Wild—who was just over a metre and a half tall—was a domineering ogre who abused and tormented him to his wits' end. A man who claimed he was verbally belittled and forced to change his surname to prove his love, Sherna said his entire life was controlled by Susie— to the point where she told him what to wear, rationed his cigarettes and money, smelled his clothes for the odour of imagined love affairs and limited his TAB phone account bets to $1.50 a piece. She even stole Christmas, he said.

'In our eighteen-and-a-half year relationship we never had a Christmas tree,' Sherna told a Supreme Court jury. '[One year] Susie was upset with something or someone and she said, "You take those bloody tree and decorations back, we're not celebrating Christmas."'

Sherna told homicide detectives that he strangled his wife with a dressing-gown cord after she yelled at him and scared their pet puppy. 'She was always at me,' he told the detectives. 'I reached my threshold of the horrible life that we had together. The constant put-downs of me. I just had enough.'

If Sherna's testimony was to be believed, Susie Wild was a woman more akin to Annie Wilkes—the possessive lead in Stephen King's *Misery*—than a sweet-hearted Tasmanian girl with a habit of telling tall tales. But who was Anthony Sherna? A guileless and socially awkward type, as he portrayed himself in the witness box? Or a calculating man capable of murdering a woman more akin to his mother, as was the picture painted by the prosecution? Ultimately, was he a Norman Gunston or a Norman Bates?

Sherna—born Anatoli Chernishoff on 15 July 1966—was the second-youngest of eight children. His mother, Fatina Chernishoff, was a religious Russian Orthodox woman who immigrated to Australia with her family in 1962. The Victorian Supreme Court was told her late husband was a violent alcoholic who bashed her while pregnant, injuring Sherna before he was even born. Sherna was delivered with a detached retina.

A kid keen on sports, particularly cricket and Aussie Rules football, Sherna led a fairly typical teenage life.

He developed a close group of friends at high school and studied half a year of a Bachelor of Applied Science degree before dropping out of university to join the workforce. He was working with the Department of Consumer Affairs when he met Susanne Wild on a train in inner-city Melbourne in August 1989. A man in his early twenties, he was immediately infatuated with the older woman.

'Very soon after meeting her it was Susie's birthday and I spent an entire pay packet,' Sherna said at his re-trial. 'I bought a cake, flowers, put a notice in the *Herald Sun* and bought her a Bangles cassette tape. By the time of her birthday I spent more and more time with her and less time at both home and work, and eventually I left work altogether.'

When asked how he spent their early days together, Sherna replied: 'Being really naughty. Drinking too much and just enjoying her company.'

But the days of wine and roses were to take a bitter turn.

Susie Wild was thirty-five years old when she met Sherna. Born in Launceston, Tasmania, on 6 September 1954, she was the second eldest of four siblings. She had a son to a Tasmanian policeman from whom she separated acrimoniously. She had lost contact with all her relatives apart from her mother, Lorna, still in Tasmania.

Vladimir Chernishoff said Susie did not make a good impression on their family after his brother brought her home. '[She was] dominating and also very extreme in how she approached people.'

Family friend Kellie Dower told Sherna's defence barrister, Jane Dixon, SC, in court that it appeared 'more of a dominant relationship on Susie's behalf'.

DIXON: When you say it was more dominant, what did you see?

DOWER: [She was] just barking orders for a drink one night.

DIXON: What would he do if she barked an order at him?

DOWER: Get it … It was more like Tony was a possession, not a human.

When Sherna and Susie met, he was living with a friend and a Sri Lankan boarder in a house he and younger brother Peter owned in the south-eastern Melbourne suburb of Noble Park.

'It was a true-blue bachelor pad,' Sherna said in court. 'We all enjoyed sport. We went to sporting events. We enjoyed partying.'

All that was to end when Susie moved in.

'Susie didn't like me sharing my time with others and she got really upset if I said, "I've got to go and play cricket,"' Sherna said. 'She hated it.' He gave up his favourite sport at her behest.

'It was early in the relationship and I just backed right down from any type of argument and just tried to make her happy.'

After Susie turned a Sherna family party into a disaster by alleging Sherna's brothers and friends sexually harassed her, Sherna ostracised himself from his family.

'When I was at work Susie would ring me up and say, "Your mother's snooping around. Your brothers are snooping around,"' Sherna told the Supreme Court.

My mother's Russian Orthodox and they wear scarves. Susie used to call her the old scarf woman … They [my family] did knock on the door but Susie wouldn't let anyone inside. I had to pretend that we weren't home.

According to Sherna, Susie's draconian rules applied to everyone but herself. He told the jury that she was still in touch with an ex-boyfriend, a man he named as Michael Bennis.

'He had long wavy brown hair,' Sherna recalled. 'His mother was Egyptian and his father was Greek. As such he had like an olive complexion. He had big full lips. The reason why I remember the lips in particular is because Susie used to love kissing him because of his great lips.'

Sherna told of his first encounter with the swarthy love god.

Susie didn't like the colour of the paint in the bathroom and she told me to paint the bathroom a different colour, so I said, 'Yeah, no worries.' I started painting it in the middle of the afternoon on a Saturday and I'm busily painting and six o'clock Susie rang Michael Bennis to come and pick her up, which he did. And then she went back to his place and she said to me, 'Make sure you get this done by the time I get home.' So stupid me was still painting away. I was drinking. It was ten o'clock. She still wasn't back.

Susie didn't return until the following day. When asked in court what he thought she was up to, Sherna replied: 'Ex-boyfriend all night. Put two and two together.'

Despite apologising Susie would later pull another overnighter. 'She just called me a weak little bastard for letting it happen,' Sherna told the court.

The couple rented a home owned by Sherna's mother for a short time. Before moving out, Susie cut up Fatina's lace curtains—much to Sherna's horror. 'It was like a fit of rage,' Sherna said,

> and I'm like, 'What the?' I couldn't believe it … [But] I just had to put all my eggs in the one basket and Susie was it. I had to make it work with Susie. Each of them [my relatives] had a few words to say about it and I ignored them because I was so infatuated.

At the time, Sherna began work as a clerk with Roy Morgan Research in the city.

> At the beginning I would have a drink with workmates on a Friday night … But I had to stop doing it altogether because when I got home Susie would grill me and say that I was womanising, or words to that effect, which was simply not true. She was screaming from the top of her lungs and I'd say I wasn't womanising and she'd just scream out, 'Liar!'
>   It reminded me of family dramas when I was a kid and I would be shaking like a leaf and just frightened.

The couple moved to a flat Susie had picked out. She still was not working. Sherna was the sole provider.

'My understanding of the relationship was that I had to provide a roof over our heads and not just any roof,' Sherna said. 'This place had a spa. It was unbelievably expensive. We struggled very much and had to change our lifestyle. I couldn't drink beer any more and I had to drink cask wine.'

And Susie's ex-boyfriend was still appearing every now and then.

'One day I was home and lo and behold Michael goes and knocks on the door, wearing a tank top and a pair of Speedos,' Sherna recalled.

Susie demanded Sherna change his surname to prove his love. He changed it from Chernishoff to Sherna by deed poll at the Registry of Births, Deaths and Marriages in the city. By that stage he and Susie were sleeping in separate bedrooms. There were verbal and sometimes physical disputes, he claimed in court.

> Sometimes Susie would run in [to my room], turn the light on and just call me—what did she used to call me—a rude little bastard or words to that effect for running out on her when she was arguing.
>
> I would get upset naturally and I'd throw a shoe at her or try and get her out of the room and shut the door. She would run into the kitchen sometimes, grab a kitchen knife, come belting back into my room and try to attack me with the knife. I'd fend her off nearly every time, except one time she grazed me along the shirt and actually cut me along the chest.
>
> I ended up curling on my side protecting my vital organs, and that's how I sleep to this day. I don't sleep on my back any more.

While living in the affluent suburb of South Yarra, Susie regularly drank champagne and took Sudafed and, Sherna claimed, would treat him 'terribly' and start trivial arguments. Sherna blamed Susie's bizarre behaviour on the cocktail of champagne and Sudafed. During his re-trial, Dixon asked if he tried to persuade her to give up drinking alcohol.

'I couldn't do anything like that, no,' he replied.

I couldn't tell her what to do because Susie was older and if I made the silly mistake of telling her what to do she would say, 'I'm older than you. I know better.' I felt so low and miserable it was just demoralising. I felt so helpless because I had no one. I had no family. No friends. My life was just one insult after another from Susie. It got so bad that I actually thought about ending my life.

I cried myself to sleep, and while I was crying myself to sleep I'd look across the hallway and there would be Susie flaked on the bed on her champagne and Sudafed. I was that heartbroken. It was terrible. I was holding down a job as a supervisor in the meantime.

Sherna became a team leader in a print room at National Mutual across the city. The only problem was his little yellow Mini Minor—with a top speed of 80 kilometres an hour—couldn't be driven along the freeway. Susie suggested they move to Burwood East to be closer to his workplace. Susie lived like a hermit there, before they moved to a brand new unit right across the road from the sprawling Box Hill shopping complex. Sherna's life turned into an *expensive* nightmare after that. 'She went from recluse to shopaholic,' he told the jury.

DIXON: What happened in terms of expenditure at that time?
SHERNA: Brand new unit got full of brand new furniture and accessories and more.
DIXON: In terms of the money, who was controlling the money at that time?
SHERNA: Susie controlled the wages … I would withdraw the entire week's wages, hand the money to Susie and she would then hand out the cash as

needed according to groceries that were required.

DIXON: Were you able to keep up with the spending at that time?

SHERNA: No. Actually, I had no idea how much she was spending but I had to get a second job … I was doing shift work plus overtime, then I got a second job working at Safeway Liquor on a casual basis. Susie kept wanting more things to buy and it was getting out of hand, all the spending.

DIXON: How were you coping with that level of working hours?

SHERNA: No, didn't last too long. I couldn't cope. I ended up leaving Safeway and National Mutual … and got my old job back at Roy Morgan—less money.

Less money meant unpaid rent which meant a move to a nearby 'cold and damp' two-bedroom townhouse. Susie caught viral pneumonia there. With cap in hand, an ashamed Sherna made contact with his long-lost mother and asked for $2000.

'It was Susie's idea,' he told the court.

The money went towards a bond and four weeks' rent in advance for a villa unit in Mount Waverley. By that stage Sherna had changed jobs again, and was working at a company called SNP Ausprint five kilometres away.

DIXON: How did you get to work?

SHERNA: The mini broke down at the Box Hill address and Susie told me to sell it and just catch a bus or taxi to work from then on.

A rat problem forced the couple to move to another villa unit, this time in neighbouring Glen Waverley. Dixon asked Sherna: 'What was her general attitude to you in that period? How did she treat you?'

Sherna replied, 'I was basically just the bloke who brought the income in.'

Sherna, by then, was sleeping on what he described as a camp bed.

'I slept on a camp bed for many, many years,' he said. When asked why he didn't just buy himself a new bed, Sherna replied: 'She wouldn't let me.'

> **DIXON**: If you wanted to go and buy something for yourself were you able to go and just do that?
>
> **SHERNA**: Oh, no, no, no. Susie held all the money. She held the credit card, ATM card, bank book, cash.
>
> **DIXON**: Did you try and express affection to her from time to time?
>
> **SHERNA**: As the years progressed I'd try and be affectionate and all she would say is, 'You want to get in my pants.'
>
> **DIXON**: Did she have an attitude about your hygiene, your general hygiene in the house?
>
> **SHERNA**: Put it this way, apparently my 'number twos' were filthy and I stunk and I should be doing those at work and shopping centres. I wasn't allowed to defecate in the toilet [at home].

During his first trial (which ended with a hung jury), Sherna admitted that, while he trained himself in the art of bowel control and the use of toilets other than his own, long weekends 'were a problem'. It was a startling statement from a grown man. Prosecutor Andrew Tinney, SC, who took Sherna to task on several aspects of his evidence during the re-trial, grilled him about his toilet claims.

TINNEY: Some of these things that you claim about Ms Wild are treatment by her of you that would be nothing short of demeaning.

SHERNA: Absolutely.

TINNEY: For example, for a wife to insist of a husband that he never use the toilet in their house if he wants to do anything other than urinate ... that would be quite demeaning and bizarre, would it not?

SHERNA: I didn't have personal space to use the toilet how a human being should be able to ... I had to go to shopping centres and work.

TINNEY: How many years or months or days was it that you were not permitted to use the toilet at whatever house you were living in?

SHERNA: I'd say maybe five years.

TINNEY: [It's not in your police interview] because it is a lie, isn't it?

SHERNA: Hell no. Why would any person stand in the dock and tell the world that?

TINNEY: You were telling the police about your life and you did not tell them anything about this very notable claim that you now make of not being able to use your own toilet?

SHERNA: Yes ... to me that was everyday. That wasn't unusual.

Sherna's next job, as a highly paid laser printer, led him to suggest to Susie they purchase a home-and-land package they could call their own, rather than living like rental gypsies. After Susie reneged on a first home deal, they bought in Hogans Road, Tarneit. Their future neighbours had no idea what trouble was about to move in. Sherna would often visit the house in development, while trying to break the ice and build a rapport with people living in the street. Despite his best efforts to add his own touches to the place as it was taking shape, he still managed to get into trouble.

'I bought wooden blinds from the Kmart catalogue to match the windows of the plan, and of course when we got to moving day, the blinds that I'd bought didn't fit,' he said in court.

> The house plan windows—a lot of them were incorrect. Susie called me an idiot. She was absolutely livid, furious at me. I'd tried to do the right thing. There was a thirty per cent off sale. Lo and behold the windows are different. It wasn't my fault.
>
> Any time there was any sort of responsible decision that went pear-shaped it was *moi*'s fault.

Of Susie's alleged common abusive taunts, Sherna said: '"Low life" was her favourite in probably the second half of our relationship. "Weak bastard" was the favourite for the first half. "Grow some balls." That used to happen a lot.'

He also said: 'Susie used to comment that I didn't have a full deck. The put-downs were basically part of everyday life. They were just routine.'

Sherna and Susie moved into Hogans Road in June 2002. It did not take them long to make an impression. Neighbour Claudia Cortez would often see Sherna working in the garden under a figurative whip. '[Susie would say], "You missed that weed" and do that and do this and do that. It was a domineering … just a weird kind of relationship.'

Mark and Anthea Rose were the first couple to meet them. The Roses were walking their dogs and introduced themselves while Sherna was out gardening. The Roses got around to telling their new neighbours they were expecting a baby. After the birth, Sherna and Susie took over a bottle of champagne. The cork was popped and the couples began to talk. Everything seemed to be going fine until Susie began a lecture about the Roses' dog and the danger it posed to the infant. An argument broke out between the two women; Sherna appeared to try to placate his wife as he continued sipping on champagne. The Roses asked them to leave.

'Susie said something that got the pair of us offside with the Roses,' Sherna would tell the court:

[and] goodness me did I cop it when I got home. I was called disloyal and it was just terrible because I was truly trying to support her. [She said] that I was a weak little bastard and I should grow some balls.

In November, not long after Susie managed to get 'offside with the Roses', Sherna was retrenched from his high-paying laser printing job.

I was absolutely shattered because it was a brand new house, I had a mortgage. It was out of the blue. Susie was livid and said to me, 'That's why I didn't want a house in the first place', and she made me look and feel rather foolish about it.

Being the provider, Sherna scoured the local newspaper for work. He picked up a job as a casual bottle-shop attendant at a hotel. A couple of months later, in March 2003, he gained employment as a laser printer at a company called Security Mail in nearby Laverton. On top of the two jobs, he took on a third—as a casual bottle-shop attendant at another hotel. His work hours were long—days, nights and weekends. About eighteen months later, around November 2004, he started working normal business hours with the company after an upgrade to customer service. He worked with a team of fourteen people, twelve of whom were women. Those numbers didn't go down too well with Susie.

'I had a business unit leader of Rachel Kasupee and my team mate that worked on the same account was Elisha Blake,' Sherna explained. 'Susie was insanely jealous of those two.'

Phone calls to Sherna's desk became incessant. Sherna explained: 'Susie rang many times every day. She would say, 'Who are you screwing?' and things of that nature. These ladies were just my team mates and Susie actually made me feel bad.'

Despite the phone calls, life at work was a luxury for Sherna compared to his regimented existence at home where he slept on the camp bed in the back study.

'[Susie's bedroom] was a no-go zone for me,' he told the jury. 'That was Susie's private area.' Sherna claimed during the 2009 retrial that he had last had sex with Susie on Valentine's Day 2004 after buying her a partner desk as a gift for her front study.

'That was a reward for purchasing the desk,' he said of the sex. 'Every time I tried to be affectionate she'd say, "You just want to get in my pants," and she would make me feel dirty, like a sleaze.'

Sherna told the jury that he was only ever allowed into the kitchen to grab a beer.

'He did mention that he was very rarely allowed in the kitchen,' workmate Elisha Blake said in court. 'That it had been years since he'd made a cup of coffee in the kitchen. He wasn't allowed in the kitchen.'

Sherna described the situation in this way:

[The kitchen] was [Susie's] office, I suppose, and as luck would have it that was the exact middle of the house. If Susie had a topic that was on her mind I had to stand on the other side of the bench and listen. If I had the audacity to walk away I would just cop the biggest tirade and she would say, 'You come back here and you listen.' It was like she was the head master telling you off.

It was strict routine in Susie Wild's home, according to Sherna. He told the Supreme Court that on workday mornings, Susie would grant him one of his twelve daily cigarettes. During his re-trial, Dixon asked, 'So what if you wanted to smoke more than the daily quota?' Sherna's response: 'Too bad.'

Sherna would smoke his morning cigarette in the back courtyard and then return inside to be sprayed with some sort of medical aerosol. While he showered, Susie would make his breakfast—toast and coffee only. Lunch was always three sandwiches a day, Sherna said.

> **SHERNA**: One was to be eaten for morning tea. Two for lunch.
> **DIXON**: What about if you wanted to buy lunch at work?
> **SHERNA**: No, no. I was never given any money, especially any lunch money.

While Sherna brushed his teeth after breakfast, Susie would lay out his clothes for the day.

> **DIXON**: Did you ever disagree and say, 'No, I don't want to wear that. I wore that yesterday or last week?'

SHERNA: I made that mistake a few times but she'd explode at me [and say] that she is older than me and she knows the corporate world.

By ten past eight Sherna would be out the door with his briefcase, and a grocery list with an estimated amount of money to cover it.

SHERNA: As far as the ATM card, credit cards— Susie held on to those. They were her property. That money she gave me was purely for that grocery list. I was not to spend any of it, absolutely not one cent of it.
DIXON: What would happen though in terms of using them to withdraw money?
SHERNA: I had to withdraw $600 or $800 a week at Susie's request. I would then have to hand her the money and ATM receipt, and look out if I didn't have the ATM receipt.

Of an evening after work, Sherna arrived home and— after taking his shoes and socks off and putting on his 'indoor thongs'—he placed any groceries and the receipt on the kitchen bench.

'Then I would have to empty my pockets of any change, mobile phone, keys, cigarette case, lighter … Susie would grab the change, receipts, make sure that it was all there.'

DIXON: When you got home did you go and turn on the telly? What did you do to relax at home after work?
SHERNA: Well I loved sport. I love current affairs, and like any person, you want to watch the news

when you get home. But every time I tried to watch the news, because Susie used to control the remote, she would flip the channel. 'I've already watched the news.' Bang.

DIXON: So in terms of relaxing at home, what did you do to relax at home of an evening?

SHERNA: I didn't. I sat on the couch. I tried to watch TV but they were all Susie's shows.

Pre-prepared meals would be heated in the microwave and eaten for dinner. Susie would drink up to a bottle of red wine and Sherna about eight cans of beer. After tea it was lights out on Susie's say-so, according to Sherna. 'In our relationship, if Susie was tired, the household was tired,' he said in evidence.

'Off with the telly. We are going to bed.' That was it. Didn't matter if it was the last quarter of the Grand Final. Too bad. Bed … It was best to let her be when she was on her bandwagon. There is no way I was going to cause trouble at that time of night.

On weekends, Sherna said, it was his primary role to play chauffeur. 'If Susie wanted to add a piece of home decorating that she wanted to buy, regardless of where it was in Melbourne, I had to drive her there.'

He said he would then have to wait in the car and listen to the radio as Susie shopped her little heart out. 'Didn't matter if it was four hours. I wasn't allowed to drop her off and come home. I had to wait outside the store.'

On Friday evenings to welcome in the weekend, Sherna's workmates would regularly head to the pub for a few beers.

DIXON: Did you ever go?
SHERNA: No. Wasn't allowed and I didn't have money.

According to a former workmate, Sherna referred to his wife as 'the thumb' or 'the boss'. When asked in court if he ever confided with workmates about his tempestuous relationship, Sherna said:

I confided in nobody … because with Susie loyalty was her number one motto. I was never to discuss any of our relationship with anyone else. It had to remain within those four walls … I had to be loyal out of fear of what may happen if I broke that loyalty. I was terrified of what she was capable of doing.

Sherna made a mistake one year of attending a work Christmas party, held in a restaurant at the Victorian Arts Centre. Roadworks and traffic jams on the West Gate Bridge caused him to miss his home curfew by twenty minutes.

'Susie was in a massive, massive rage,' Sherna told the jury.

She was throwing full cans of beer at me, right at my head. She was calling me a womanising toe rag. It was just an incredible tirade of abuse and it was so uncalled for. You can't help traffic delays … Lucky she was drunk and not a good aim.

Sherna's working role required him to travel interstate occasionally. On the first occasion, Susie allowed him to go to Sydney for one day, instead of the required two. Sherna was not to stay overnight interstate.

Despite his only travelling the one day, Susie called three times to check up on him.

> **DIXON**: What was the nature of the calls?
> **SHERNA**: Well obviously I had to pull my pants up. She was checking who I was screwing.

Susie Wild appeared to be disgusted at the thought of fun, as neighbours learned after putting a gazebo, veranda and spa in their backyard. Susie abused them constantly.

'It was always a hassle to be in the backyard,' Claudia Cortez said in court. 'She would always say, "Get out of the spa you lazy bastards," and so on. "Go and get a job."'

Sherna told the jury: 'They were nasty, abusive remarks. She would call them things like trailer trash. She just thought they were having sex orgies.'

Susie falsely reported other neighbours, like Mauricio Perez, for wasteful water usage. Perez also found human faeces in his letterbox several times. Susie was abusive to Perez and his young daughter whenever they were out walking or playing.

'She used to just come out and start abusing the hell out of us,' Perez said in evidence.

> She used to come out swearing, insulting me and that kind of thing. It got out of hand when my daughter was around. I told him [Sherna] to put her on a leash … because she looked like she was out of control.

Susie would even yell at children who dared pat horses in an adjacent paddock.

'I'd been trying to build a rapport with neighbours and it didn't matter what I said to Susie,' Sherna told the court.

If I told her 'stop it', she would scream things out at me like, 'You disloyal little bastard.' She loved saying that.

When Susie had a bee in her bonnet she was the boss. You just didn't mess with her.

To try to improve his 'marriage', Sherna accepted a free pup from a work colleague. It was a Jack Russell–Maltese cross. Sherna called him Hubble. He brought the dog home on 24 December 2006.

'I brought Hubble home to compensate for not having children and also to make Susie happy,' he recalled. 'We treated him like a kid, like a child.'

In August 2007, Sherna was required to travel to Sydney for work again. The court was told that Susie packed his suitcase and gave him his orders.

DIXON: Did Susie tell you anything about what you were to do in Sydney?
SHERNA: Well, I had to behave. Susie rang me heaps and heaps and heaps of times.
DIXON: What was the nature of the calls?
SHERNA: She was in a massive panic. She was one hundred per cent certain that I was screwing [my work colleague] Elisha, saying, 'Put that bitch on the phone.'
DIXON: What about when you came back?
SHERNA: When I came back from Sydney it was awful. The taxi pulled up. I got my suitcase out and Susie was screaming at me that I was a womaniser and words to that effect. When I got inside, to my horror, she grabbed my wallet and started searching for women's phone numbers. I mean, come on.

DIXON: What happened with your suitcase?
SHERNA: What she did, and this is even more disgusting, is she picked up every piece of clothing and smelt them for women's scent … She was adamant that I was having an affair.

Sherna said life was like a pressure cooker for him. Desperate for a normal married relationship, he decided to throw his career away and seek a sea change with Susie. Maybe that was the tonic: a change of scene away from Melbourne. He quit his job at Security Mail in November 2007, but Susie pulled out of the plan to move to the seaside.

'I was at home. I'd given up,' Sherna said in evidence. 'Just lost all motivation. Just sat around mucking around with Hubble. Susie called me a lazy bastard. "Get yourself a job and stop playing with that bloody dog."'

Sherna did as he was told, and found employment with QM Technologies in Port Melbourne as an account manager. At Christmas 2007—two months before he was to strangle Susie to death—he took Hubble and visited his cancer-riddled mother.

Fatina later told police: 'I asked him if they did anything together or had any friends. He said they never went out or did anything outside the house. I told him he was like a slave to Susie and he agreed.'

There was a 20/20 cricket match at the MCG between Australia and India on the night Susie Wild was to die. One of Sherna's workmates had invited him to the game, but he had politely refused. He knew it wasn't worth the trouble it would have caused. That day Susie had told Sherna that a bill for his mobile phone had arrived two weeks earlier. His phone had since been disconnected.

To add to his frustration, Susie had demanded to know exactly who he had called. According to Sherna, Susie was 'very, very frosty' when he arrived home that night.

'Susie had already been drinking and she said to me, "Skol, catch up," so I had to skol beer,' Sherna told the jury. 'She seemed to be in a real mood for stirring up trouble. I don't know what got on her pip that day, maybe it was the mobile phone bill.'

Sherna continued to drink. Some time around 10 pm he went out the back for one of his twelve daily cigarettes. He let Hubble out for his 'toilet business'. Susie, meanwhile, made a 'distressed and afraid' phone call to her mother in Tasmania.

'She was crying a lot and I asked her what was upsetting her and she said she couldn't tell me,' Susie's elderly mother Lorna Brazendale told the Supreme Court. 'I said to her, "Have you had a fight with Tony?" She said, "I can't tell you that." When I said, "Why?" she said, "You call it discretion."'

Lorna changed the subject and asked about Hubble the dog. That seemed to cheer Susie up. 'Towards the end of the conversation she said, "I feel like God's sent Hubble to me for somebody to love me,"' Lorna said. 'I said to her, "Well, I love you and pray for you every day."'

The phone call ended at about 11.45 pm. Susie Wild had no more than twenty minutes to live.

Sherna was in the laundry rocking Hubble to sleep to radio tunes—as was his usual practice of a night-time—when Susie stormed in. 'Turn that bloody thing off and come and sit down,' she yelled. 'I've got to talk to you.'

Susie's yelling scared Hubble in Sherna's arms. Sherna told police: 'Susie came in ranting and raving. It was loud and Hubble was shaking like a leaf. I was really angry.'

On the way from the laundry to the kitchen, Sherna grabbed the cord from his dressing-gown and followed Susie. 'I was just so angry ... because I was drunk ... I grabbed the cord to kill her,' he later told Homicide Squad detectives Nigel L'Estrange and Vic Anastasiadis.

'She was in the kitchen heating up her red wine in the microwave. I stood there and just listened to what she was saying ... I was angry but I was calming down.'

Susie then went on to taunt him about the mobile phone bill.

'Susie said I would never find it,' Sherna told the jury. 'And at that inexplicable moment I had a surge of emotion. It's impossible to explain. And I lost all rationality ... It was the final taunt.'

Sherna 'stormed' into the kitchen, raised the cord and wrapped it around Susie's neck. She uttered: 'Tony, no. Don't do it.' He ignored her plea.

L'ESTRANGE: Was she making any sounds?

SHERNA: At the end it was horrible.

L'ESTRANGE: What do you mean by that?

SHERNA: Because she was dying. The blood, oxygenated blood come up through her mouth.

L'ESTRANGE: How was that making you feel?

SHERNA: At the time nothing was going into my head.

L'ESTRANGE: At any time did you think that you should stop?

SHERNA: No, because I thought if I stopped ... I just didn't want to stop.

When asked what went through his mind as he stood over his wife after what was a two- to three-minute death throttle, Sherna said: 'I was in shock. I couldn't believe what I had done.' In court, Dixon asked him: 'Did you intend to kill Susie?' Sherna replied: 'No way in hell, no way. No way.'

Tinney aggressively cross-examined Sherna on that point.

> **TINNEY**: You had ample time to think about what you were doing. Ample time to stop short of killing her, but that killing her was exactly what you had in mind and was exactly what you were intending to do.
>
> **SHERNA**: No way. I had absolutely no intention of killing Susie.
>
> **TINNEY**: If you had no intention of killing Susie … first of all could I ask you why did you wrap a dressing-gown cord tightly and twist it tightly around her neck?
>
> **SHERNA**: That is something that I have been asking myself ever since. I cannot provide an answer to that. All I can tell you is I wasn't acting rationally. I had a surge of emotion.

After the killing, Sherna stood and took a drink. He knows exactly what time he killed his wife because he spied the oven clock as he rocked his head back to take a slug of Toohey's Red. He threw on some clothes and got 'the hell out of there'. In what Tinney described as 'entirely frightening' behaviour after the killing, Sherna went and played with poker machines and a prostitute:

> He grabbed some clothing, got himself dressed and he left his de facto wife dead on the kitchen floor, sort of crumpled there, and his dog asleep in the laundry and he went out drinking and gambling at a

pokies venue at the Werribee Plaza. After a few hours and many drinks there he went off to a brothel called Whisper's Studio, where he spent some time with a prostitute.

Tinney grilled Sherna about his actions, post-death.

TINNEY: Why did you not [go to the police] straight away after you had killed your wife?
SHERNA: Because I was in shock. I had no one to confide in. I didn't know what to do.
TINNEY: So you confided in the good folk down at the Werribee Plaza Tabaret pokies venue. Is that right?
SHERNA: I wouldn't have said it like that, but yes, I did attend there.
TINNEY: You went down there and kicked up your heels a bit did you? To celebrate what you'd done?
SHERNA: Definitely not.
TINNEY: And your thought process was, 'I've killed my wife. I'm going to go and have a drink?'
SHERNA: I was getting the hell out of there, and that's the first thing that came into my head … I was drinking and obviously gambling as well.
TINNEY: And then you went off to see the prostitute for an hour?
SHERNA: That's correct … It was totally out of character. I never do that and my dear old mother would be so upset with me.

According to the police summary, Sherna arrived at the brothel at 3.25 am on Saturday, 2 February, 'utilising the services of one of the girls initially for half an hour then extending this to one hour'. After the brothel, Sherna drove home and passed out on his bed close to 5 am. He woke up about noon.

'I let Hubble out again and then it hit me,' he told Homicide detectives during his record of interview.

> I went, 'Shit. What the hell have you done?' Because I didn't have family or friends I didn't know what to do. So what I did is I grabbed her under the arms and I dragged her body from the kitchen and somehow I managed to put her on [her] bed. Not out of any spite, or anything, but she ended up face down on the pillow and that's where she remained.

During the afternoon, Sherna made several phone calls. And none of them was to the police. The first number he dialled at 4.48 pm—about seventeen hours after killing Susie—was a sex chat-line. It gave him this recorded message: 'Hi babe, I was waiting for your call. Welcome to Australia's hottest chat-line.' He called that same number again.

> **TINNEY**: Your wife was still lying dead on her bed not more than a few metres from that desk [from where you were calling]. Is that right?
> **SHERNA**: I'd never rung them before and it was a stupid thing to bloody do.

Sherna's next call was to a different sex chat-line. That call lasted 23 minutes and 42 seconds and cost him $41. Tinney asked him, 'Were you not happy with the service you got during the first two calls?'

Sherna also called Whisper's Studio brothel.

TINNEY: What were you doing calling a brothel at 5.20 in the afternoon?

SHERNA: I don't know. I don't know. I was acting so irrationally. I'm just so ashamed.

TINNEY: You keep on saying you're acting irrationally but you killed a woman with whom you hadn't had sex for three years. Within hours of that you went off to a brothel and had sex, and later that day phoned sex chat lines and then phoned the brothel again. I mean were you particularly interested in sex during this day, the day that you had killed your wife?

SHERNA: No.

TINNEY: And after you had killed her?

SHERNA: No way. That's what I'm saying to you, I wasn't acting rationally.

Interspersed between the calls to sex chat-lines and brothels, Sherna steadily punted on the horses through his TAB telephone account.

'I think I had the radio on the horse channel,' he admitted.

Susie Wild lay on her bed all Sunday. It was February and the summer heat was unkind to her.

'On Monday the rigor mortis and smell was really hitting,' Sherna told detectives L'Estrange and Anastasiadis.

In that time I had the evaporative cooler going to keep the temperature down because it was very hot weather. I went and got Glen 20 disinfectant spray, or whatever it is, and I also got a rose scented candle for two reasons. Number one reason was for the smell.

Number two is because Susie is Catholic and I knew candles and deaths are associated with each other.

On the Monday morning, Sherna rang his supervisor Lucy Mariani and asked for a week off because his wife had 'left' him.

'He was very apologetic,' Mariani said in court.

Despite Sherna's efforts to mask the smell of death, the stench emanating from his home had the closest neighbours complaining. He had no option but to bury the body. To save Hubble from the trauma of seeing one of his owners burying the other one, Sherna took the puppy to a pet resort kennel.

'I didn't want Hubble to smell or see anything,' he told the detectives. 'I didn't want him to be traumatised.'

Sherna stopped in at a Safeway store and bought 20 metres of orange nylon rope. He wrapped his wife in bed sheets and plastic from his garage. It was amateur hour.

'It [the smell] was terrible,' he told the detectives.

I slid the plastic somehow over her from the feet up. I tried to make her dignified. I pushed her legs together, her arms together and I wrapped her in the plastic bag and tied it up to keep the smell away.

While drinking beer, he tried to dig a grave in the hard backyard clay with nothing more than a spade and a pitchfork. Amateur hour continued.

You could clearly see that I was digging a grave-like hole. I was out in the open and I was digging for hours and hours because it was clay. [The weather was] boiling hot and [the ground] rock hard … I could only dig the hole approximately two to three feet deep because I hit an easement pipe.

At about 1 am on the morning of Tuesday, 5 February, he dragged his wife's wrapped, decomposing body and dumped it in the shallow grave.

'I knew I had to take the body outside somewhere because it was just stinking,' he told police. 'It was decomposing … I had been drinking very heavily and I lost a right thong. That's in the hole as well.'

He covered the body with dirt. Tinney described it as if Sherna had disposed of Susie 'as though she was some sort of animal'. After sunrise, Sherna planted rose bushes along the edge of the garden. Even in death, Susanne Wild was still on the wrong side of the roses.

After cleaning the floors with disinfectant and throwing out the clothes he had been wearing, Sherna went and picked up Hubble. He later rang his mother and told her what he'd done. Sherna went and picked her up and drove her to Tarneit.

'I walked in the house and just stood by the kitchen bench near him and dropped my head and just cried,' Fatina said in her police statement. 'Tony was holding his puppy dog and crying. He was telling me not to cry and he said he would calm down a bit, call the police and it would be all over.'

Sherna never called the police. That duty was left to brother Vladimir, after Fatina told him what had happened. On Saturday, 9 February, his last day of freedom, Sherna drank, played with Hubble and placed a dozen bets on the horses via his phone account.

Tinney questioned Sherna about his so-called state of shock and grief at that point.

TINNEY: You were at home listening to the races were you?

SHERNA: Yes, no doubt.

TINNEY: Putting on bets at your leisure?

SHERNA: I wouldn't have put it like that, but yeah. I was putting on bets.

TINNEY: I would suggest that you didn't really have any particular regret about what you had done other than in respect of how it was going to affect you.

SHERNA: I had absolutely heaps of regret.

Senior Constable Graeme Rayner and his constable partner arrived at the Tarneit home for a welfare check on Susanne Wild about 9.30 pm on Saturday, 9 February. They found Sherna asleep on the couch in front of a flickering TV in a dark lounge room. They roused him with torchlight and he came outside. The cops then questioned him.

RAYNER: Mate, we're here to do a welfare check on Susie.

SHERNA: I know. I've been expecting you.

RAYNER: Where is she? I need to speak to her.

Sherna dropped his shoulders, sighed and replied: 'She's dead. I killed her.' He was arrested and read his rights. Rayner then continued. 'Where is she?'

Sherna told him. 'In the backyard. I buried her. I just had enough. I strangled her to death then buried her.'

Sherna led the two cops to the shallow grave. 'She's just over there,' he pointed. 'About two feet off the corner of the house; three feet down. I hit a stormwater pipe and couldn't go any further.'

Forensic examiners later dug up the body.

'The body was wrapped in three bed sheets and the head of the deceased had a pillow over her face,' the police summary states. 'Inside the grave underneath the body, crime scene examiners located a blue-and-white thong.'

Sherna's first Supreme Court murder trial ended with a hung jury. During the re-trial in October 2009, forensic psychologist Jeffrey Cummins said he believed Sherna fitted the profile of a victim of battered woman syndrome.

Cummins told the jury:

> The battered woman syndrome was first described in the late 1970s, early 1980s, and it was characterised then, as it is now, by a set of psychological phenomena where a person who is subjected to physical and or emotional abuse over an extended time period acquiesces to that and becomes depressed.
>
> [They have] concentration difficulties, their self-esteem deteriorates, they often report feeling isolated, feeling a sense of loss of control. In my opinion this man, Mr Sherna, ended up effectively having a symptom set identical to that described in the battered woman syndrome.

Tinney was obviously sceptical, and cross-examined in that fashion.

> **TINNEY**: Well at the heart of the condition, if there is such a thing, I'd suggest to you is a history of pretty much constant and severe violence?
> **CUMMINS**: When the condition was first described in the late 1970s it was described in the context of women who had been subjected to repeated

physical violence … And progressively the
definition has been broadened to include people
who perceive they have been emotionally abused
and or physically abused.

Later in his cross-examination, Tinney asked
Cummins: 'How many women you have assessed over
the years who could be said to be suffering from such, or
experiencing such a syndrome?'

CUMMINS: Fewer than one hundred.
TINNEY: Fewer than one hundred women. Over
how many years are we talking about?
CUMMINS: Thirty years of practising.
TINNEY: How many men?
CUMMINS: I would say two.

Sherna spent several days in the witness box. His
evidence ranged from poignant to darkly comical. He
was asked why he simply hadn't walked out on the soul-
destroying relationship.

'The only thing I knew is that I couldn't leave her …
because I couldn't break that loyalty aspect that she had
on the relationship; the hold that she had on it because I
didn't know how she would react,' he said. 'She was five
foot tall, sure, but goodness me she knew how to use the
phone and she had connections. If she had a bee in her
bonnet she used to make things happen and I used to be
bloody terrified.'

Tinney accused Sherna of exaggerating the extent
of his tormented life, but Sherna was adamant. 'No way.
No way in hell. That was my life. That happened. It was a
horrible damn life and I had to live it. I had to endure it
every day.'

Tinney told the jury that Sherna's crime was the result of the 'voluntary, conscious and deliberate' actions of a drunken man who lost his temper.

'Now we all know, I suppose, that there are good ways and bad ways of ending a relationship,' Tinney said in his closing address.

A good way might have been for the accused to go up to Susanne, sit her down and tell her, 'Susanne, for eighteen years we've been together. I've worked at this relationship. I've loved you, I've done my best to make a go of it. But honestly I've reached the point where I can go no further. The relationship doesn't give me what I need. I'm sorry. I'm leaving you. You can stay in the house. I'll continue to make the mortgage payments until we can arrange our financial affairs. Goodbye.' That would be a good way of ending a relationship.

If I was to put forward a bad way of ending a long-term relationship then perhaps what the accused did to his wife on 2 February 2008 would be a reasonable sort of blueprint. A bit on the extreme side. Even if every single negative thing he said about this woman or any of the other witnesses in this court said about this woman were the truth, it would not have given him any justification whatsoever for killing her; for doing what he did. She could be the worst and most unpleasant and controlling person in the world, but she deserved a bit better, members of the jury, than to be strangled to death in her own house, wrapped up and buried in her own backyard.

He could have been the most sad, the most ineffectual, the most under-the-thumb figure imaginable—but it did not give him the right to do what he did.

Dixon told the jury that it was a spontaneous killing that happened due to a sudden eruption after 'many, many years of abuse'.

The accused man was so totally overborne by the deceased that she essentially had him completely in her thrall to the point where he had lost the capacity for sensible independent judgment about his situation. It had really become more like a parent and child relationship.

Manslaughter is the true verdict in this case, in my submission to you. The defence says there was certainly no premeditation about this killing. This is a man who never in his wildest dreams imagined being here in the Supreme Court on trial for murder.

After just over a day's deliberation, the jury acquitted Sherna of murder but found him guilty of manslaughter. Justice David Beach sentenced him to a maximum fourteen years' jail with a minimum of ten. It was a substantial sentence for manslaughter.

'I accept that the deceased was both controlling and domineering of you and that, from time to time, this involved significant episodes of unpleasantness on her behalf,' the judge said.

Nonetheless, even if everything you said in evidence concerning the deceased and your relationship with her was true, it would not justify or excuse killing her.

This is not a case where someone in a fit of anger lashes out and kills with one blow. This, on your own evidence, was a case where you took two to three minutes to strangle the life out of the deceased. It was, on any view, a brutal attack perpetrated by you on a person who was smaller and weaker than you were.

In her victim impact statement, Lorna Brazendale said she would never be able to come to terms with her daughter's death.

'The emotional trauma and ongoing anxiety is probably the worst aspect,' she said. After the sentencing, Lorna told this author:

> I think the sentence is justice, in a way. I don't think we could have hoped for much more … but nothing will ever bring Sue back. My counsellor said only a cold-hearted person and callous man could do what he did. This is the most horrible thing that can happen to your child.

Sherna sought leave to appeal against the severity of his sentence. After consideration, three Court of Appeal judges refused the application.

'The sentence imposed here was at the very top of the range but in my view it was not outside the range,' Justice Simon Whelan stated.

3
The Facebook Killer

*'You know those shows on Foxtel that you
watch on the crime channel with the psycho
people? I feel like one of them now.'*

TO HIS TWO-YEAR-OLD DAUGHTER YAZMINA, RAMAZAN
Acar must have looked like the devil. Crazed, drunk and
armed with a large ornate knife, the spiteful father had
nothing but sinister intentions as he approached his little
girl while she played outside his car in a suburban reserve.
Yazmina had done nothing to enrage or provoke her dad.
No. She was as innocent and naïve as the day was long.
Ramazan Acar—the bricklaying son of a hard-working
and respected Turkish father—was being fuelled by the
pure loathing of another: his former girlfriend Rachelle
D'Argent. In his resentful, alcohol-soaked brain, Rachelle
was nothing but a bitch. A slut. Of that he was convinced.
So convinced, in fact, he'd once carved that description
into a wooden pillar next to Rachelle's front door for all to
see. Rachelle was the mother of his child; the mother who
had left him and was denying him access to his precious
daughter. So precious was little Yazmina that Acar was
about to sacrifice her for the most selfish of reasons. To put

it simply, he was going to murder his daughter to torment Rachelle for the rest of her life. Yazmina, or Mimi as her mum affectionately called her, was the pawn in Acar's sick and twisted game of revenge.

According to the experts, Ramazan Acar was no dill. Not stupid in the true sense of the word. He had an above-average IQ of 106. But, as Supreme Court judge Justice Elizabeth Curtain would accept, he was an immature young man with anger-management problems and 'very fixed views'. A history of drug use—including substances like cannabis, speed and ice—only exacerbated what a psychiatrist would diagnose as Acar's 'mixed personality disorder with borderline antisocial and narcissistic traits'. Ramazan Acar was a bloke who could not accept rejection; could not accept being told 'no'.

Born 24 February 1987, Acar dropped out of Fawkner Secondary College after Year 9 and pottered around as a panelbeater, painter and tiler. He and Rachelle had known each other since their mid-teens.

'I first met Ramzy when I was fifteen or sixteen years old at an underage Metro, which was an underage nightclub in the city,' Rachelle said in a police statement.

> We did not have any friends or family in common, we just met there and he continually pestered me there all night until I gave him my phone number. We started off just talking to each other for around three months and then we started a relationship … For the first eight months of our relationship, it was perfect.

But trouble soon brewed in paradise. About eight months later, according to Rachelle's statement, Acar punched her to the floor at a billiards club 'because I was playing pool with other guys'.

'I woke up and he was trying to kick and spit on me and his brother and a mate were trying to pull him away,' Rachelle told police.

I did not tell my mother about this, or report it to the police … A few days later we spoke about this and he apologised and told me that he is not like that and it is not him. I forgave him and our relationship continued.

Needless to say, their de facto relationship was destined to be a turbulent and volatile time marked, as Justice Curtain would say, by Acar's 'jealousy, possessiveness, violence and, it appears, drug use'. Acar's true colours again rose to the surface in January 2006 while he and Rachelle were living with her father. At a barbecue, according to Rachelle, 'Ramzy drank too much alcohol too quickly and became drunk and aggressive.' Armed with two steak knives, Acar stabbed himself.

'Everyone ended up out in the street,' Rachelle said in a statement. 'He grabbed me and held the knife to my throat and said something like, "If I am going you are coming with me."'

Police stormed the home and showered Acar with capsicum spray. He ran off and was later arrested.

Upon his release from custody, his family returned from Griffith, New South Wales, where they had been residing and working on a farm. In late 2006, the Acar clan moved back to Victoria and settled into a home in the northern suburbs. (A magistrate would later hand Acar a three-month suspended jail term for unlawful assault, making a threat to kill, threatening to inflict serious injury and criminal damage for the knife incident.)

'They would spend nights together, weekends together, but would live separately at their respective parents' premises,' Acar's barrister, Gavin Meredith, would tell the Victorian Supreme Court. 'He was working as a bricklayer—not a qualified bricklayer—but working in the industry. Ultimately, he and Rachelle commenced to live together in or about July of 2007.'

By that stage, Rachelle was pregnant.

'This was not a planned pregnancy,' she told police.

When I told Ramzy that I was pregnant he was shocked and couldn't believe it. He thought that I was joking. He is five months younger than I am, so he would have been nineteen at the time. He said to me that he was too young to be a father. After a couple of phone calls with him, he came around to the idea. I will say that he was working and saving money. He came to my medical appointments with me and came shopping for baby clothes and other stuff. At the eighteen week ultrasound we found out that I was pregnant with a little girl. I was so happy when I found out. Ramzy said that he thought it was going to be a little boy, but he was over the moon that he was going to have a little girl. When I was pregnant we lived apart, however, once I reached seven months he moved in with me and my mum in Narre Warren.

Ramzy and I went to the pre-natal classes and he seemed to be loving it. In the class he was like the clown. He loved it; he couldn't wait to be a dad. He was always interested in what they were showing—like how to bath the baby and stuff.

Their daughter, Yazmina Micheline Acar, was born via an emergency caesarean on 23 November. 'I did not see my baby at birth as during the procedure she swallowed meconium and did not breathe,' Rachelle explained in a statement. 'She was resuscitated and rushed by ambulance to the Royal Women's Hospital. She commenced breathing unaided after twenty-four hours.' The little girl was a survivor.

'Yazmina, or Mimi as we used to call her, was and still is my everything,' Rachelle wrote in a victim impact statement after her daughter's death. 'She was my reason for getting up every morning.'

In June 2008, Acar went to jail for three months after committing serious driving offences in breach of his suspended unlawful knife assault and death-threat sentence. On his release he returned to live with Rachelle.

'Two weeks after Ramzy was released we held our engagement party at mum's house,' Rachelle told police. 'Ramzy had proposed to me before Mimi was born— when I was eight months pregnant. I had accepted straight away. I wanted to marry him, even though we had had our troubles.' The couple split around January 2009, with Acar moving back in with his family.

'This was because he hit me again,' Rachelle said in her police statement. 'Mimi was crying and he got pissed off with it.'

Acar underwent some counselling and Rachelle resumed her relationship with him, ironically so as not to deprive her daughter of a father figure. 'I grew up without really having a dad and I did not want this to happen to my daughter,' she explained to police. 'We were living with our respective parents during the week and Mimi was living with me. I would drive to [Acar's parents' house] on the weekends and we would spend the weekends together.'

In June that year the two started living together yet again, with Acar participating in a male family violence program this time. One of the program workers found Acar to be 'a young man with very strong views that will require ongoing work in the area of change'. But it appeared to Rachelle that there was no change.

'It was hell,' she said in her statement.

> I was just a housewife. I cooked, cleaned and laid his shoes out for him. All he did was eat, shower and go out. I have been asked why I stayed with him, and one reason is that I was bloody scared, but also the smile on my little girl's face when she saw her dad come home from work was priceless. I don't have memories of my dad and I did not want that for her.

In November 2009 Acar was convicted of recklessly causing injury to Rachelle by hitting her. For that offence he received another suspended sentence—a two-month term suspended for twelve months. When their lease ended in July 2010, the couple split again, Acar moving back in with his parents and Rachelle into her own unit in the outer south-eastern suburb of Hallam. According to Gavin Meredith, Acar was hitting the drugs at that stage.

'There was a period where his amphetamine usage became fairly heavy, his [bricklaying] work sporadic,' Meredith told the Supreme Court.

Acar visted Rachelle and Yazmina once every weekend.

'And then he would start coming during the week and he would be fried,' Rachelle told police.

> By this I mean that he was obviously taking drugs. I confronted him about using drugs and he denied it. One other day he turned up to my home with flowers and chocolates. He never in eight and a half years

bought me flowers and chocolates and when I spoke to him he was just off his head. Again he denied it. He was constantly frustrated and yelling at me over trivial little things and getting angry because Mimi was crying. He would sit up all night just watching TV.

Rachelle told police that during one of Acar's visits she found a crack pipe and what she believed to be drugs in his bumbag. She said it was in August 2010 when she 'stood up to him'.

One rule I always had is that he doesn't bring drugs into my home. This was my home now. I paid all of the bills. I told him that it was over and he could just get his stuff and get out. I recall that we were watching the footy on TV at the time. He didn't say anything. It was like he did not believe I had spoken to him like this. He picked up his wallet and his keys and went into the room where Mimi was playing. He kissed his daughter and then he went outside, got into his car and drove away.

The following month Acar appeared to try to clean up his act. Rachelle had changed her phone number and Acar had no access to his daughter. According to a relationship counsellor, Acar was 'wanting to commence family dispute resolution and indicated that he wanted to sort himself out, clean himself up, go through the appropriate legal channels and re-establish access for his child'. Acar expressed interest in a family dispute resolution program operated by the Family Relationships Centre at Broadmeadows, but he failed to attend one session. Centrelink referred him to a psychologist named Peter Stanislawski. According to Justice Curtain:

That referral had identified what was said to be three barriers to your [Acar] employment, noted as follows: your limited employment history, your social isolation and anger. It appears that you attended four sessions and the discussions concerned your cannabis use and dependence, which Mr Stanislawski said you appeared to be motivated to address. You told Mr Stanislawski that you regretted being violent towards your ex-partner and that you wanted to be a good father to your daughter.

Acar continued to try to contact Rachelle in an effort to resume a relationship with his daughter.

'[Acar] was denied permission by Rachelle to have access to his daughter,' Crown prosecutor Peter Rose, SC, told the Victorian Supreme Court.

In November, Acar contacted Rachelle through her mother.

'Eventually Rachelle returned his phone calls and he indicated he believed he was likely to go to jail in the near future as a result of driving offences and he claimed he wanted to see his daughter before this occurred,' Rose told the court.

Rachelle agreed to let Acar see the child. 'He wanted to see Mimi before he got locked up,' she explained in her police statement.

Mother and daughter met him at the Fountain Gate Shopping Centre: a busy public place where nothing violent or untoward was likely to occur. They walked around the plaza; Acar gave his daughter shoulder rides and bought her presents. It ended as a good day out.

'He looked actually refreshed,' Rachelle told police.

I can tell when Ramzy's been on stuff however he had a new look about him. He was clean and fresh, he had money in his pocket. He was carrying Mimi on his shoulders and was playing. He bought her things. I thought maybe he was getting better. We talked about him seeing Mimi and I said that he could see her every fortnight. He said to me that he loved me but he knew that we could not be together, as it was too complicated for us. He was so polite and grateful for me letting him see Mimi that day. It was a real shock.

After a forty-three-minute phone call on 13 November, Rachelle allowed Yazmina to spend the night at Acar's family home.

'He begged me and told me that he would look after her and that his mum would be there and help with the food and everything,' Rachelle recalled. 'I told him that it was something very big that he was asking of me but I said, "Well, how about next weekend?" He was so grateful and surprised. It was a whole different Ramzy that I was seeing.'

In a show of public joy, Acar posted several pleasant messages on his Facebook page. He was dearly looking forward to the sleepover, he posted. 'He had all toys and stuff for her,' Rachelle said. 'It was again a whole different Ramzy, or so I thought.'

The night went well. Acar and his family enjoyed their time with little Yazmina. The stay ended all too quickly and the next day it was time to wave the little girl goodbye. Acar dropped Yazmina back to Rachelle on the Sunday afternoon, and then went to a park and smoked dope.

'He began ruminating about the fact that he'd have to give his daughter back,' Meredith told the Supreme Court.

That he did want to continue to see his daughter and then would he be able to see her, and so on. He also indicates that he became aware of the fact that Rachelle, he believed, had commenced seeing another man and he didn't necessarily view that in a negative sense but indicates that he commenced to have feelings that he would probably or potentially be squeezed out of his daughter's life—that Rachelle was moving on with hers.

Acar started calling Rachelle several times a day. Rachelle tried to pull his reins in a bit, telling him that he could call—but not as frequently as he was. Around this time, Acar met a new girl. We shall call her Talia. He took her out for drinks on the Monday night. Went to work and smoked cannabis on the Tuesday before paying Talia a visit at her mother's place of work. Talia told him he was becoming a little overbearing and was rushing their relationship. She told him to slow down and back off a bit. Acar took the advice badly. Meredith described the situation: 'She noticed a discernible change in his demeanour once she said that to him. He left and sent her a text in Turkish: "You were my last breath, but I'm not shit. You've burnt my heart."'

Meredith went on: 'That is a window, it seems, into the way he was feeling at that point in time and he instructs, Your Honour, that he felt overwhelmed, that he felt like crying, that he felt worthless.'

After that disappointment, Acar drove to a bottle shop and bought a six-pack of Scotch and Coke, which he guzzled down. He smoked some dope. Cut himself with his knife. Relatives had to drag him home before he instigated an ugly confrontation with cops at the Broadmeadows police station. Meredith again: 'He felt that the best thing for him was either to get himself locked up or get himself shot by the police.' That night he stayed in his younger brother's garage. In the early hours of 17 November Acar went to work but did little on site that day. That afternoon he bought some grog and cut himself again. He travelled to Fawkner Cemetery and sat by his grandmother's gravesite, as well as that of a fallen friend.

'He says he was crying,' Meredith told the Supreme Court. 'Was speaking to his grandmother and his friend. He got more to drink.'

That afternoon, at around one o'clock, Acar sent Rachelle a text: 'RIP Ramazan Kerem Acar 1987–2010'. It was to be the first of a barrage. At 2.02 pm he sent another: 'U wanted 2 convert ma kid. Do it. U wanted 2 lock me up. I did it. U wanted 2 b independent. Do it. U wana take full custdy. Do it. U wana 2 kill me. I'll do it. Wat eva makes u happy.' About an hour and a half later, Acar was seen driving erratically along the Monash Freeway near the Heatherton Road exit, which was only a couple of kilometres from Rachelle's home. He was abusive to other drivers. He fired off his next text at 3.37 pm: 'Can I talk 2 mim.'

Rachelle was obviously concerned about the tone of Acar's messages. She responded via text, explaining that Yazmina was at creche and that she would be arriving home in about twenty minutes. At the same time, Acar texted: 'Hurry I need 2 talk 2 u plz babe.'

Rachelle pulled into her driveway at 4.15 pm. Acar was parked out the front.

'He had a Toyota Hilux, like a 4WD—an old one all battered and bashed,' Rachelle explained to police. 'Ramzy was sitting in the driver's seat.'

She asked, 'What are you doing here?'

Acar replied, 'I'm just here to see Mimi.'

Rachelle noticed a large knife in his lap.

'It was about thirty centimetres long. It was thick and it had like a sharp pointy end along one side of it. Along the blade it had holes in it.'

Rachelle asked him why he had it.

Acar replied, 'I've had enough of life.'

Flaunting the blade and with superficial cuts on his arms, Acar told Rachelle that he didn't 'have the guts to do it'. He said he wanted to see his daughter. It appeared that he had been drinking. Rachelle and her friend left and picked Yazmina up from the creche. At 4.40 pm, Acar sent Rachelle another text, asking where she was. She responded by telling him that she was on her way back. Upon their arrival home, Yazmina appeared elated to see her dad, running towards him yelling, 'Bubba! Bubba!' (her nickname for her father).

'My kid ran up … she ran to my car with a big smile,' Acar would later tell detectives. 'She was happy to see me, and I put her in my car and she was playing in my car and she was just scribbling with pens and stuff … with mum standing next to the car just watching over us 'coz I don't think she trusted me.'

At about 6.15 pm a friend of Rachelle's—a woman by the name of Sonia-Rita Mardirossian—arrived at the home. Rachelle told Acar that his time with Yazmina was up. He asked if he could take Yazmina for a quick spin down the shops to buy her a chocolate—a Kinder Surprise to be exact.

The nearest milk bar was about a minute away by car from Rachelle's house.

'Do you trust me?' Acar asked Rachelle.

'Yeah,' she replied.

'I wouldn't take her away from you like you took her from me,' Acar said.

This moment will no doubt haunt Rachelle D'Argent for the rest of her life—the moment she allowed Acar to drive off with their daughter. She was acting in good faith.

'She had stars in her eyes when she ran up to him,' Rachelle told police of her daughter.

That's why I let her go with him. I did it for Mimi. He made a point of saying he would bring her straight back and even offered for me to keep hold of his phone while they were away. I told him to take his phone in case of an emergency and once they had been to the milk bar, to bring Mimi straight back. I think every child deserves to have their mum and their dad. During Mimi's whole life, Ramzy had never been violent at all towards her. He got frustrated with her crying and took it out on me, but was never aggressive to her.

That evening outside her home was the last time Rachelle would see her darling little daughter alive— although she would get to speak to her over the phone.

In her victim impact statement, Rachelle would later ask: 'How do I even begin to write about the horror of losing my child: someone more precious to me than life itself?'

Acar told detectives he was surprised that Rachelle allowed him to drive off with their daughter.

'All she had to do was call the cops and like, nothing would have happened—fucking idiot,' he said in his police record of interview.

The night before this I was going to hand myself into the cops 'coz I was cutting myself. I was just fed up, man: just fed up with everything. Nothing goes my way. I didn't know why she let me go.

He would also admit to the fact that the promise of a chocolate was a lie.

I really wanted to take my kid with me. I just wanted
to take her … I asked Rachelle 'Do you want anything
from the shops?' just to make her believe me, so she
thinks I'm really going there 'coz I'm not—so she
thinks that I'm not lying.

Nearing 6.30 pm, Acar told Rachelle over the phone
that their daughter had asked for McDonald's and that he
had taken her to the Fountain Gate restaurant.

'Get the food and bring her back,' Rachelle ordered.

'Yeah, no worries,' Acar replied calmly. 'We'll be back
soon. We're just grabbing the Maccas.'

A short time later, Rachelle rang Acar from
Mardirossian's phone. Mardirossian took the phone and
warned Acar that the police would be alerted if he did not
bring Yazmina back. Acar told her where to go, and hung
up. At 6.50 pm Rachelle rang back. Acar said: 'How does
it feel not to have your child when I did not have mine
for three months?' He then pretended he was joking and
promised to bring Yazmina home.

'Ramzy, stop joking around,' Rachelle pleaded. 'Just
bring her back man.'

There was still no sign of them by 7 pm. Rachelle,
panicking now, rang back. Using his daughter as
collateral, Acar demanded she go to the Narre Warren
police station and withdraw previous statements she had
made against him.

Justice Curtain: 'This she refused to do, and you told
her that you would do her no favours.' Infuriated, Acar
hung up in Rachelle's ear. Rachelle called back some
fifteen minutes later. Acar told her: 'Payback's a bitch.
How does it feel?' Rachelle begged for Yazmina's return.

Acar replied: 'Guess what baby, you're not getting her
back. I loved you Rachelle and look what you've made me

do.' Holding all the power, Acar gave her two options—he could kill their daughter by driving at high speed into on-coming traffic or cut her throat with his knife. Acar told her: 'I loved you more than her and that's why I'm doing this.'

What had become an apparent kidnapping was reported to police. In the meantime, Acar was upping the ante on his Facebook page. 'Bout 2 kill ma kid,' he posted. He then sent a text to Rachelle: 'It's ova I did it'. Two minutes later Acar was back on Facebook: 'Pay bk u slut'.

A distraught Rachelle responded with a desperate text: 'Ramzy please just bring Yazmina back. We can work things out, just bring our daughter back.'

At 8.21 pm, in the presence of a police officer, Rachelle rang Acar. Acar said: 'I'm going to kill her.' Rachelle pleaded with him. Acar replied: 'It's too late, I'm going to do it. I'm going to do it. Do you have any last words for her?' As a cruel taunting gesture he put Yazmina on the phone to speak to her mum.

'I love you,' the little girl said.

'I love you too,' Rachelle replied.

They were the last words ever exchanged between mother and daughter.

After more communication via Facebook, Acar spoke to Rachelle over the phone for more than eight minutes. During the conversation he confirmed that he had murdered his daughter.

'I've killed her,' he said. 'She's just lying there next to me in her leggings, her top covered in blood, and her guts are hanging out.'

A disbelieving Rachelle told him not to be stupid, and pleaded with him to tell her where Yazmina was.

'It doesn't matter any more,' he said.

All I need to know is should I dump the body somewhere and how much time do you think I'm going to get for this? I killed my daughter man, I killed her. I killed her to get back at you. I don't care. Even if I go behind bars I know that you are suffering. I've killed her. I swear to God I killed her. You know those shows on Foxtel that you watch on the crime channel with the psycho people? I feel like one of them now.

By that stage, Acar was at his parents' Meadow Heights home, where he stayed in his car. After an argument with a relative, he drove off. His newest flame, Talia, had been apprised of the situation and joined the text fest, asking Acar about Yazmina's location. 'Dead,' he said in a reply text.

Acar met up with Talia at the Campbellfield McDonald's store around 10 pm. He confirmed that his daughter was dead before trying to change his story. Prosecutor Peter Rose told the Supreme Court:

Acar told [Talia] that he'd done something and he couldn't leave his vehicle where they were, and he told her to follow him. They drove in convoy to the Merri Creek Concourse at Campbellfield. This is an area of light industrial premises. Whilst [Talia] remained in her vehicle, the prisoner set fire to his own vehicle.

Acar then told Talia to drive him away. At 10.24 pm, Acar rang his mother, repeating 'It's all over. It's finished.' When asked about Yazmina's whereabouts, he said: 'She's in safe hands.' His mother begged him to return his daughter home.

Sixteen minutes later, Acar sent another text to Rachelle. 'I h8t u.' He then rang her and told her he was going to hand himself in at the Broadmeadows police station. He told a petrified Rachelle that Yazmina was in heaven.

'You've got a copper sitting right next to you, don't you?' Acar then said knowingly. 'Say hello to the copper.'

Texts to Rachelle then followed. 'She's in heaven I feel lyk shit.'

At 11.20 pm, he posted on his Facebook page, 'I lv u mimi'.

Special Operations Group police intercepted Talia's car with Acar on board at about 11.30 pm. (Talia, who told police she believed Acar was just seeking attention, would not be charged with any crime.) Detective Sergeant David Butler asked Acar if he knew why police had arrested him. He replied that he did.

> **BUTLER**: Why do you think that is?
> **ACAR**: Because I've done something really bad.
> **BUTLER**: What do you mean by that?
> **ACAR**: I killed my daughter.

He told police he'd dumped Yazmina's body at Shannon Rise at Greenvale, near a display home. On the way to locate the body, Acar told police he had stabbed the toddler multiple times in Providence Road, Greenvale, not far from the airport. He said he had dumped her around 8 pm, 'when the sun was going down', and that he had thrown the knife away at a different place. As police searched for Yazmina, with the help of their Alsatians, Acar was left sitting in the back seat of a canine unit vehicle, one police dog barking in the cage. Weeping and babbling, Acar turned to a young police constable.

'Just put me in a room to rot,' Acar said. 'That dog's psycho, you should put me in there with him. I deserve a belting. Can you give me a belting? Can you guys give me a hiding please. I want to die now.'

And then he changed his tune. 'No,' he muttered. 'I want to live so I could suffer the pain for it. Ah, this is scary. What the fuck did I do? Why?'

He went on to ask the constable: 'Am I going to be on the news? My face and all?'

Acar then expressed concerns for his own safety in jail.

ACAR: Is this murder?

CONSTABLE: What do you think?

ACAR: Yes, but I was drunk when it happened. I can't believe it … How long do you think I'll get? Do you reckon it may be life?

According to Justice Curtain: 'This was the beginning of the realisation of the enormity of what you had done.'

It was 1.37 am on Thursday, 18 November, when police found Yazmina Micheline Acar's tiny stabbed body dumped in scrubland at the Greenvale Reservoir Reserve. The little girl had been six days short of her third birthday.

Prosecutor Rose:

She was lying on her right side, fully clothed, with multiple stab wounds to her chest and abdomen, which had exposed her organs … A number of crime scenes were established and eventually a large 'fantasy' style knife was located in the scrub.

Rachelle: 'I will never forget the night sitting at the police station and receiving the news of my daughter's passing. My ears went blocked, I could barely see nor breathe, and my whole body went numb.'

A forensic medical officer deemed Acar unfit for interview and he was allowed to sleep for six hours. During his eventual record of interview, he told investigators he had thrown the knife away to try to hide it because he was embarrassed by the size of the blade compared to the size of his little girl.

'I just got it and threw it,' he stated. 'I didn't want youse to see it because the size of the knife and the size of my daughter: the knife's bigger than her. It's a fucking embarrassment.'

He remarked that he'd wanted to kill himself but didn't 'have the balls' to do it. He also spoke of Rachelle. 'She took that kid away from me and I went through hell, man,' he bleated. 'She won't understand what I went through like I wanted her to feel it.'

Rachelle's world had spiralled into despair.

> After the news of Mimi's death the next five days were hell. Not only did I barely know any details of what had happened, but every time I switched on the news, horrific headlines would appear and the story would come on and I stared in disbelief that that was my child.

Two days before Yazmina's third birthday her mother, grandmother, and two hundred relatives and friends congregated where the toddler had been dumped. Those gathered released pink balloons and sang 'Happy Birthday'.

'She is still with us,' a resolute Rachelle told the media. 'She was looking forward to her Dora [the Explorer] cake and to her balloons—and she got it. She would have wanted us to be smiling and dancing because that is what she would have been doing.'

Four days later, Rachelle stood outside the Our Lady of Help Christians Catholic Church in Narre Warren, hugging a framed photo of her dead daughter and the little girl's favourite teddy bear. Father John Allen had told those present that Yazmina's death was a 'tragedy beyond comprehension'. A family friend told the service that Mimi was no doubt laughing and dancing in heaven, and probably bossing the angels around, as well.

After he was charged with murder, and before he was to plead guilty, Acar spent the majority of his time at the Metropolitan Remand Centre where he was classified as a protection prisoner. As media coverage of his crime intensified, so too did the heat in jail. Defence barrister Meredith explained:

Apparently there is a box within the unit whereby prisoners can put request forms to see different people, and so on. His picture had been cut out from the newspaper, and it had in effect written on it that the dog was to be taken out of the unit. There was a reference to one of his texts about pay back being a bitch and in effect the view was taken by him, and presumably by the prison authorities, that his life was in jeopardy and he couldn't remain there.

For his own safety, the child killer was transferred to Port Phillip Prison where, at the time of his Supreme Court plea hearing in June 2011, he was housed in special protection.

'He finds his position within the prison very difficult, given that there has been the degree of media coverage,' Meredith told the plea hearing.

Given what occurred at the other unit, [he] feels effectively that he is a marked man within the system and so, to that extent, presents as being concerned, fearful, worrying about what ultimately might happen to him within the prison setting and … in combination with him ruminating over what he's done … he is finding the going pretty tough.

Meredith told the hearing that Acar had engraved tear drops on the skin under his eyes whilst in prison as some form of self-punishment: prison-style self-flagellation.

'He felt it was appropriate that he should carry [them] for the rest of his life as some form of remorse and repentance for what he had done,' Meredith told Justice Curtain.

CURTAIN: What, he's had tear drops tattooed under his eyes?
MEREDITH: He got the phosphorous end of match sticks and set about engraving those shapes under his eyes … He also on his stomach has engraved by the same method the initials of his daughter.

A brave Rachelle D'Argent read her own victim impact statement to the court during Acar's plea hearing. Unlike others who had gone before her in different murder cases, she managed to read it in its entirety before breaking down. Sometimes, understandably, grieving relatives find the task of voicing their impact statements too traumatic an experience.

'My name is Rachelle D'Argent, and I am the mother of Yazmina—Mimi—D'Argent,' she began.

I was horrified the night that I found out my one and only daughter Mimi had been taken away from me, neither for a few minutes nor a few hours—but for life ... Since Mimi's death I have felt so many emotions. The first few weeks I cried every day. I yelled and I screamed, begging everyone to please bring her back to me. Then it turned to frustration. I realised that all the crying and shouting in the world could never bring my Mimi back to me.

She finished:

I will never be able to take her for a first haircut, for a first day of school or having her lose her first tooth—so many firsts that I have been robbed of. Yazmina Micheline D'Argent will always be my daughter, my love, my life, my everything and even though I can't see her, I know she's watching over me every day and giving me strength and courage to get through everything. It was always and always will be mummy and Mimi for life.

Rachelle's mother Micheline D'Argent—Yazmina's maternal grandmother—wanted her impact statement read out on her behalf. She had written:

Yazmina was my life. I miss her so much ... We spent so much time together as she was always at my house. Since her birth, I used to sing a French song for her every night and by the age of two she was singing the song by heart. Rachelle recorded it for me and I always listen to it and that breaks my heart.
I have her pictures everywhere in my house and I'll talk to her all the time pretending she's around me ... I can't cope. I have visions of her all the time ... Now I hate this house. I'm so hurt. I can see her in every

corner. I will say my life is over, but I have to be strong for my daughter Rachelle.

Micheline said she spent an hour every week sitting at Yazmina's grave.

'I talk to her and always bring a little toy for her,' she wrote.

Acar had told consultant psychiatrist Dr Danny Sullivan that when he decided to kill Yazmina, she was outside the car playing. He described the murder as a slow-motion event, remembered a feeling of rage and noted a worried look in his daughter's eyes.

Sullivan told the plea hearing that he believed anger played a significant part in the murder. 'I think that his inability to find more constructive ways of manifesting his anger or of addressing his anger were germane to the offence,' Sullivan said, as if that was some sort of revelation.

Rose cross-examined Sullivan, confirming Acar was not hiding behind mental impairment or psychosis an excuse.

ROSE: Dr Sullivan, do you say that this man had no sign of significant cognitive impairment?
SULLIVAN: Yes, that's correct.
ROSE: And there was no indication of psychotic illness or psychotic symptoms apparent at the time of the offence?
SULLIVAN: Yes, that's correct.
ROSE: And this man was capable of understanding that to stab his child multiple times was wrong?
SULLIVAN: Yes.
ROSE: His situation was that he was consumed, was he not, with a hatred for his ex-partner?

SULLIVAN: Yes, it would appear so.

ROSE: And that he was consumed with hatred for his ex-partner and sought to punish her—all of those are statements you made?

SULLIVAN: Yes.

ROSE: And that's the overwhelming picture here, isn't it—a man who had just become so consumed with punishing his ex-partner that everything else falls by the wayside.

SULLIVAN: Yes, that's my perception.

In his final submission, Rose told Justice Curtain:

This was an angry young man who was consumed by hatred for his former partner and who wanted to punish her and that, all consuming, has overtaken any thought for the welfare of his child and we say this is quite horrific. This is the man who is the father of the child, who is charged with the responsibility of looking after that child, and we say this is one of the most horrific type of killings you can have … And [then there is] his description of the worried look of the child: the fact that the child is playing and then he comes out of the car with a knife … He has got to understand the consequences of his actions and the horrific consequences that they are.

Meredith asked for a minimum term, citing his client's young age, early plea and remorse.

Curtain questioned the issue of remorse. 'You'd be hard pressed, really, to find any remorse in [his] record of interview,' Her Honour stated.

Meredith also mentioned this as a sentencing factor: 'At lockdown of a night he finds it very difficult because that's

when his thoughts go to what he's done and indicates that
the hours are very long throughout the passage of the
nights when he's in his cell.' (As if that wasn't the aim of
jail time.)

Curtain made mention of several matters. Of Acar
allowing Yazmina to speak to her distraught mother on
the telephone, Her Honour said:

> It is a callous and ruthless act—ruthless is probably
> not the right word for it—but it certainly bespeaks
> that he really at that time really understood the nature
> of what he was doing in that he knew not only was he
> about to kill his daughter but that this was the last
> time the child's mother was ever able to speak to her.
> It shows a callousness. It is quite breathtaking, really.

She also made mention of the fact Acar was serving a
suspended sentence for assaulting Rachelle at the time
of the killing, saying 'That effected no deterrence upon
him.'

Curtain sentenced Acar to life in jail with a thirty-
three-year minimum term.

'I am satisfied that what was impairing your judgment
at the time was your hatred and your desire for revenge
in the context of you having consumed alcohol,' Curtain
said.

> Certainly I accept the evidence that you are an
> immature young man with very fixed views. You
> have had problems with anger and, indeed, you seek
> emotional release from self harming and I accept
> that in the days leading up to this offence you had
> been drinking heavily, at times smoking cannabis, and
> appeared to be suffering a degree of emotional turmoil.

Curtain agreed that Yazmina's death was a 'chilling and horrific murder'.

'More than that,' she said,

> the victim was your infant daughter and she was killed by the one man in the world whose duty it was to love, nurture and protect her. As such, your conduct was a fundamental breach of the trust that reposes between parent and child; a fundamental breach of a parent's most fundamental obligation. Further, you committed this murder for the worst possible motives: revenge and spite. You killed your daughter to get back at her mother. You used your daughter, an innocent victim, as the instrument of your overarching desire to inflict pain on your former partner.

Acar sought leave to appeal against the length of his sentence, on the grounds both the head sentence and minimum term were manifestly excessive. His application was refused.

'This was a brutal and callous murder which, in my view, should be characterised as one of the worst cases of its kind,' Justice Mark Weinberg said in his Court of Appeal judgment. 'It was aggravated by the applicant's behaviour towards Ms D'Argent, which was both cruel and sadistic.'

Outside court after the judgment, a relieved Rachelle said justice had been seen to be done. Her victim impact statement said it all.

> There is not a day that goes by where I don't think of my daughter and wish she was still here by my side. I miss her face, I miss her smile, I miss her voice, I miss her laugh, I miss her smell, I miss her hair, I miss

her cheekiness, I miss her getting ready for childcare, I miss giving her a bath, I miss singing and dancing with her, I miss her lying next to me at night and her playing with my fingers so she could fall asleep. But most importantly I miss her running up to me and jumping into my arms and hugging me while she tells me that she loves me.

While Yazmina's grandmother, Micheline, was not there for the ruling, the last words of her victim impact statement hung in the minds of all.

'My last dream of her?' Micheline had written. 'She was crying and told me, "Grandma … I'm so cold. Come and get me."'

4
Slaughter House

'I was trying to picture it as like just the life has gone. She's dead … Work on it like a piece of meat. Make the cuts. Separate the joints.'

FORMER VICTORIA POLICE HOMICIDE SQUAD DETECTIVE Andrea Turner is not a religious woman. Doesn't believe in angels. Or spirits or the supernatural. But strange events that occurred at a house on Phillip Island in which a young woman was strangled and painstakingly dismembered still send a shiver down her spine. Turner, an experienced Victorian cold-case murder and homicide investigator, was no stranger to kill scenes by 2009: whether they were bathed in gore or had been cleaned to some extent by killers. But 'the creepy, creepy little house', as she calls it, where innocent victim Raechel Betts met her awful demise will be etched in Turner's mind forever.

Turner was part of Homicide's Crew Two investigating the Betts disappearance-cum-murder. Fine work led investigators to the killer—a depraved Svengali-style drug dealer named John Leslie Coombes. He had murdered twice before. Turner remembers Coombes as simply 'a creep': a suspect who had a habit of flicking his tongue at a female detective. But Turner's most vivid memories of that particular investigation centre on the slaughterhouse where Coombes sadistically reduced Raechel to garbage-bag fill. It was Melbourne Cup Eve—the night of the annual Homicide Squad social function in the city—when Turner was processing the house with a male crime scene examiner and a female crime scene trainee. Turner would have much preferred to have been at the squad party. The Phillip Island house belonged to one of Coombes's playthings, a naïve interstater named Nicole Godfrey. Coombes had brought Raechel back to the house, strangled her in a bedroom and spent a night and a day cutting and pulling her body apart in a bathtub before disposing of it. Turner recalled Godfrey's pet rabbit and Staffordshire terrier. During the crime scene examination, Turner said, the rabbit was 'going crazy' in its indoor cage and the dog, with swollen eyes, seemed to stare at them through a back window. And then the power cut out, the impromptu blackout plunging the house into darkness while every other home in the street remained lit. Some twenty seconds later the lights flickered back to life and with them a music track on the CD player. Turner turned off the music.

'We looked at each other and thought, "Shit, that was a bit freaky,"' Turner recalled.

Fifteen minutes later the power died again. Darkness. An eerie silence. Turner felt some sort of presence.

'The rabbit was going crazy.'

The lights came to life again—and so did the music. The same music. Again Turner turned it off. Ten minutes later the power died again. The rest of the street remained lit. And then the lights came back to life, along with that music.

'I don't know what it was but I still remember the music,' Turner admitted. 'In all my years of policing it was the most bizarre thing I'd experienced. The house was horrible. There's no question in my mind that Raechel was there while we were there that night. I just can't explain it.'

Raechel Renee Betts was born on 5 January 1982. In her teenage years she left her mother Sandra's home in Lismore, New South Wales, and moved in with her grandparents, Neville and Doreen Betts, in the Melbourne suburb of Ivanhoe. After high school she completed a Bachelor of Education at RMIT.

As a young woman engaged to be married, Raechel Betts was told she would have extreme difficulty bearing children. That news hit her hard, and left her bitterly disappointed.

'She wished to have her own children but was worried her troubles with polycystic ovarian syndrome and cervical dysplasia would prevent this,' Sandra Betts said in her victim impact statement.

As a substitute, Raechel channeled her energies towards other people's children. She became a qualified school teacher and earned additional early learning qualifications. Up until the end of 2008 she worked at a childcare centre and oversaw an after-school program.

'Raechel could have earned a much higher wage as a teacher in primary or high schools,' Sandra wrote in her impact statement, which she recited in full in the Victorian Supreme Court. 'She chose to work in early childhood education because she loved the rewarding affection and loyalty that little children would show her. Raechel kept every picture, letter, card and note given to her by any child.'

Raechel also took on the role of primary carer of two teenage girls—whom we shall call Kylie and Kate. The two teens came to Raechel 'with troubles', according to Sandra Betts.

'These two young friends had been expelled from their school and had family problems,' Sandra said in her statement.

> Raechel got them back into schooling and helped them study. She arranged dental appointments for them, fed them and clothed them. She ensured they continued their sports activities, organised their birthday parties and drove them to school. One of the girls began to improve so well at school that she was put up a year level.

Raechel, who also sponsored a child through World Vision, was described as a mother-figure to Kylie and Kate. With their parents' permission, the teens moved into a home in the middle-class suburb of Heidelberg with Raechel and another woman. By that stage Raechel's engagement had ended and, for reasons only known to Raechel, she waded into the world of drug dealing. At first she was a small-time dealer but later moved bigger quantities. The murky realm consumed her and by the end of 2008, Raechel had quit her cherished childcare job to traffic methylamphetamine, ecstasy, cannabis and other illicit drugs. By February 2009, Raechel and the teenage girls had moved to a house in Doncaster East. According to a Supreme Court judge, Raechel sold drugs from that address with a bloke she was having sex with.

'I thought she was very interesting,' that male friend, whom we shall call Vince, said in a police statement. 'She liked drums. She liked music. She liked cars. She was like a female version of me … I know she liked fishing. Her Facebook site has lots of photos of her fishing with the girls.'

Vince had a long-term girlfriend during the time he was sleeping with Raechel. He was a drug user, but denied to police that he ever sold drugs.

'I tried some of Raechel's ice at one stage,' he told police.

> Raechel was using marijuana flat out at that stage and she was into pills, maybe a little bit of ice. She kept telling stories about people who were selling cocaine, who had gone missing. It was like an episode of *The Sopranos*. She would message me things that didn't make any sense.

One of Raechel's suppliers was John Coombes, a paroled double killer by that stage. He had an ability to charm younger, impressionable people.

'I knew that Raechel knew John previously,' Vince said in his police statement. 'Raechel had told me that her dad knew John from when they were in the army together. I didn't know if this story was true.'

According to Sandra Betts, Coombes 'recruited' her daughter at a vulnerable time in her life. 'She was under financial duress, supporting and assisting two young women and having to quit one job due to fatigue and losing the other,' Sandra wrote in her impact statement. 'She was suffering emotional stress since the ending of her relationship with her fiancé and the loss [on medical advice] of the child she wished to have.'

John Leslie Coombes was a sadistic killer. He was into mutilation and disintegration. He liked to see his victims end in pieces.

Coombes was born on 14 September 1954; his mother abandoned him and his infant twin brother in a boarding house. After his brother was adopted, according to prison psychology reports, Coombes's father returned from overseas to claim him. His father remarried and moved the family to inner-city Richmond. According to reports, that marriage failed and Coombes's father moved himself and the boy to the idyllic bayside suburb of Edithvale. But things were not so idyllic. Coombes did not get along with his dad's new partner.

'Mr Coombes reported that he had significant problems with that lady, indicating that she was an aggressive and evil lady whom he hated,' the prison psychiatrist wrote.

That woman killed herself when Coombes was seven. He practically celebrated the death.

He left school after Year 10 at age fifteen and joined the army three years later after a failed apprenticeship as a mechanic. He served as an army truck driver in the Royal Australian Corps of Transport until age twenty-one. According to his story, he was discharged in 1974 after sustaining a head injury in a trucking accident. He had married at the age of twenty and had two children. He worked numerous jobs over the following years, including as a chef and hotel manager in Sydney. He was an avid fisherman.

At home, he was violent towards his wife and kids. Sandra Coombes was sometimes taken to hospital with fractured bones.

'Our marriage was not a happy one,' she once told detectives. 'John would also threaten that if I left him he would find us and he would kill the children in front of me and then he would kill me.'

Coombes's first murder victim was a man named Michael Peter Speirani. He killed Speirani on 26 February 1984.

Coombes and a mate of his took Speirani, aged twenty, out on a fishing boat with a plan to bash him and throw him overboard because he was dating the mate's sister. Supreme Court judge Justice Geoffrey Nettle said:

> According to a version ... which you gave to prison authorities in 2004 when you were seeking parole, you killed Speirani because he had sodomised [your friend's] 15-year-old sister. In any event, the plea ... was that, after you had thrown Speirani overboard you would then pick him up and rescue him and warn him to stay away [from the girl].

But, while out on the boat, Coombes lost control and stabbed Speirani to death. After throwing the body into the water he then took pleasure in driving the boat's propeller into Speirani to mutilate him. The remains would never be found.

'John said they had run over Michael with the propeller and that they had dragged his body to the side of the boat and that John had sliced Michael up a bit so that the fish could finish the job,' Sandra Coombes told police investigators at the time.

Coombes made his wife clean the boat the next day.

'I felt sick and scared,' Sandra Coombes told police. 'I saw there was dried blood on the gunnel rails. There were splotches everywhere but the majority of the blood was on the starboard side and there was also a handprint in blood on the rear wash wall.'

Nine months after murdering Speirani, on 17 November 1984, Coombes killed forty-four-year-old Henry Desmond Kells. Coombes and a friend held a grudge against Kells because he had been drinking with the friend's landlady.

Coombes and his pal drank heavily before travelling to Kells's bungalow to bash him. Coombes again lost self-control, stabbing Kells multiple times and mutilating him. In 1985, Justice Barry Beach sentenced Coombes to life imprisonment without parole for the sadistic Kells killing. Three years later, at the age of thirty-four, Coombes and another prisoner—a convicted double killer—escaped from Ararat Prison by placing a water pipe across the inner and outer security fences and crawling to freedom. The pair managed to elude a dragnet, and were found three days later armed and hiding out on a goods train near Mildura. Coombes was returned to Pentridge Prison rather than the less-secure Ararat jail.

In April 1990, Coombes applied for a minimum term on the Desmond Kells murder sentence. A psychiatrist found that a head injury Coombes had received in the military truck crash back in 1974 caused a traumatic nervous condition that in turn triggered aggression. That aggression, combined with drugs and alcohol, according to the psychologist, led to Coombes's murderous actions. A senior corrections officer stated in a report: 'In spite of his offence, which did not seem to be premeditated, he does not seem to pose a substantial threat to the community.'

Hearing the application, Justice Beach considered as a mitigating factor the fact that Coombes was a heavy drinker and hardcore prescription drug user at the time he killed Kells. 'I think it would be fair to say that at the time Kells met his death, the applicant was not in a normal and rational frame of mind.'

The judge—who at that stage was unaware that Coombes had already committed murder—also cited Coombes's 'disturbed' life as a youngster and his marriage break-up as other mitigating factors. He fixed a minimum term of eleven years. Coombes was released on parole in October 1996.

Two months later he was arrested and charged with the 26 February 1984 murder of Michael Speirani, thanks to fresh information provided to police. In 1998 Justice Bernard Teague had a chance to jail the evil Coombes for good, but instead handed him a fifteen-year maximum term with a ten-year minimum. While Teague agreed that the two murders were 'high in the scale of what is horrifying and abhorrent', he decided that they 'lacked the chilling, cold-blooded premeditated elements of the most abhorrent'. Teague was told that Coombes's prospects of rehabilitation were good and, like Justice Beach before him, found that Coombes's moral culpability was reduced by his mental condition.

'There is also other evidence which suggests that what you did [to Speirani] in 1984 was to some degree the product of alcoholism and other health problems no longer pressing and, more significantly, that there are clear indications of your having been rehabilitated,' Teague said.

> Put shortly, the evidence indicates that the period of imprisonment between 1988 and 1996 has had a strongly maturing and stabilising effect upon you. You had only a limited period on parole from November 1996 but the indications during that period were favourable ... Although I do not propose to go into the details, I would also note that I have had regard to other matters affecting your position as at February 1984, including your difficult upbringing, your chequered employment history, the head injuries suffered in a 1974 motor vehicle collision and your alcoholism.

Unfortunately for Raechel Betts, Coombes walked from jail on parole in early 2007. He weaseled his way into the drug scene and established himself as a supplier. Due to his corpulent figure, florid cheeks and white beard, he became known around the traps as 'Santa'. He started seeing an older woman, although her daughter took an immediate dislike to him. For Coombes, it seems, women were his playthings.

'There is some suggestion that you sought to persuade Raechel Betts to become your mistress, too, although there is insufficient evidence of that for me to conclude it was so,' Justice Nettle would later say.

Coombes moved into a public housing flat in Preston upon becoming eligible. While there, he started up a cottage drug industry.

'Coombes had many customers attend this address to either collect drugs to distribute or drop off drugs to be distributed,' the police summary stated. 'Coombes also had the users attend to make purchases.'

In April 2009, while living in Doncaster East, Raechel asked a platonic male friend, David Gould, if he could get her some 'hardware'. Gould knew she meant a pistol.

'I know weapons very well as I was in the navy reserve cadets,' Gould said in his police statement.

> She told me that she needed guns for protection. I told her that I don't deal with anyone who deals in firearms. She wouldn't tell me any more as to why she needed protection. She was a bit flighty but not scared.

Raechel started making claims that she, Kylie and Kate had been burgled, drugged and sexually assaulted.

She claimed their food had been tampered with and the sexual assaults filmed and posted on certain websites.

'Raechel called me and was hysterical and crying,' Gould stated. 'There was self loathing and fear … They felt that nowhere was safe and that they were being followed.'

Gould took Raechel and the teenage girls in and collected a sample of the supposedly laced food. Gould's wife took Raechel and the teenagers to a local medical centre for examination. Fearing Raechel was possibly suicidal, based on a letter she had written, her grandfather, Neville Betts, contacted a Crisis Assessment Team. They detained Raechel on 11 June 2009 under the provisions of the *Mental Health Act* and involuntarily admitted her to the Northern Hospital as a patient suffering drug-induced psychosis. The food that Raechel claimed was laced was tested and found to be normal. No images of her or the teenagers could be found on any suggested websites.

Raechel was discharged on 18 June into the care of her mother. After holding a party at her mum's home—which Sandra closed down due to drug use—Raechel and the teenagers moved in with Kate's mother in a north-western suburb. On 10 August, Raechel spent the night with an old school friend named Donteaba Gunn, who later said Raechel acted strangely. The next day Raechel took a call from a man she called John. Raechel told Gunn that John said he had a 'surprise' for her. Raechel told Kylie that she was going fishing with John.

'[Kylie] took that to be code for going away to do "drug business",' Justice Nettle would say.

In her police statement, Kylie said:

She told me that she was going away with John but she didn't really want to go. She seemed a bit fed up. She was getting fed up with the way John had been treating her. She felt like she was previously the favourite drug runner for John but now, because she couldn't off load as much product for him, she felt like a failure. She believed that John wasn't happy with her. She believed that she would be replaced ... I got the impression that Raechel may have been right and that John didn't think as much of her towards the end.

There was also the suggestion that Coombes wanted to pull Raechel on as a mistress.

Kylie recalled a list Raechel once showed her. It consisted of three names: names of people Raechel was said to have not liked very much. According to one of Kylie's police statements, one was a bloke Raechel described as 'creepy'. He was said to carry child pornography on a laptop computer and alleged to have stolen drugs from Raechel. ('He never hurt me in any way,' Kylie said.)

The second name on the list was that of a woman who was said to have smoked ice in crack pipes in front of her small boy, and made wild accusations about her boyfriend locking her and the child up, and also urinating on them. That woman was also said to have shot up heroin at Raechel's house, only to later deny doing so. 'Raechel was offended by that,' Kylie stated. 'She hated heroin users.'

The third name was that of a man who was said to have made sexual advances towards Raechel and the two young teenagers.

'Raechel told me that she wanted [those three] to be sorted out,' Kylie said in the police statement. 'She told me she'd given a list of names to John Coombes. I can't remember the exact conversation in relation to the list but I was under the impression that she had asked him to sort out these people for her.'

Kylie said she was shocked by a conversation she overheard in which Coombes explained to Raechel different ways to dispose of bodies. Kylie said she was 'gobsmacked'.

> They talked about dismembering bodies. They talked about popping out limbs and then using fish wire to cut the skin right open. They discussed how to dispose of bodies as well. I was just gobsmacked as to how they could think of such things to do to a human body ... One thing they talked about was putting say an arm into a container full of something like acid, which kills all forms of DNA. John mentioned this. He talked about meat grinders and using them to dispose of bodies. He talked about cutting off fingers and then cauterising the hand so it doesn't bleed out.

Sandra Betts had pleaded with her daughter to leave Coombes and her other northern-suburbs associates behind. Sandra's gut told her they were bad news. It seems Raechel may have felt the same and had decided to leave their circle.

'Raechel had sought the assistance of a financial advisor with Anglicare to have her superannuation released so that she could pay off debts, particularly to John Coombes, and probably then leave Melbourne,' Sandra Betts explained in her victim statement.

> She had plans to go to Queensland where her father had bought a property, to work in Queensland at a school or childcare centre. She had also discussed with me her plans to do a course in business management. This qualification would have put her in an excellent

position to run childcare centres, rather than just work in them as an employee—a career move that I was encouraging her to take.

She was only days away from being free of any association with John Leslie Coombes and others she was worried about being associated with. She was very close to implementing her plans to get back on a successful path with her career and life—away from danger.

I had advised Raechel to not have any contact, even by phone, with anyone associated with drugs or debts and to keep quiet about her whereabouts … I especially believed it was not safe for her in Melbourne's north and told her to come home to my house where I believed she would be safe. My last words to her were, 'Please come home. You are not safe in that part of Melbourne … Please come home. You are not safe over there. I love you.'

On the afternoon of Tuesday, 11 August 2009, Raechel Betts packed a bag and told Kylie and Kate that she would be back in forty-eight hours after the 'fishing' expedition with Coombes. That was the last time the teenagers saw Raechel. It was about 6 pm when Betts met with Coombes, as planned. Strangely, she left her wallet in her car before she climbed into his Nissan Pulsar sedan. He drove her to a house at Wimbledon Heights on Phillip Island— some 140 kilometres south of Melbourne. It was a three-bedroom weatherboard rented by a woman by the name of Nicole Godfrey. In her twenties, Godfrey was another of Coombes's acolytes. Born in Queensland, she had moved to Melbourne some time between 2003 and 2006.

'Your life appears to have been rather aimless,' Justice Paul Coghlan would say when dealing with her in the Supreme Court.

Nicole Godfrey worked as a barmaid and had experienced at least one abusive relationship. A woman with veterinary nursing experience, Godfrey had returned to Queensland mid-2008, only to return to Victoria later that year—when she met Coombes while living in shared accommodation. She should have stayed in the Sunshine State. Godfrey, working in a clothing shop in 2009, looked upon Coombes as a kind man who had helped her in Melbourne. Coombes was the classic wolf in sheep's clothing.

What happened after Coombes and Raechel arrived at Godfrey's Phillip Island house is not entirely known, other than Raechel, at age twenty-seven, met an untimely and grisly death.

In a nutshell, Coombes strangled her on a bed and moved the body to the bath where he dismembered her with knives. The process took over a day, during which time a salesman, or similar, visited the home.

'I don't think he was an insurance salesman,' Coombes later told Homicide Squad detectives. 'I think he had something to do with the power or gas or something. He wore a brown-coloured suit. I do remember that.'

Coombes stuffed Raechel's body parts in garbage bags and drove them to nearby Newhaven Pier. The bags were thrown into the bay. The full gory details of the murder, dismemberment and dumping of the body parts would later shock all concerned.

Later in the week after Raechel left, Kylie and Kate began to wonder when she would return.

'I didn't think too much of it because I knew Raechel was away with John,' Kylie said in a police statement.

We certainly trusted John at that time. It was around
the Friday when [Kate] and I had lots of chats about
what to do and we decided that we wouldn't tell the
police—or the 'popo' as we called them—[that she
had gone to see John] because this would definitely
get Raechel into trouble and there would be a million
questions asked … I just expected Raechel to walk
back in the door, although I was becoming worried.

Kylie rang Coombes. 'I found it odd at the time that
John had answered his phone no problem but that
Raechel's phones were all "out of range",' she said in
her statement. 'He then invited us to come down on the
Friday night for dinner.'

The two teenagers went to the Preston flat.

'I remember seeing in John's unit behind the couch,
next to the window, a hedge trimmer, a chainsaw and a
whole heap of cloth tied up in butcher's string,' Kylie stated.

I didn't say anything to John about it and I didn't
discuss it. I wondered at the time whether he might
have used that stuff on Raechel but didn't want to
think about it. I was really stunned and didn't know
what to think.

As the mystery of Raechel's whereabouts deepened,
some of her body began to surface. A lone jogger ran
across a severed left leg, less than a kilometre from
Newhaven Pier, on 16 August. Detective Tom Hogan, of
the Homicide Squad, travelled to San Remo police station
and liaised with other Homicide members and local
detectives. The following day, the captain of the Sorrento
ferry spotted the other leg floating in the water. Despite
the water police and police helicopter scouring the area,

the limb was never recovered. Less than three weeks later a different jogger found two pieces of Raechel's flesh—one sporting a distinctive tattoo—on nearby Ventnor Beach. Police had themselves a homicide. A gruesome one. A pathologist decided Raechel's killer was skilled in the use of knives.

'I was deeply shocked to see the tattoo from her left foot in the news,' Sandra Betts recalled. 'I was intensely fearful that it was her leg that had been found at Newhaven Beach. I acted immediately after recognising the tattoo to try to contact her, to check on her safety and whereabouts. I became increasingly distraught.'

It was 20 August when Hogan was briefed about a missing persons report filed that morning. It related to a Raechel Betts—a twenty-seven-year-old Epping woman. Hogan and Detective Sergeant Steve Martin travelled to the Epping address with forensics officers. While the detectives took statements from Kylie and Kate, the forensics team collected DNA samples from Raechel's room for comparison with the recovered leg.

'Waiting for news of the DNA results to confirm or deny her death, mutilation and dismemberment—I had a sense of dread and of surreal disconnection from people and events,' Sandra Betts stated.

Kylie knew that Raechel's return date was well overdue. There had been no word from her but, out of a misguided sense of loyalty and a well-founded level of fear, she and Kate felt they had to stay silent about John Coombes.

'Raechel wanted me to "cover her arse" when she was gone,' Kylie said in her police statement.

> What I mean by that is, [a family friend] didn't know that Raechel was heavily into selling drugs, nor did

Raechel's grandparents. I knew my job was to tell the truth about Raechel's whereabouts during the time she was to be away ... [but] I wanted to be loyal to Raechel and didn't want to get her into trouble. [Kate] was basically doing what I was doing: covering for Raechel.

Kylie's fears for her own safety, and that of Kate, grew.

As time went on, I became more paranoid that there were going to be repercussions for me if I told police exactly what I knew. John obviously knew that I knew from the beginning that Raechel had gone away with him. John, at least after that dinner on Friday 14 August, knew that [Kate] knew as well. I was scared also because John knew so much about us—where we lived, what school we went to. He'd met most of our friends. He knew so much about Raechel's grandparents. He knew where they lived. It seemed a lot safer for all concerned to play dumb and not admit to what I knew ... I also believed my input about my knowledge to police wasn't hugely important because it appeared that they were investigating John at that stage anyway. It may sound strange, but I was worried that John may have somehow bugged the house and may have been listening to my conversations to the police when they were asking about Raechel's disappearance. I felt that if I said the wrong thing, it wouldn't take much for John to jemmy my window and kill me too. I knew John knew a lot of people and had a bit of influence in the drug using/selling community and he could have got people to harm us or even lie for him. Around this time my dad got hit by a bit of wood by someone. It might have been a burglary gone wrong but I thought to myself maybe it was related to Raechel's disappearance.

Rather than try to avoid Coombes after the grisly murder, Nicole Godfrey maintained contact with him. They even started having sex.

'In one call they discuss what Coombes did to Godfrey with breakfast cereal,' a police document stated. 'The sex talk continued for some time ... at the end of the call she says she will let him know when the GP bikes are on at Phillip Island.'

Saucy text messages also flew between the two. The document continues: 'Other text messages between them occur in which they discuss missing each other.'

Homicide Squad detectives first questioned Coombes on 21 August. He denied being at the island on the nights of 11 and 12 August. The following month, on 29 September, Raechel's family said goodbye to her at a funeral service attended by some four hundred mourners. All they had to bury was a leg and some flesh.

'Her life has been stolen from her and stolen from us,' Sandra told the congregation. 'I have lost my true love; my first true love. Her sisters have lost their mentor and confidante. For us the hurt is almost unbearable.'

Sandra also pleaded for information. 'I think there could have been some people who might have known more than they have said,' she said,

and it would be a hell of a lot better if they came forward and informed the police about what they know. When something like this remains unresolved, your faith in society, your faith in police and your faith in so many things is rocked.

But the investigating detectives were not rocked. Hogan and detective Leigh Smyth paid Coombes a visit on 30 October. He again denied being at the island, adding that he helped Godfrey with her car, which he said broke down somewhere near Cranbourne. Homicide detectives and forensic examiners combed Godfrey's Wimbledon Heights house in late October. They arrested Coombes on 2 November and placed him in the squad car.

'Coombes paused for some time and appeared to be attempting to say something, but couldn't bring himself to do so,' Hogan said in his statement. 'He appeared to be attempting to control his emotions.'

Smyth spoke up in the car at that point.

SMYTH: The hardest part is actually saying it.
COOMBES: She just pushed my buttons.
SMYTH: Once you say it, it gets a lot easier. It's just the first words.
COOMBES: Yeah, I know … I killed her. She got me so fuckin' angry. She taunted me.

In the Homicide Squad interview room, Hogan provided Coombes with a cup of coffee and asked if he wanted a lawyer.

'It's too late for that,' Coombes replied, before opening up.

Coombes gave two records of interview: one at the Homicide Squad office and the second at Barwon Prison—during which he agreed to draw a diagram of how he dismembered Raechel's body. He admitted having taken Raechel to the Phillip Island house. He claimed they went there to discuss a plan to kill or maim three men Raechel said had sexually assaulted her and the two teenage girls. Coombes told the detectives that he and Raechel arrived there just after midnight and that he introduced her to Godfrey before all three drank coffee and listened to music. He said Raechel later went to bed in the spare room but called him into her room to further talk about the claimed kill plot, which he described to police as a 'plan to either cut someone's balls out or cut their fucking heads off'.

According to his first version given to police, he sat next to Raechel with his arm around her and she admitted that she had allowed Kylie and Kate to be sexually tampered with in order to pay off debts. In that version Coombes claimed he became angered by the alleged comments. In his second version to police on 23 December, he claimed that he and Raechel went to Phillip Island to 'organise drug stuff' and that Raechel told him she could set up Kylie as his sexual plaything if he played his cards right. In a secretly recorded phone conversation with the woman he had first moved in with after being paroled in 2007, Coombes said he could not remember what Raechel's last words were. Coombes would later tell a consultant psychologist that they went to Phillip Island because he thought it would be a good spot for Raechel to establish herself as a drug dealer, but made no mention of the claimed kill plot.

'As in the first version [you gave Homicide detectives],' Justice Nettle would say when sentencing Coombes,

> you said that the deceased [Raechel] showed you some pornographic images while you were en route to Phillip Island but, in contradiction to the other versions, you

added that later, as Raechel lay on the bed at Phillip Island, she showed you further images of young women being sexually abused and told you that, if you played your cards right, you could also be involved. You implied it was that which triggered the killing.

Justice Nettle disregarded the notion that Raechel would have subjected Kylie and Kate to any harm or degradation.

'The weight of evidence is that the deceased was deeply attached to both girls and spent what money she had in providing for them,' Nettle said.

Indeed, it appears reasonably possible that the main reason she gave up her work as a teacher and took to drug dealing full time was to provide for the girls while spending more time with them. Among other evidence to that effect, the deceased's good friend, David Gould, expressed the opinion, based on his observations of the way in which the deceased cared for the girls, that it was inconceivable that she would have allowed them to be sexually abused for financial advantage. Mr Gould's observations were that the deceased devoted herself to the girls' welfare to the point of her own personal detriment.

Gould told police:

I heard that the guy charged with Raechel's murder said he did it because Raechel allowed the girls to be raped in order to make money—this would be absolute rubbish. I know that Raechel had these girls' best interests at heart. She wanted to be a mother so badly … She loved children and devoted her life to looking after them. This was why she started to sell drugs as she needed money to look after the two girls.

Regardless of Coombes's fabricated reasons for killing Raechel, he did describe the process.

> She lifted her chin, like she wanted a cuddle and then I straddled her … put a fuckin' sleeper hold on her and I just fuckin' hung on. I was so fuckin' angry. How could you fuckin' cuddle that?

He added that Raechel kicked a bit as he strangled her. In cold fashion he described his technique.

> It's a figure-four leg lock, they call it in wrestling. It's across the front and you take them around the neck, the other hand up and tilt the head over. I believe it … cuts off the air if you push it correctly with the palm of your hand. It prevents anything from getting through there. It's fairly quick. That's what they say. In reality it's a little bit longer.

Coombes reckoned he may have broken Raechel's neck. He said he choked her so hard that his hand cramped up.

> I'm not a pathologist and that but from what the army tells us, if you're strangling someone and they take quite a while to die, the bladder, the bowel, everything goes. But there was only a small amount of urine on her jeans.

Coombes was left lying with a warm corpse.

'I know it is a human being, but the soul was gone,' he told police. 'And I know I am responsible for taking that fucking soul.'

He described what he did next.

I pulled her through to the bathroom. I got her
clothes and everything off. I put 'em in the bath …
I think I got Nicky [Godfrey] to make me a cup of
coffee … or some fuckin' stupid thing. I think I tried
to pick her [Raechel] up. Yeah. One stage there she
was dead heavy. I thought, 'Oh fuck'. That's when I
decided then to—I went out and had a look in my car.
Fuckin' found a set of—in a box, a set of knife blades.

When I came back inside I asked Nicky if she had
garbage bags … and put her [Raechel] into the bath
and then just stopped and thought, 'What the hell am
I goin' to do here? How the hell do I go about this?'

Using sash-type cord he had also brought in from his
car, Coombes said he tied Raechel's feet to the taps.

'It was cheap Chinese shit … but it was strong enough
to hold her feet up onto the tap and suited what I had to
do,' Coombes continued.

He then started cutting through skin, muscle and
bone, hacking Raechel's body into pieces and pulling her
apart. Godfrey told police that Coombes asked her if she
would like to watch. She said he asked her at one point,
'Do you want to come in and do a dissection?'

'I know she was chopped up in the bathroom,' Godfrey
admitted to detectives. 'He took her in the bathroom
because I was in bed and I had the TV on a little bit and I
had my hands on my ears.'

But Godfrey was not able to block out everything. She
could still hear sickening 'pops' and 'cracks' as Coombes
pulled Raechel apart.

'[There was] like popping,' Godfrey would explain.
'I've had my arm dislocated before and I know damn well

what it sounds like when you pop a joint—and I could hear it.'

To sate a depraved desire, Coombes hacked off Raechel's breasts. He became excited, or his anger rose, as he mentioned this to the police.

'"You don't deserve to die as a fucking woman," I think I said to meself,' he recounted. 'There you go. I'm getting me anger back again.'

In his second version to police, he tried to justify the dismemberment.

> I had no other way of doing it … I was trying to picture it as like just the life has gone. She's dead. It's a piece of meat. Do it that way. Work on it like a piece of meat. Make the cuts. Separate the joints and do what you could there … I've given her a quick release. It's more than she fuckin' deserved.

The disposal job proved a tiring task. Coombes said he had to turn on the water periodically to drain away the blood.

'I'm not sure how far in I was,' he told the detectives, 'but I started getting pretty crook. I had to spew in the dunny and in the end I just had to stop.'

Coombes had a sleep, lying next to Godfrey, before rising some time on 12 August to continue the dismemberment.

> I had a bit more coffee and got some garbage [bags]—I think I've already said I got the garbage bags. I got those garbage bags and with the pieces, I was puttin' em in. Two or three and puttin' them in.

Around 3 pm that day, Godfrey's neighbour—a local panelbeater named Shayne Gislingham—returned

Godfrey's car to her home having repaired its brakes. Hearing noises inside, he knocked continuously on the front door because he needed a lift back to his workshop. Coombes, in a dressing-gown, finally opened the door. He made Gislingham wait while he got changed and then drove the guy back to work.

'Gislingham described Coombes' demeanour as calm and not anxious,' the police summary stated. 'That he engaged in conversation, but that he didn't get a good feel about Coombes and consequently wouldn't accept the $400 Coombes offered as payment for the job on Godfrey's car.'

Godfrey described Coombes as looking a little tired on the night of 12 August but 'pretty normal like nothing had happened'. Godfrey just wanted Raechel's body out of her home.

'I just told him I want it out of my house,' Godfrey told police. 'I didn't want it there. Just get rid of it … it was making me sick.'

Coombes packed five full garbage bags into Godfrey's car and drove to the pier in the early hours of 13 August. He tossed Raechel's mobile phone, clothing and the knives into the water along with the bags containing the body.

'I'm pretty sure there was only five. There was the torso and the head, and the arms and legs were in separate bags.'

An experienced fisherman, Coombes knew a thing or two about dumping offal at sea. He admitted to cutting open the bags and, before tossing all the body away, slicing through Raechel's abdomen.

'I did open the abdominal area but that was only to, sort of, pierce the intestines to let the gases out so they didn't float.'

Afterwards, Coombes drove back to Godfrey's home and scrubbed the bathroom clean with bleach-based cleaning products. He returned to his Preston flat, all the way concocting a false alibi. In a secretly recorded telephone conversation, he would later tell a lady friend it was his 'cleanest' kill.

'It was just click. It's over. Gone.'

In her police interview, Godfrey told how the sexual relationship with Coombes had bloomed after Raechel's murder.

> [We were] just talking one night and he just said, 'You know we get along really good, not mattering about our age differences, we'd make a good partnership.' I sort of thought about it and I said, 'Yeah, you're right. We sort of do. You know, we get along really well.'

Godfrey described the relationship this way: 'I don't know if it's love or a fear.'

She would go on to plead guilty to attempting to pervert the course of justice for 'knowingly making false statements to investigating police as to the whereabouts at particular times of John Leslie Coombes'. It was established that Godfrey remained in bed when Coombes and Raechel had arrived at her home—and never got up to greet them.

'In the early hours of August 13, [Coombes] used your car to transport the remains of Ms Betts to Newhaven Pier where he threw the body parts into the fast-moving current,' Justice Paul Coghlan confirmed.

> You told police, who you knew were investigating the murder, that on the night Ms Betts disappeared

Coombes had fixed your broken-down car near Cranbourne and then, after having done so, returned to his home in Preston. Eastlink records of Coombes' car were able to assist the police relatively quickly to show that your statement of your car breaking down at Cranbourne was false.

Coombes had threatened the naïve Godfrey that she would be in 'big trouble' if she ever told the truth about what she knew. Coghlan sentenced the twenty-eight-year-old to three years' jail, all of which was suspended but for the fifty-one days she had spent in custody on remand.

'You told the police you were petrified of Coombes when you made the first [false] statement, although you got along well with him both before and after the murder,' Coghlan told Godfrey when he sentenced her.

Your involvement in this offence and your relationship with John Coombes remains unexplained. Why you commenced a relationship with a man whom you knew to have murdered … is not easy to comprehend.

I accept that you regret what you did in supporting Mr Coombes.

In a surprise move, Coombes pleaded guilty to murdering Raechel during a morning of pre-trial argument in the Victorian Supreme Court on 2 May 2011. That afternoon, Neville Betts told the *Herald Sun*'s Russell Robinson that the parole system had to be reviewed after allowing a beast like Coombes back on the streets to murder again. During his plea hearing, Coombes claimed his psychological problems had stemmed from childhood when, he dubiously suggested, his mother served him up to a paedophile ring run by a headmaster of a primary school. In another effort to avoid responsibility for his horrendous crimes, he also blamed the prison hospital system for failing to diagnose the extent of his claimed psychological problems.

'You have demonstrated in the past that you are a liar,' Justice Nettle told him.

> It is also apparent that, in the past, you have not hesitated to lie about your lifetime experiences and state of mental health in order to advance your interests. One striking example of that is that in the past you have claimed repeatedly to have suffered trauma symptoms, including intrusive recollections and disturbed dreams, the result of fire fights in which you said you were involved while on active service in Vietnam. More recently, you have felt the need to admit the fact that you never saw any military service in Vietnam.

It was submitted that Coombes deserved a sentencing discount due to his guilty plea. It was claimed that Coombes had shown remorse and had prospects of rehabilitation. Nettle slammed the lid on any chance of a sentencing discount.

'I am satisfied beyond reasonable doubt that the nature and gravity of your offending, your lack of remorse and the absence of a significant prospect of rehabilitation render the idea of any discount on sentence in this case inappropriate,' Nettle said.

> In my view, the dreadful nature of your crime; the consequent need for denunciation, deterrence and just punishment; and the requirement for community protection; combine to dictate that a sentence of the

utmost severity is proportionate to the gravity of the offence.

During the pre-sentence plea hearing, Sandra Betts stood strong in the dock and eyeballed Coombes while telling him—and all present—of her family's real life sentence. As she read from her victim impact statement, she spoke of her family's anguish. The need for medication and visits to a psychologist. And ongoing grief, night terrors and nightmares.

> I have had many nightmares and dreams, initially of very disturbing scenes of torture, then of the many unique expressions of Raechel's face, then of her murderer's amateur, inept and difficult dismemberment of her body reported to have taken twenty four hours and possibly having taken much longer … Recently I have had many dreams of a baby—my baby girl—which I cannot hold on to.

It was said that Raechel's death had also affected her dog, Chloe. 'She was Raechel's companion for over seven years, sleeping on the floor beside her bed every night … Now she sleeps on the floor beside my bed,' Sandra told the court.

Sandra said she and her family would, understandably, remain haunted for the rest of their lives.

> People ask me about closure. I can assure you there is never really any closure when your loved child has been murdered. She will be missed at every family function, every Christmas, on every birthday—whenever I think of her I know I will be deprived of the chance to see her, hold her, talk with her. I think of her many times

every day. The heartache is pervasive and repeated and will be with me and her family for the rest of our lives.

Sandra pleaded for Coombes to be locked up and the key to be thrown away. 'Coombes represents a definite threat to society—of further murder and mutilation—should he ever be released,' she told the court.

Although the 'justice system' has failed Raechel and her family, it should be certain not to fail another person again by ever allowing this man to walk free in the world. I do not want to find, in eleven years or so, that John Leslie Coombes has again been released and again murdered another person. My heart goes out to the Speirani family and the relatives of Henry Desmond Kells, who must be experiencing renewed trauma at the news of a further murder committed by the man who killed a member of their family.

In August 2011, Justice Nettle sentenced Coombes to life imprisonment with no chance of release. He said Coombes lacked remorse and harboured a 'frightening predilection for homicide'.

'The nature and gravity of your offending places it in the worst category of cases of murder,' Nettle told him.

Although you have alleged that the deceased provoked you to kill her by telling you that she was involved in the sexual assault of young girls, I am satisfied beyond reasonable doubt that a substantial part of what you told police and others about the deceased's death, and particularly your allegation that she claimed to have been involved in the sexual assault of the young girls, is a fabrication or confabulation calculated to conceal the true nature and gravity of your offending … The gravity of your offending is made worse by the way in which, immediately after the killing, you hacked up the deceased's body and cast the pieces into the sea.

It passes understanding that a sane human being could hack up and destroy the body of another as if, to use your own words, she were just a lump of meat. The heinousness of that conduct is shocking. It bespeaks an utter disregard of the law and basic norms of society and depraved inhumanity towards Raechel, her family and her loved ones.

Nettle said he had to protect the community from a man beyond rehabilitation and redemption.

Given that you have now murdered three people, given the manner and circumstances in which you killed them, and given that you killed the last of them after spending almost half your life in jail for killing the first and second of them, I am persuaded there is a real risk that, if you were afforded the opportunity to kill again, you would kill again.

Outside court after the sentence, a shaking and exhausted Sandra Betts branded Coombes a 'cruel monster'. She said she believed he murdered Raechel because she refused to become his mistress.

'Murder to him is better than sex,' she said. 'May he never be released and never have a chance to harm another human being.'

While Coombes did attempt to appeal the severity of his sentence, he had correctly summed up his ultimate fate during one of his police interviews.

'Even though I was still trying to throw off, I knew that I was a monty to be looked at [for the murder],' he'd said. 'Believe me, I haven't lost sight of the fact that, you know, three strikes and you're fuckin' out, boy.'

Coombes was refused leave to appeal the length of his sentence. Justice, albeit late, had finally been delivered.

5

A Heart of Darkness

'We are perhaps indeed fortunate that he didn't throw all three children over the bridge.'

ARTHUR PHILLIP FREEMAN WAS AN ORDINARY MAN. HE was what most would have classed a common man: a father of three with no particular standing other than within his small group of friends and in the eyes of his parents, siblings and children. His commonality had stretched across every aspect of his life—from his days as a university geek–cum–IT 'slacker' with a penchant for Playstation games to his role as a crestfallen suburban dad who looked forward to weekly social tennis games with his mates. A thirty-something 'computer nerd good with spanners and tools', according to a former family associate, whom we shall call Michael, Freeman dearly missed the sweet taste of an affluent life he had once lived in the United Kingdom. It was a brief taste in the scheme of things. Michael told this author that Freeman enjoyed personal trainers and fine lunches during his employ with a major company, while embarking on weekend trips to France and ski jaunts on exotic mountains. Freeman longed for that life again—a life that had ended because his then wife, Peta Barnes, had preferred that they move back to Melbourne for the sake of their children's education. A one-time king of his own tiny slice of England, Freeman was a mentally worn divorced dad living an *ordinary* life in a cluttered rented flat in Melbourne when he committed his most *extraordinary* crime—a crime so chilling in its heartlessness, it would leave his defence barrister with no other option but to admit the 'horror' of it all.

'It would be impossible for any of us in this community not to have heard of the events on 29 January [2009] when they happened,' David Brustman, SC, told a jury of Freeman's peers in the Victorian Supreme Court. 'It galvanised us all. It was splashed across every paper, every television station, with updates, almost like an international event—and for good reason.'

It was a crime that still needles the minds and stomachs of those unfortunate enough to have been driving across the West Gate Bridge the moment Freeman tossed his innocent little girl over the railing and into the cold water 58 metres below. It still affects motorists who cross the bridge to this day.

Traffic crossing the West Gate that fateful morning was bumper to bumper. It was just past 9 am and the mercury had already hit a searing forty degrees. The day was to prove a harbinger for a string of insanely hot days ahead, on the back of which would ride the killer Victorian Black Saturday bushfires. It was to be Darcey Freeman's first day of school. By all accounts the four-year-old was excited, but her dad—a thirty-five-year-old unemployed computer programmer—was struggling with arrangements. Freeman, described by some as a loving dad, was driving against the clock. He knew his former wife, Peta Barnes, would be impatiently awaiting their daughter's arrival—along with that of her two sons—at St Joseph's Primary School in Hawthorn. Still smarting and distressed after a bitter negotiated settlement the previous day that restricted his access to his kids, Freeman had left his parents' Aireys Inlet holiday home with the children around 7.30 am. His father, Peter, had been worried enough to suggest he accompany his son and the children on their journey. The offer was rejected. Peter Freeman, a former schoolteacher, had then thrown up another suggestion.

'I was concerned that Arthur was very stressed and I suggested that he and the children miss a day of school and stay home,' Peter recalled in a statement later made to police.

Freeman's Toyota Land Cruiser was stacked with the kids' toys, bikes and clothes. The three little ones had just spent several days with their paternal grandparents. Ben, aged six, was already dressed in his school uniform. But Darcey was not. Her school dress was back at Freeman's flat on the other side of the city. There were concerns that her new shoes would not fit. The traffic slowed to a crawl across the West Gate. The clock in Freeman's head was ticking like a time bomb. According to a psychiatrist's report, he described experiencing a 'feeling of being trapped' and 'a rising sense of anxiety and hopelessness' atop the bridge. *Tick-tock. Tick-tock.* The setting could have been compared to the opening scene from the 1993 film *Falling Down* starring Michael Douglas—the tale of a socially awkward, unemployed divorced father whose mental state implodes while sitting stationary in gridlock. While it was never suggested that Arthur Freeman's crime of throwing his daughter off the bridge was committed because of his 'falling down', his barrister would suggest he simply fell apart and was unaware of his actions. Crown prosecutors Gavin Silbert and Diana Piekusis, on the other hand, said Freeman's crime of murder was a voluntary and deliberate strike at his former wife's heart.

Arthur Freeman met Peta Barnes in 1998 through friends while employed at Colonial Mutual in Melbourne's CBD. The two lived together in the inner Melbourne suburb of Richmond. Friends noted that Peta seemed the dominant half of the relationship.

'It was around this time that I noticed that Arthur was beginning to be called "Artie", and not the "Ardy" we had always known him as,' former family associate Michael told this author.

Arthur Phillip Freeman had been called many things during his life. One of four children, his primary school days (while living in the working-class suburb of Whittington, on the outskirts of Geelong) were unremarkable—although he did spend a short stint at a school for kids with behavioural problems. In her police statement, his mother hinted there were troubled times.

'In his primary schooling, Arthur was reluctant to go to school,' Norma Freeman said.

Professor Graham Burrows, a veteran psychiatrist who gave evidence on Freeman's behalf at his murder trial, was able to uncover some other truths.

He contended that he had some difficulties at school. He was shy. He had problems in establishing relationships. He was bullied. I note that he moved from school on five separate occasions in an attempt to improve his performance. He suffered with a lot of incontinence through most of his primary school years.

It was at Newcomb High School where, it has been confirmed, Freeman received cruel treatment. According to fellow students he was ostracised and bullied. He was a different sort of kid. Not a frail or oversized schoolboy, the most prone to intimidation and extortion, but a loner who skirted the fringes. He was said to be the only student at the school named Arthur, a point of difference in itself. Some students recalled that he smelled. His nicknames were interchangeable. Some called him Ardy Dunger— possibly in reference to Paul Hogan's thong-wearing, pot-bellied 'yobbo' character named Arthur Dunger. Others called him Ardy Monster. Fellow students remember torture sessions where he was made to stand on a rock, sometimes for twenty minutes at a time. He rarely stood up for himself or fought, but when he did it was frightening. Witness accounts suggest a teenage Freeman was prone to placing tormentors in headlocks, forcing onlookers to pry free his arm from the victim's neck. An insight into Freeman's bruised psyche can be found within the words of a poem entitled 'Feelings', printed in the 1986 Newcomb High yearbook. Freeman, aged twelve or thirteen when he wrote the piece, described fear as 'when you're in a maze with a tiger behind you'. One former student told *Herald Sun* senior feature writer Patrick Carlyon that he remembered Freeman as a 'ticking time bomb'.

'He copped it for his name, his look, and the way he acted,' the former fellow student said. 'He had zero people skills.'

Another former classmate told Carlyon that Freeman 'was like a Martin Bryant type'. (Bryant, at age twenty-eight, shot dead thirty-five people—including children— during a gun rampage at Tasmania's Port Arthur in 1996.)

'He'd get that stare,' the former classmate told Carlyon. 'It was scary. It was when he got bullied a bit and he'd had too much. They picked on him because he was harmless. But everyone knew he had that ability—that something inside him that could explode at any time.'

At Deakin University, Freeman studied aquatic science for a year before transferring across to information technology. For the first time he found like-minded comrades within the IT field. Those friends included a young man named Anthony Luscombe, who would also go on to work at Colonial Mutual. During his university years, Freeman lived with other students and developed a mutual interest in autocross car racing.

'They would buy Ford Escorts and prepare them for racing or get what parts they needed and then sell the rest as parts,' said Michael, who first befriended Freeman in the early- to mid-1990s and agreed to provide information on the guarantee of anonymity.

For most university students, time on and around campus is a time spent learning theory as well as expanding life experience—sexual awakenings and experimentation included. But Freeman was not overly interested in the female student body. He seemed more content tinkering with cars than with women. He never took on a girlfriend, leading some to question his sexuality.

'[Another relative] said that he was hurt by a girl while at high school, which is why he was probably taking things cautiously,' the former close family associate said.

After graduating with a computer science degree, Freeman gained work in computer programming and data collection. 'Arthur had a fairly simple life [at that stage],' said Michael.

Not a lot was expected of him at work. So Arthur enjoyed staying up late—and I mean very late. He

would be playing Playstation until at least 5 am and be
ready to head off for work at 8 am. I am sure that he
would catch up for some sleep in his office only to do
it again the next night.

Freeman's interest in cars continued. His first car was a
simple make and model, reflective of his own personality.
'It was nothing special,' Michael said. 'It was certainly
not an attractive car, with a number of panels having
had previous repair. But to Arthur, that little yellow Ford
Escort was just fine.'

In the year after they met, Freeman and Peta Barnes
married on the eve of the new millennium. The ceremony
was in Perth, where Peta's family lived. Guests described
the wedding as 'not overdone' and a 'semi-casual affair'.

Michael still raises his eyebrows at the chosen date.
Maybe the marriage was jinxed from the beginning. 'It
was ironic for a computer nerd to get married when the
world was set to fall apart due to the Y2K bug,' he quipped.

Three weeks later and the newlyweds relocated to the
United Kingdom. Their first son, Ben, was born February
2002. Darcey was born February 2004. Second son, Jack,
was born February 2006.

The family lived in Maida Vale, north of London, and
Freeman and Peta made friends with locals like paramedic
Charles Leahy and Aussie expat Elizabeth Lam, with
whom Peta worked. Freeman worked as a computer
programmer and data collector for a major company.

'Arthur enjoyed working for that company,' Michael
told this author.

In this job he had a personal trainer and could call
the kitchen and order meals, as they had a dedicated

chef. He would also get maybe one or two [movie] CDs a month. It was the simple things like this that kept Arthur happy. While in the UK, Arthur and Peta would enjoy going to pubs, travelling to France for the weekend and loading up the car with bottles of wine. As you can imagine, both were on a very good income.

At Peta's behest, the family moved back to Melbourne in June 2006. Insiders say she wanted her children to have an Aussie education. According to relatives, Freeman was annoyed about coming back to Australia early, as they hadn't obtained their British passports as planned.

Charles Leahy thought the family 'left in a bit of a rush'. 'I don't know that Arthur felt he'd tied up everything as he would have liked before they left,' Leahy said in a police statement. 'I think there were disagreements as to whether to sell their London home. Arty wanted to keep it and rent it.'

Freeman's good mate Anthony Luscombe also sensed disappointment. 'Ardy had loved living in England and was living the life over there before he returned.'

Elizabeth Lam wouldn't be quite as subtle. She told police: 'Arty loved being in England and had mentioned that Peta had dragged him back to Australia just when he had settled into a job that he really enjoyed.'

After arriving back home in Melbourne, Freeman and Peta rented a flat in Hawthorn—an affluent inner-eastern suburb. She found work quickly. But Freeman remained unemployed and lived the life of a stay-at-home dad. Trouble was brewing on the home front.

'Peta told me she was unhappy and was thinking about leaving Arthur,' Freeman's sister, Megan Toet, said in her police statement. 'She was in two minds about it. She told me she was unhappy about him not being employed.'

Freeman claimed that Peta was verbally abusing him because he did not have a paying job.

'Arthur wanted either Peta to look after the kids or [to do it] himself, but he didn't want strangers looking after them,' Megan said. 'Peta seemed to be more interested in the potential earning capacity if they both worked than having one of them stay home to look after the kids.'

According to Megan, money was never her brother's major concern.

In Peta's mind, Freeman experienced a 'lot of difficulties' upon their return to Melbourne. 'Arthur struggles with change and we had difficulties as a result,' she told Detective Acting Sergeant Damian Jackson in a statement. 'Arthur and I had a lot of arguments.'

Freeman's mother visited him several times in Hawthorn to see how he was coping full time with the children. 'I found Arthur was going well,' Norma Freeman said in her police statement, 'though with three children, and a wife working long hours, I thought they sometimes didn't understand each other's positions.'

Fissures in the matrimonial relationship were set to crack wide open. Peta packed up the children and left Freeman in March 2007. Norma Freeman, who was present on the break-up day, recounted events in her statement.

Ben and Darcey were out in the yard, while Peta was washing the baby in the laundry. Arthur had told Ben to stop bouncing on the trampoline as he wanted to give Ben a drink of water. I couldn't see what happened, but Ben yelled out. Arthur later told me he had splashed the water on Ben because he wouldn't stop bouncing to take the cup. On hearing Ben yell out, Peta said, 'That's it. I'm not taking any more of this.' She decided to take the children with her.

Arthur protested, and refused to move his car to allow Peta to drive away.

'He wouldn't move his car and she wouldn't walk away with the children so she called the police,' Norma stated. 'They told Arthur she could take the children and that is what she did.'

In her police statement, Peta said her husband had personality problems. She described him as 'rigid and inflexible'.

> Arthur has quite large mood swings so he will go from anger and vengefulness to remorse and back again. Unfortunately it took me until I left him for me to recognise that he may have been suffering a depression of some sort.

Peta revealed she had once spoken to her doctor regarding fears about Freeman. 'I told [the doctor] that I believed [Arthur] would kill my children and that I believed he was vengeful enough to kill my children to get back at me.'

After the separation, Freeman rented a Hawthorn flat to stay close to his children's school and child-minding facility. During school holidays, the kids would spend some time with Freeman's parents at their Aireys Inlet holiday home. But the hostile relationship between husband and wife continued, and boiled over when Peta and her mother, Iris, visited Freeman at his rental property. The women had baby Jack with them.

'Arthur just wanted to berate me for all of the things that I had done wrong,' Peta said in her police statement.

> Arthur was incredibly resentful in the time since we had come home [from England]. Mum and I went to leave with the baby and as we were walking out Arthur grabbed the baby off me and I thought he was going to throw him against the fireplace and kill him. Mum and I fought him and I bit him to get him to let the baby go because he is incredibly strong and he wouldn't let go.

A scuffle ensued. The police were called.

'The police convinced me to allow him access to the children and I didn't know my rights, so we established a contact routine,' Peta said. 'I agreed to the contact regime because the police left me with a clear impression that if I did not allow him access the children would be placed [in state care] and to me this was an unforgivable situation.'

A shared care arrangement was established. To his sister, it appeared Freeman was coping well with the separation and shared care deal. But not so in his dad's eyes.

'I found it hard to believe some of the things that he was doing,' Peter Freeman said in his police statement.

> It was a very strange thing that was happening. He had a system going with his dishes and his food and dishwasher and all that stuff was super efficient, yet the rest of his life was in confusion. He was starting to collect hard rubbish and he would collect every receipt. He had a box full of them in the kitchen … every receipt relating to the children. The place was overflowing with toys and clothes and stuff. Norma

and I were constantly trying to bring that back into order.

The couple's divorce was finalised in June 2008. Two months later, Freeman returned to England in a desperate bid to secure a British passport. While there he stayed with and confided in old friends. Freeman asked Charles Leahy if he could stay with his family for a couple of weeks.

'We agreed, and he came over,' Leahy explained.

He told us he actually was going to stay for three months. He planned to apply for residency and had to be in the UK for at least three months every two years to fulfil the requirements. I believe he planned to work in block periods and return to Australia in between. He felt he would get better work in London and had been doing a lesser quality of work in Australia.

In Leahy's eyes, Freeman seemed 'clearly depressed'—a situation not helped with apparent efforts made back in Melbourne to prevent him from talking to his children. 'He cried a lot and was emotional a lot,' Leahy said. 'It appeared it was made hard for him to contact the kids. By this I mean they weren't available when he called.'

By that stage, Elizabeth Lam had divorced her husband. She and Freeman came together as kindred spirits. They talked a lot about their failed marriages. 'Although Arty was extremely upset about the breakdown of his marriage and was very bitter about Peta's behaviour towards him, he was still good company,' Lam recalled in her statement. 'Arty kept himself very active, doing odd jobs for friends of mine, playing tennis, cycling and socialising with friends, among other activities.'

No amount of activity could fully distract Freeman from his family situation, however.

'Arty was a fairly introverted person but was becoming emotional, which I think shows how stressed he was,' Leahy suggested in his statement.

> He was also becoming paranoid. He thought his mail had been tampered with. He also wouldn't answer the door because he thought he'd get served with something [like legal documents]. I don't know what he thought he would get served with.

Freeman was also starting to show signs of obsessive and—more disturbingly—heavy-handed behaviour. Leahy told of a day Freeman accompanied his family, and their young goddaughter Kayla, to London's National History Museum. Kayla misbehaved and Freeman lifted her into her pram.

'She continued throwing her arms and legs about and screaming,' Leahy recalled. 'Arty went to her and physically restrained her. I thought it was an over-reaction. I noticed Arty was shaking … He was worried about his finances and the custody arrangements and was so wrapped in these problems.'

Elizabeth Lam also noticed a change in her close friend's behaviour. 'Towards the end of his stay in London he became anxious and expressed his worries … Arty definitely felt that Peta was not going to provide the best role model for his children.'

Anxious to see his kids, Freeman arrived back in Melbourne in late 2008. Michael told this author that Freeman spoke of his bitter resentment towards Peta during an early family Christmas dinner at Aireys Inlet in November 2008.

'Arthur and I were discussing things about his children,' Michael recalled.

> During this conversation Arthur said that she [Peta] would regret it if he lost custody of the children. That comment has gone through my head over and over. I am not sure [what he meant], but it did suggest that he would make her life hell.

Elizabeth Lam, originally from Melbourne, brought her own children back for a four-week holiday in December. She stayed with her sister. Freeman and their children spent time with Lam and her kids. Apparently he seemed relaxed.

'My sister commented on how much Darcey loved her father,' Lam recalled in her police statement.

> Darcey came up for cuddles from her father during the time they were there. Arty met up with me and my family on three other occasions and on one occasion he and I went out for dinner together. Over dinner Arty seemed very relaxed and was talking about getting on with his life and looking forward to his future.

For Christmas, Peta took the children to Perth. Freeman flew to Western Australia on Christmas Day to spend a couple of hours with the little ones, before flying back to Melbourne the same day. The kids stayed with him in early January for the second half of the school holiday period. They spent some of the time at his Hawthorn flat, and the rest at the Aireys Inlet holiday house. It appeared to friends, like Anthony Luscombe, that Freeman was coping well. Luscombe and Freeman saw each other weekly when they caught up for social tennis. The two talked about the future.

Clinical psychologist Dr Jennifer Neoh was asked to complete a report on Freeman's fractured family. She met with Peta and the children and Freeman and his parents. A major focus of Neoh's appraisal was to consider Darcey's needs during her first year at school. It would be fair to say that Freeman blew it. For starters, he arrived late. During the consultation, Neoh decided that he was a man who had difficulty following directions and answering questions, had difficulty accepting responsibility for his behaviour and sought to deflect to others. She also determined that he tended to be irrational and contradictory and, in summary, 'demonstrated passive/aggressive traits that seemed to cause chaos around him'. Here's what Neoh wrote, in part:

> I am ... not convinced that Mr Freeman's behaviour and personality style does not expose the children to the conflict between their parents. I believe these factors have combined to produce a potentially harmful environment for the children ... I consider that all the children need a greater sense of security and predictability in their lives.
>
> I also have doubts about Mr Freeman's capacity and inclination to promote effective and successful communications. I consider that it is likely he has chronic personality and interpersonal problems that are caused by a tendency to irrationality, contradiction and denial of responsibility. His presentation showed passive/aggressive traits which does not auger well for successful parental communication and cooperation— or the facilitation of the children's relationship with their mother.

Neoh's report was released to both parties on 19 January. Freeman decided he did not like Neoh, or her attitude towards him. He reckoned she treated him unfairly and was biased against him.

'Arthur wasn't yelling or screaming but he was disheartened with the lady's behaviour towards him,' Norma Freeman said in her police statement. 'Arthur was of the opinion that he hadn't provoked the psychologist, even though he was late. He was worried about the outcome.'

Freeman's family also criticised Neoh's attitude. Peter Freeman told police: 'My wife, my daughter and myself were shocked at the attitude of the clinical psychologist, and her approach seemed deliberately structured to create conflict. I believe the report did not accurately reflect what had occurred during the assessment.'

Freeman confided in his few close friends. 'I think he perceived that a lot of weight would be placed on what was contained in that report,' mate Greg Jarman told the Supreme Court.

Freeman spent the Australia Day long weekend at Aireys Inlet with his parents and the three children. He played beach soccer with the kids and took them to the park.

'It was just a happy time,' his mum recalled. 'But Arthur was still concerned about [his relationship with his children].'

Freeman left the children with his parents and travelled back to Melbourne on Tuesday, 27 January. That night he hung out with friend Anthony Luscombe. The mates talked.

'It was all to do with financials,' Luscombe said in his police statement.

The two watched the Australian Open tennis tournament. One of their idols, Roger Federer, was playing centre court. The two mates spent four hours watching and dissecting the Swiss champion's game. 'I remember we discussed tennis for a lot of the night and we spoke about how we could get our tennis games similar to that,' Luscombe stated.

The next day Freeman called his mum and dad, and spoke to his children.

'He told Norma that he wanted the children to stay at Aireys Inlet until the morning due to the heat and he would take them to school the following morning,' Peter Freeman told police. In the Supreme Court he added:

> It was extremely hot weather. It was the time just prior to those bushfires. I was going to bring the children up to Melbourne the day before but it was agreed that because of that heat they would stay down that extra day and go up early [Thursday] morning.

'He wasn't yelling or screaming and was talking coherently. In hindsight, there is nothing in the conversation that gave any indication he was thinking about doing [what he was soon to do],' Norma Freeman said in her police statement.

That evening, Barnes phoned Freeman. Not to talk to *him*, though. She wanted to speak to her children and, in particular, to wish Darcey good luck for her first day of school. Freeman told her that the kids were at his parents' place, and that he would ring her the next morning so she could talk to them. Freeman rang his only female friend— who lived on the other side of the world. Elizabeth Lam was not home, so he left a message.

'He sounded calm,' Lam said.

Freeman also spoke to mates Jarman and Luscombe in separate phone calls.

Luscombe said: 'I do remember that he was not happy.'

The three mates organised to meet at a St Kilda bar the following evening.

That night, Freeman drove back to Aireys Inlet. He arrived at his folks' place around midnight. He was frazzled. Pissed off. Felt persecuted. He knew he hated Dr Jennifer Neoh.

'He was very distressed,' Peter Freeman told police. 'He felt that he had been set up. I asked him if he wanted something to eat and he said he didn't want anything cooked, but ate some fruit.'

During Freeman's Supreme Court trial, Peter said: 'He believed … that he had sort of been ambushed in this [Neoh] report.'

Freeman had a torrid night. The heat was uncomfortable and he hardly slept. Jack cried. Freeman had to get up and change the little boy's nappy.

Tick-tock. Tick-tock. Tick-tock.

Darcey Iris Freeman loved to dance. She was a cheeky butterfly with a button nose and a mischievous glint in her brown eyes.

'Even though she was only four, she was determined and strong willed,' her uncle, Tim Barnes, told this author in the weeks after her death. 'She knew her own mind and was prepared to always stand up for what she believed in.'

Tim had many fond memories and anecdotes. 'One memory that stands out in my mind was her choice of clothes,' he said. 'She would wear what she wanted to wear, end of story—even if it meant wearing pink Wellington boots to tennis.'

Her other uncle, Joe Barnes, said Darcey turned her hands and mind to many things during her short life. 'She played Auskick [football] for one season. Tried tennis. She's given us a lot fun. She was into everything. She had an effect on everybody.'

Joe also made mention of how Darcey would often dance. 'Whenever particular music came on, she'd be dancing and wouldn't even know it. She'd be off in her own little zone.'

During a prison assessment, Freeman would tell consultant psychiatrist Dr Yvonne Skinner that his daughter was 'headstrong and needed firm handling'.

'He said that she craved attention but he thought that was understandable as she was a second child,' Dr Skinner wrote in a psychiatric report. 'He was aware of his experiences as a second child and tried to make sure that she had attention. For example, he took her to the ballet so that she would have extra attention.'

On the morning of Thursday, 29 January—Darcey's last day alive—everyone was up and about early at Aireys Inlet. Freeman and his dad made breakfast.

'I went down and the children were already up, as were Peter and Arthur,' Norma recalled. 'Jonathan [Jack] was still sleeping but Darcey and Ben were up and dressed. Darcey and Ben had their breakfast, as did Arthur.'

Freeman packed the kids' bikes, toys and clothing in his car. In his parents' eyes Freeman was not himself. He still appeared distressed, and strung out—like he was in some kind of a trance—and 'unreadable', according to his dad.

'He hadn't slept,' Peter Freeman said in court. 'He looked very tired.'

Concerned, Peter offered to travel with his son and

grandkids. Freeman insisted that he go alone. Peter then suggested the children stay at Aireys Inlet.

'I thought, you know, give Peta a call,' Peter told the jury.

It was extremely hot. This was the weather prior to that bushfire. Very, very hot. I'm a schoolteacher and I understand the stresses on young children in that sort of heat and I thought it's not going to hurt [if they miss] the first day at school … [But] Arthur was focused on getting there.

Freeman buckled the children in the 4WD. It was around 7.30 am when he pulled out of his parents' driveway. He had to get Ben, and more importantly, Darcey to school on time.

'When they left, Arthur was a bit short with me, and a little stressed,' Norma Freeman told police. 'But I was in no way concerned for the children's safety.'

During the drive towards the West Gate Bridge, Freeman spoke to several people on the phone. Crying and sobbing, he called Elizabeth Lam in England and lamented.

'He was just very upset,' Lam said in the Supreme Court. 'He [said he] felt that he'd lost the children. He was so helpless. He loved his children. He loved being part of their life. He felt they had been taken away from him.'

According to Lam, Freeman was worried about 'the little things' in his children's life. 'Like putting them to bed and reading them a story. He was worried that it wasn't going to happen for them if he wasn't there. He was just very upset.'

Lam's phone battery went dead mid-call. She did not feel compelled to call Freeman back, as nothing he had said forewarned her of his cruel and deadly intentions.

'It didn't even enter my head that he would harm anybody. I felt that he was having a good cry and that the reality of the situation would settle … Arty never said anything that set alarm bells off.'

Freeman also talked to his sister Megan. He was starting to watch the clock. The pressure was mounting to get Ben and Darcey to school on time. He told Megan he was concerned about what the two eldest would have for lunch.

'He told me he was worried about being late for school and he said that he didn't think he was going to make it.'

Tick-tock. Tick-tock. Tick-tock.

Peta Barnes had decided to travel with her mother to school to see Darcey off on her first day in prep. As her watch ticked past 8.30 am, Peta rang her former husband on his mobile to see where he was with the children. Freeman told her to say goodbye to her children and hung up in her ear. Peta frantically redialled several times. Finally, Freeman answered.

'I think he said, "Who is it?" and I said, "It's me",' Peta recalled in court. 'He said, "You'll never see your children again."'

Freeman hung up for the last time. A worried Peta phoned her solicitor and explained what had just happened. She also informed the school principal. She then called the police. She and her mother drove to the nearest police station and reported the situation. A police officer told her they might need photographs of the kids, so Peta and her mother went home to collect some. Word of the phone conversations reached Freeman's solicitor, who phoned Peter and Norma Freeman.

'I thought he may have been thinking of taking the children out of the country,' Norma recalled thinking at the time.

She and Peter began to drive from Aireys Inlet back to their Whittington home, desperately hoping to find their son and three grandchildren safe and sound there.

It was 9.15 am when Freeman pulled over in the inbound emergency lane atop the West Gate Bridge. He had the presence of mind to flick on his hazard lights before asking Darcey to climb over into the front seat. Amid the stalled traffic he hopped from the car, walked around to the front passenger side and lifted his daughter from the vehicle. Calmly and with purpose, the 'loving dad' carried his little girl to the railing.

Motorist Barry Nelson was driving to work with his wife, Michelle, at the time.

'It was busy … [and] very hot,' Michelle later told the Supreme Court.

> We were busy talking in the car and my husband said something like, 'Oh my God, I think that guy's going to throw his child off the bridge'. I remember trying to look to see what was going on and my face and hands were up … against the passenger window.

Michelle thought the man was just scaring the child and was going to pull her back to safety. Instead, Freeman dropped the little girl.

'It was like he was holding a bag and tipped it over,' Barry Nelson recalled. 'There was no aggression, or anything. There was no struggle, no noise, no screams.'

Motorists Greg Cowan and Michael Costello—travelling in one car—saw the child go over.

'He [Freeman] put both his arms on the railing, looked over the side of the railing for a couple of seconds—then just casually walked back [towards his vehicle],' Cowan said in court.

In his police statement, he said: 'He was walking like he didn't have a care in the world … He just took his time.'

Barry Nelson pulled over and leapt from his car. He approached Freeman and asked: 'What are you doing?' With not a hint of emotion on his face, Freeman failed to respond.

'The overriding impression was he was totally neutral,' Nelson said in court. 'It was just like it was an everyday event, like he may have been posting a letter and was walking back from the post-box to his vehicle. That's the only way I can describe it.'

The event had, understandably, shocked all witnesses to the core. Freeman sat back behind the wheel, calmly rejoined the traffic and drove away.

'I was trying to comprehend what I'd seen and just trying to understand what I'd seen; what I thought I'd seen,' Greg Cowan told the jury. 'Comprehension just wouldn't allow it … I told Michael, I said: "I think he's just dropped a child off the bridge."'

Barry Nelson immediately called 000. His wife, back in their car by that stage, was not prepared to believe a man had just thrown a child over the edge.

'I started to tell myself it may have been a toy because I didn't want to believe it was a child,' Michelle Nelson told police.

> So I got back out of the car and looked over the edge again. That is when I saw the child's body lying face down on the river. I got back in the car and said to my husband, who was on the phone to police, 'It was a child. It's definitely a child.'

Another witness, Paul Taylor, had also pulled over with mobile phone in hand. He tried to dial 000 but his hands were shaking too much. A woman ran up to him and asked: 'Did I just see what I thought I saw?'

As Freeman drove on, his son Ben found his voice. The boy asked him to turn around and go back because 'Darcey can't swim'. Freeman allowed Ben to climb over into the front seat and then drove into Melbourne's CBD.

At 9.20 am, water policeman Acting Sergeant Alistair Nisbet received the first report of a little girl being thrown from the bridge. The police crew jumped in a launch and cut across Port Phillip Bay towards the iconic structure.

'As I got closer I began to make out a figure of a child, much like a doll lying in the water,' Nisbet said in his statement.

Leading Senior Constable Andrew Bell dived in and retrieved Darcey, whose body was brought on board. The police tried frantically to revive her. Darcey was taken ashore, where paramedics and a chopper had arrived. The paramedics took control, and Darcey was airlifted to the Royal Children's Hospital.

Freeman parked his vehicle. Carrying two-year-old Jack—in a T-shirt and wet nappy—and with Ben in tow, the killer dad shuffled his way into the Commonwealth Law Court building. With a blank expression he entered the foyer and stopped at the security point. For reasons only known to him, he tried to hand baby Jack to security guards Brian Skilton and Rao Aziz.

'He pushed the young child he was holding in his arms towards me and said to me, "Take my son. Take my son,"' Skilton recalled in his statement. 'He seemed quite stressed and was visibly shaking.'

Aziz told Freeman to keep hold of his child and asked him to walk forward through the metal detection scanner. Freeman said and did nothing. Aziz asked him if he was all right. Freeman began to cry. Skilton called a 'Sierra 1'—code for supervisor Ian Davis to attend.

'The older boy, who later told me his name was Ben, was wearing a blue school-type shirt and grey-coloured shorts,' Davis remembered.

> [The younger boy] Jack was standing yanking on his father's pants and pulling his wallet out of his pocket. It appeared to me that he was trying to get his father's attention. The father was not reacting at all to this.

Staff member Ilana Katz was called upon. Freeman stood rooted to the spot, his body shaking and trembling. Both Ben and Jack tried to hug him and hold his hand at different times. They were ignored. Katz told a colleague there was a problem with a 'catatonic' man in the foyer.

'He shook,' Katz told the Supreme Court. 'Tears ran down his face and he seemed to have lost control of his bodily functions.'

Katz decided a Crisis Assessment Team was required, and suggested the police be called in. CCTV footage of Freeman in his 'catatonic state' was shown during his trial. While not in the presence of the jury, Justice Paul Coghlan commented that the killer dad's behaviour looked a lot like regret.

Concerned for the children's welfare, counsellor Christine Bendall ushered Freeman into a side room. Katz placed Ben and Jack in the childcare facility. Bendall changed Jack's nappy. She again tried to communicate with Freeman, now slumped in a chair.

'Are you all right?' she asked.

Freeman remained mute.

'Can you hear me?' Bendall continued, kneeling down and grasping the man's arm. 'It will be all right.'

Freeman replied 'no' and sobbed more loudly.

Senior Constable Shaun Hill attended the court complex at 10.26 am to try to unravel the story behind the mystery man. Freeman was sitting in a chair outside Witness Room 25 with head in hands, crying and rocking back and forth.

'His nose was running heavily,' Hill recalled. He asked Freeman: 'Can you hear me? What's happened today?'

Freeman did not respond. Hill turned to young Ben. 'What's your name, buddy?'

'Ben.'

'Is this your dad?'

'Yeah.'

'Are you and your brother okay?'

'Yep.'

Hill turned his attentions back to Freeman. 'What's happened?'

Freeman stood. 'Take me away,' he said, sobbing even harder.

Hill and his offsider were ordered to keep the man detained, as he was a suspect for an unimaginable crime committed on the West Gate Bridge that morning.

Peta Barnes was still at home collecting photographs of her children when her lawyer rang. The two boys were safe, Peta was informed, but there were news reports circulating that a man had dropped a girl off the West Gate. Peta and her mother raced back to the police station.

Peter and Norma Freeman were also told the sickening news. Norma said: 'Just before [we'd reached] Anglesea we were telephoned by [the solicitor]. She said that she had some really bad news; that she believed Arthur had been arrested and that he had thrown Darcey off the West Gate Bridge.'

Freeman's sister Megan caught the breaking news on TV. She rang her parents. Her dad answered.

'He told me he was on the way to my place and that he had some terrible news. It was then that I knew that the incident on the West Gate Bridge had involved Arthur and the children. I just burst out crying.'

As Arthur Freeman sat in a Homicide Squad interview room at the St Kilda Road police complex, Peta was given time alone with her daughter at the Royal Children's Hospital. The little girl had been revived, but was not going to survive.

'I spent time with Darce before she passed away,' a stoic Peta said in her police statement.

Back at the police complex, medical officer Justin Du Plessis arrived to assess Freeman's fitness to be interviewed. The time was about midday.

'He was hunched over in the chair,' Du Plessis told the Supreme Court. 'He was crying. He was non-verbal. And he was shaking, or trembling.'

Du Plessis grew concerned for Freeman's wellbeing: he was concerned the suspect might harm himself. Freeman needed to be psychiatrically assessed. The only problem was he was not answering any questions. He was deemed unfit to be interviewed. Peter and Norma Freeman arrived and were allowed to see their son.

'He didn't say anything and was in a psychiatric state that I have never seen him in before,' Peter told the Supreme Court. 'He was all hunched up, down on the ground … like a newborn child. With no communication:

no reception to anything that we would say. It really disturbed me.'

Peter and Norma told their son they were there for him.

It would be more than a year later when Freeman would tell Dr Yvonne Skinner he had 'little memory of events' after Wednesday, 28 January 2009. He told Skinner he felt 'frustrated and distressed' by his family situation. He said he remembered being at Aireys Inlet and telling his dad how frustrated he was.

'He recalled that he was worried about getting everything ready for the children for school,' Skinner wrote.

> Darcey's school shoes were big. He had purchased them earlier thinking her feet would grow and he had not had time to change them. Her school uniform was back in the house at Hawthorn. He had planned to take the children back to Hawthorn and prepare them for school a day or two before starting ... He did recall feeling rushed.

Freeman claimed he did not remember talking to his ex-wife but, according to Skinner, 'thought it was plausible that Peta would have telephoned and "berated me for not being there"'.

'Mr Freeman again referred to arguments with Peta after they separated and said that the arguments were mainly about finances,' Skinner wrote. Freeman told psychiatrist Dr Lester Walton during a separate assessment that he recalled being worried he was running late to deliver the children to school and that once on the bridge he felt trapped. According to Skinner:

[He told Dr Walton] he could recall thinking, 'We are never going to make it' and it seemed like an enormous failure to him that he would not deliver the children on time. He remembered the traffic on the bridge was travelling quite slowly and: 'It felt like we were not moving at all.' There was a rising sense of anxiety and hopelessness.

The weekend before Freeman's murder trial was to begin, former family associate Michael visited Freeman in jail. He was immediately taken aback.

When Arthur came out, I greeted him then said, 'What's with the hair? You look a bit like Krusty the Clown [from *The Simpsons* cartoon].' I asked Arthur to arrange to get his hair cut at least three times during that visit.

The Supreme Court trial, before Justice Coghlan and a jury of fourteen, started in March 2009. Despite a suit and tie, Freeman presented to the jury like an extra from the asylum-based film *One Flew over the Cuckoo's Nest*. His ginger hair exploded in tufts from his balding scalp. His beard was bold and grizzly. A solid man, he lumbered as though made of concrete; permanent furrows looked like they'd been etched across his forehead with a hammer and chisel. Patrick Carlyon described it aptly when he wrote in an award-winning *Herald Sun* feature piece: 'Mostly, he stared with wide eyes, like a zoo exhibit who could not grasp how he'd arrived where he was.' Chief Crown prosecutor Gavin Silbert, SC, suggested he'd adopted the 'Rasputin-like appearance of a mad monk' for the benefit of the jury.

Freeman's appearance worked well for his barrister's opening address. David Brustman hit the jury with a simple proposition—was Arthur Phillip Freeman mad or was he bad?

'The actions of Mr Freeman were the actions not of a sane mind functioning properly, but of a highly disordered mind; a mind suffering mental illness,' Brustman told the jury. 'What I say is possibly a little bit trite but it's about as succinct as we can get. Was Mr Freeman mad or was he bad?'

The trial ran for nineteen days. The case was conducted on the basis that only two verdicts were open: that Freeman was guilty of murder or not guilty of murder on the grounds of mental impairment. It all boiled down to the expert opinion evidence of psychiatrists. Six in total had assessed Freeman at different times after the bridge incident. Only one of those six backed his defence that he was mentally impaired and therefore not aware of his actions at the time. That man was Professor Graham Burrows. He had assessed Freeman at the Metropolitan Remand Centre on 22 March, and 13 and 29 September 2010. In evidence, Burrows told the jury it was his belief that Freeman suffered a major depressive disorder and was in a 'true dissociative state' at the time of the crime.

'Dissociation … is the split between the feeling, the emotion and intellect and what's going around you,' the professor explained. 'What we're talking about here is a man who in fact moved not just from the usual dissociation that you can see in major depressive disorders but severe-end dissociation, where in fact he didn't really know what was going on.'

Burrows likened the state to that of a sleepwalker. 'They can get up and go to the fridge and eat things and do things and go back to bed and they can't remember anything about it.'

BRUSTMAN: Are you able professionally, in your opinion, to give an opinion about whether there was a catalyst—a final clincher or something—which … could have or would have tipped Mr Freeman?

BURROWS: Well, I think [his family situation] was the cruncher …

BRUSTMAN: Could he in any way understand, in your opinion, the nature of what he did on that day at the time?'

BURROWS: I don't think he still does. I haven't been involved in his therapy, but as I have said in my reports, he still doesn't believe that it occurred. He still doesn't believe that he could have done it. But he believes that people have told him he's done it, so he accepts that.

During his cross-examination, Silbert referred to Burrows as 'effectively the psychiatrist of last resort'. Brustman objected.

'On what basis is this put?' he asked.

'I'm about to put the basis,' Silbert responded, before turning back to Burrows in the witness box.

The jury should be aware, professor, that this accused man has been seen by a minimum of six psychiatrists … And it is fair to say that you are the only one of the six who's been prepared to find mental impairment?

Burrows did not miss a beat. 'If you want opinions from psychiatrists you'll get controversy,' he answered.

In rebuttal to Burrows, the prosecution called two psychiatrists. The first was Yvonne Skinner who, during her career, had treated more than eighty people—both mothers and fathers—who had killed their children. That crime is called filicide. Skinner assessed Freeman on 22 November 2010. In a nutshell, she believed there was no indication that Freeman acted unconsciously or was suffering from a psychotic mental illness.

'He was able to discuss plans with his parents, to organise the children to prepare for the journey,' she wrote in her report.

> He drove from Aireys Inlet to Melbourne. He spoke to the children on the journey. He was able to make and receive telephone calls … His actions and the alleged telephone conversations indicate that he was acting voluntarily and consciously.
>
> I believe that the alleged offences can be explained to some extent on the basis of underlying psychological dynamics. Mr Freeman had been involved in ongoing acrimonious disputes. On the day prior to the alleged offences he had been … disappointed and frustrated by [his family situation] which he regarded as unfair. He had suffered a number of significant losses and had expressed his frustration and distress to his father and witnesses. The victim, his daughter Darcey, reportedly presented some challenges in the management of her behaviour. The psychologist has reported that Darcey was close to her mother and had enjoyed being with her mother in Mr Freeman's absence. Mr Freeman was reported to have had a past history of poor anger management and occasional aggressive behaviour.

In evidence, Skinner agreed with Silbert in that the facts and circumstances of the case were consistent with 'spousal revenge'. Brustman challenged Skinner.

BRUSTMAN: You would agree, would you not, that this extraordinary act—the actual act of throwing this child off a bridge—not only is extreme but it's profound in any which way we imagine that term, correct? It's extraordinary.

SKINNER: It's extraordinary, yes.

BRUSTMAN: All of a sudden and I stress that—all of a sudden, doctor. It's not that he gets out of the car and bashes someone. It's not that he gets out of the car and behaves like an idiot. Runs across the lane. Literally takes his child—and we must be talking seconds by everyone's account. Takes his child and hurls her over the bridge. As you have said, an extraordinary event. Right?

SKINNER: Yes.

BRUSTMAN: Now what I am suggesting to you is this—that without some severe psychiatric episode occurring, without that, there is absolutely no reason for it.

SILBERT: Well, Your Honour, I object to that question. The phone call to the wife says, 'Say goodbye to your children.' There is a reason for it.

BRUSTMAN: Well … no, no. Just answer my question.

JUSTICE COGHLAN: No, but you have left that out, Mr Brustman. It seems to be pretty significant … There is difficulty in this case in talking about, in parts, Mr Brustman. That's all I will say to you.

BRUSTMAN: What I am suggesting to you [Dr Skinner], is that this event could not by any way have occurred without Mr Freeman being seriously mentally ill and disturbed at the time. Seriously ill. No person does that. What's your answer to that?

SKINNER: I think it's an extraordinary event that can be explained, perhaps not understood, but explained in terms of the psychological sequence of events that happened preceding and on that day.

BRUSTMAN: Yes, and it can also be explained simply by saying that here was a seriously ill, mentally ill man, behaving in a seriously ill manner. Not at one with anything: himself or anything else. Doing just that with no reason … Could be that too, couldn't it?

SKINNER: If there had been a history of mental illness or a history and evidence suggesting that, it might have been. But that wasn't the case.

Dr Douglas Bell was the prosecution's second expert witness. He had interviewed Freeman at the remand centre on 26 May 2009, and 2 February and 11 March 2010.

'It is in my view, Your Honour, that there is minimal evidence to support the view, the conclusion, that Mr Freeman in any way had a psychosis—a paranoid illness—and that he was in any way delusional,' Bell told the trial.

In his report he felt Freeman became 'severely distraught' and 'overwhelmed' as the pressure mounted against him in gridlock on the bridge. He said it was obvious Freeman was aware of his surroundings when he threw Darcey over the edge.

Bell told the court:

Mr Freeman, in pulling across to the side of the road, putting on his hazard lights, walking his child across and lifting his child the way he has to overcome the barrier of the bridge is demonstrating an awareness of the environment and engaging in behaviour to overcome an obstacle to his course of action.

In his closing address, Silbert told the jury it was 'an overwhelming case of murder'. He advised them to reject Burrows's evidence on the basis it was evasive and contradictory.

'Freeman was upset,' Silbert instructed.

He was angry. The threats to Peta Barnes in the two phone conversations related by her indicate that his anger management problems were about to bubble over. What it amounts to, ladies and gentlemen, is that in a paroxysm of anger with Peta Barnes he stopped on the bridge and threw Darcey over the rail … The threats to Peta Barnes minutes before the murder demonstrate he knew the nature and quality of what he was about to do. We are perhaps indeed fortunate that he didn't throw all three children over the bridge.

Brustman, in his closing, admitted the crime was 'truly horrible'. There was no way he could resile from that fact.

'Very few cases could induce more prejudice against a person,' he said.

There in the dock sits a man who flung a four-year-old girl—his own daughter—to her death. Is this simply the face of pure evil? It is very easy, ladies and gentlemen, to think it is … We fully understand that it would be a Herculean task to set aside thoughts of prejudice and sympathy [for Darcey's family] in this case. We ask you to do just that.

We, on behalf of Mr Freeman, say to you that his head was simply elsewhere. We say to you that he was mentally impaired in the manner Professor Burrows described. That his impairment meant he was not acting consciously, voluntarily or intentionally.

> There is no question that this is an indecent act.
> It is an insane act ... What decent person would not
> recoil at the events that took place that day on the
> bridge. But what we say is, it is a mad mind.

After the jury was culled by ballot from fourteen down
to twelve, the seven women and five men took five days
to reach a unanimous decision, after some time spent in
deadlock. Coghlan had told them while he did have the
power to discharge them without verdict he believed they
had the resolve to work through their differences.

'Experience has shown that juries can often agree if
given more time to consider and discuss the issues,' the
veteran judge said. 'And we wouldn't say it to juries if it
was not our experience that sometimes extra time works.'

It was about 8 pm on Monday, 28 March 2011, when the
jury returned with a guilty verdict. Peta Barnes showed
no emotion in court. Her father, Wayne Barnes—a hard-
boiled Western Australian ex-copper who had spent parts
of the trial gripping the wooden seat in front of him—
had a tear in his eye.

The entire Barnes family returned for Freeman's
pre-sentence hearing. Before it began, a still-unkempt
Freeman sat looking as though he'd just undergone a
lobotomy. His eyes flitted around the courtroom, as if
following an invisible butterfly. During the proceeding,
Peta rose to read aloud her victim impact statement. Up
until that point she had maintained a stoic facade. It was
finally about to crack.

'I am an intensely private individual when it comes
to my emotions and thoughts,' she began. 'I provide this
information in the hope that a small measure of the pain
and loss I have suffered since the passing of my little
girl ...' She began to cry and had to stop. She composed

herself and tried again. She could not read on and returned to her seat, allowing Crown prosecutor Diana Piekusis to read on.

Since the loss of Darcey I grieve on a daily basis and realistically do not see how that can ever change. The saying 'time heals all wounds' is not true for myself and I don't ever expect it to be. Not a day goes by where I do not constantly think of Darcey, where I don't miss her and wish with all my heart that she was with me.

I can feel her little hand holding mine when I walk down the street or drive in the car. I lie in bed at night and hold her in my arms. I talk to her and think of her daily, wishing she was participating in the activities that were happening at that time. No words could ever truly describe the loss of a child to a parent. The emptiness that sits within you, the piece of you that no longer exists, the fact you no longer go on in life as a complete person.

Seeing little girls who have similar traits or looks to Darcey heightens my already active emotions. Holding myself back from giving the child a hug is always a struggle of self control.

I have now and forever only memories of Darcey when I intended to have a lifetime of love and laughter.

I can never erase from my mind the thought of my beautiful girl so willingly and trustingly going to her father at his request on top of the West Gate Bridge. Of her falling to her death and what her last thoughts must have been. The nightmares and sleep deprivation I suffer around this are too horrific to detail.

No one can erase the thoughts and associated feelings I have of sitting in the hospital and having to tell the hospital staff that they were allowed to turn the life support machine off. Of holding Darcey in my arms as she passed away and knowing that this decision would take her from me and knowing that there was no other option available to me.

Other impact statements were tendered, like that of paramedic Kristine Gough.

I have been to dead children before—SIDS, accidents and suicide. But nothing has impacted me more emotionally than this incident. I have been to hundreds of people who died, but the only funeral I felt the need to attend was this one—and I went. I have performed CPR on hundreds, but this is the only time I can recall talking to my patient as if my words of 'don't give up on me' would make a difference.

I now hate that bridge ... I was sent to the job from hell and I, like everyone there that day, have to live with the fact that despite every effort we couldn't save Darcey.

Police officer Colleen Spiteri shared lingering torment. She performed CPR before the paramedics arrived, and had also felt compelled to go to Darcey's funeral.

My sadness for little Darcey has not diminished ... I have a panic attack when I have to cross the West Gate Bridge. My heart takes a plunge every time I see it, or even a picture of it. I have recently changed police stations. This keeps me away from any jobs near the bridge. I cannot understand why this has happened.

Other police officers say that it was the worst day of their career and they weren't even there. I joined the police force with high expectations of helping people. I could not help Darcey. There was a pulse at the scene. A small one. Or did I imagine that? I hoped and hoped. She was tiny. Miracles have happened before. Kids have fallen into frozen lakes and come out alive after twenty minutes. I could not help Darcey. I pleaded with her to wake up. She didn't.

Throughout the hearing, Freeman showed no feeling. Maybe he was thinking about his jailhouse tomato plants. He had told his relatives he loved his little prison garden.

Justice Coghlan sentenced the killer father on 11 April 2011. Before he learned his fate, Freeman's blank eyes again meandered across the ceiling of the nineteenth-century courtroom as if still following that invisible butterfly.

'This was the killing of an innocent child,' Coghlan told him.

The circumstances of the killing were horrible. The throwing of your four-year-old daughter from a bridge more than fifty metres above the ground could not be more horrible. What Darcey's last thoughts might have been does not bear thinking about, and her death must have been a painful and protracted one. Your conduct is a most fundamental breach of trust and it is an attack on the institution of the family which is so dear to the community. The killing was in the presence of your son, Benjamin, who was then six, and your son Jack, who was two. The community hopes Jack will be too young to remember.

Any motive which existed for the killing had nothing to do with the innocent victim. It can only be concluded that you used your daughter in an attempt to hurt your former wife as profoundly as possible. You chose a place for the commission of your crime which was remarkably public and which would have the most dramatic impact. It follows that you brought the broader community into this case in a way that has been rarely, if ever, seen before. It offends our collective conscience.

Coghlan said he accepted that while the crime was not premeditated it was driven by Freeman's anger towards Peta and his frustration at running late for school.

'You are yet to say sorry to anyone for what you have done,' Coghlan told him. 'I am satisfied that you continue to lack any insight into your offending and I regard your prospects of rehabilitation as bleak.'

Coghlan turned to the length of sentence. It had not been an easy case for him. 'I understand that many will say that your crime is so serious in so many respects that I should not impose a non-parole period, i.e., you deserve to be locked away forever,' he said.

I see the attractiveness of that argument, but the sentencing process is not as simple as that ... I am obliged to have regard to the fact that you are thirty-seven years of age. Whatever happens, you will spend what may be regarded by many as the best years of your life in prison ... I have taken into account your previous good behaviour. I have taken into account the references tendered on your behalf and the support which you have from your direct family.

Coghlan handed Freeman life with a minimum term of thirty-two years. That meant Freeman would stay in jail until at least 29 January 2041. By that date he will have turned sixty-seven.

'One of the very unfortunate features of this case is that others seem to blame themselves for what you have done,' Coghlan told Freeman. 'They should not. You did what you did. You are responsible for it and nobody else is.'

It was then that Freeman broke his silence, yelling and accusing people of committing unlawful acts against him—as if *he* was the victim. Prison guards cuffed him and dragged him to the cells.

It is fair to say Freeman's crime shocked a nation. It has left empty to the core those who knew him and loved him. As Freeman continues to tend to his prison tomatoes, it is those people, as well as those people who loved Darcey, who are left to count the cost and simply ask 'why?'

'I wouldn't call him aggressive and I have no explanation as to why he would have done this,' his mother said in her police statement.

His sister Megan could only speculate. 'I know that Arthur was under a lot of pressure … As far as I know, Arthur loved all his kids—and he loved Darcey just like the others.'

His closest mates were dumbfounded.

'To me, Ardy was a very gentle person—so much so that in all the years that I have known him we never had an argument,' Anthony Luscombe said in his police statement.

He never raised his voice to me. In fact, if there was an argument he was usually the rational one. He seemed to be a great dad to all the children … On the weekend before [he murdered Darcey] I had been down at Aireys Inlet with Ardy and the kids and everything seemed fine.

I have no idea why what happened happened. I just know that he loved his kids. He loved them so much. He wanted to be a stay-at-home dad. Peta wanted to put them in day care which was something he didn't like at all. He didn't like the idea of strangers looking after his kids.

Former close family associate Michael received a Facebook message from a friend of his, who also knew Freeman quite well. The message summed up the conundrum facing Freeman's family and friends.

'One part of me is angry and wants justice for Darcey and then another part of me feels for Ardy who is a friend in need,' the Facebook message read. 'The conflicting feelings are like a storm churning inside. Which should rule, my head or my heart?'

Freeman sought leave to appeal the length of his sentence on the ground that it was manifestly excessive. He also contended that Justice Coghlan gave inadequate weight to his remorse and prospects for rehabilitation. It was a bold call, considering the case sparked an outcry for the reintroduction of capital punishment. If some people had had their way, Freeman would have ended swinging from the gallows in the centre of Melbourne's Federation Square. Court of Appeal president Justice Chris Maxwell refused Freeman's application.

'Leave to appeal is only granted where one or more of the proposed grounds of appeal is shown to be capable of reasonable argument,' Maxwell said in his judgment. 'In the present case, I do not regard it as reasonably arguable that the non-parole period of thirty-two years was outside the sentencing range open to the sentencing judge in the circumstances of this case.'

All Arthur Phillip Freeman has to keep him company—until his eventual release from prison—are his jailhouse tomatoes. And motorists driving across the West Gate Bridge now have high, protective metal barricades to hem them in. The cage-like fences were erected after Darcey's death to prevent another such tragedy, and to stop people using the bridge as a launching point in suicide bids, as many unfortunate tormented souls had done in the past.

6
Death Struggle

'Why did you take him away from us?
He never did anything to upset anyone.'

WATCHING A MAN BEING MURDERED, AS HE FIGHTS AND struggle in the realisation that he is actually going to die, is a disturbing event to witness. It is heart-wrenching, especially when the victim is a law-abiding harmless man and his killer an overpowering beast who controls the kill from the outset; who attacks the weaker victim by surprise with a weapon—in this case a wooden baton—before using his dominant size to pin the smaller man to the floor where he repeatedly stabs him; who continues to hold him down and then stabs him some more. It is infuriating watching CCTV footage of such a death, as the victim musters the strength to try to fight off his attacker amid the blood splatter, only to be pinned by a forearm, stabbed again and held there to bleed out while staring into the eyes of his killer. The indignity is pitiful. It is chilling to watch the blood-soaked victim looking up into the eyes of his killer to ask 'why'; blood-stained carpet around them, chairs toppled in the small office space. It is incredibly sad when the victim stops moving, his last breath leaving his lungs. The demeaning injustice of it all is overwhelming. It cannot be aptly described in words. And that is why Crown Prosecutor Mark Rochford, SC, played that very footage to a Supreme Court judge. Rochford wanted the footage to speak for itself. Although it was silent security vision, it spoke volumes.

This is not the story of the death of a Carl Williams–style gangster or a police officer in the line of duty. It is the story of the brutal and senseless murder of an Everyman and the everlasting effect his unjust death had on his family. In his trailblazing true-crime book *In Cold Blood,* Truman Capote quoted a middle-American deputy about the fate of the innocent Clutter family: 'Of all the people in all the world,' the local law man stated, 'the Clutters were the least likely to be murdered.' The same could be said of Melbourne post-office manager Dzung Nguyen. The father of two was certainly no swaggering gangster or a cop taught how to deal with angry men on mean streets. Nguyen was the typical 'little guy' of suburbia: a quiet, hard-working common man who thought more about those around him than himself.

Forty-eight at the time of his death, Nguyen had arrived in Australia as a thirteen-year-old refugee of Vietnamese and Cambodian heritage. After completing his education, he worked for Telstra for eighteen years before taking control of the running of a post office in 2006. A married father of two mature teenagers, Dzung Nguyen was a thread in Victoria's rich multicultural quilt when Riad Barbour snuffed out his life. Nguyen was the sort of bloke you would never read about in the newspapers unless, of course, he became the victim. His family was his priority. Everything he did he did for his two children. He was much liked by those within his shopping community in

Deer Park in Melbourne's north-west. As his niece Celine Cao later told the Victorian Supreme Court:

> His children were his number one priority and he only wanted the best for them. He worked hard to support them and his business was very important to him. The shopkeepers surrounding his workplace all had a connection to him. He had a positive impact on his customers and employees as he was a kind, friendly man.

Riad Barbour, on the other hand, was a brute: an illiterate ex-soldier turned failed milk-bar owner. In cowardly fashion he waited until everyone had left Nguyen's post office before he entered and attacked the meek victim. He murdered Nguyen over a batch of wholesale cigarettes he had been refused on credit earlier that day. As Supreme Court judge Justice Cameron Macauley told him:

> The specific details of your offence are chillingly simple; graphically depicted on closed-circuit television footage obtained from the premises where they occurred. Your crimes are made worse by the fact that, at that time, you were on parole for a sentence of five years' imprisonment for committing armed robbery and aggravated burglary.

Barbour was born in Syria and emigrated to Australia with his family at the age of twelve in 1991. He grew up in Melbourne's western suburbs with a younger sister and brother. According to defence barrister Christopher Pearson, the Barbour family were 'poor people'.

'His father worked as a concreter,' Pearson told Justice Macauley at Barbour's Supreme Court plea hearing.

'His father was violent and physically abusive towards [Barbour] and his siblings.'

Schooled up until Year 7, Barbour remained illiterate. 'You [Riad Barbour] were pulled out of school by your father in order that you work and earn money to assist your family,' a County Court judge, Liz Gaynor, had said back in September 2008 when Barbour appeared before her after his first foray into violent crime. (That foray had involved armed robbery.)

> As a result you are illiterate and cannot read or write— either in English or your native Lebanese. This has severely restricted your capacity to obtain well-paid employment and, in my view, has significance in terms of the lead-up and the reason for this [armed robbery] offending by you—a man with no prior history at all.

After leaving school, Barbour felt like a member of the lowest common denominator. But where many like him with a substandard educational background turn to petty crime and drug use, Barbour did not wander down that path. Well, not immediately, anyway. For a year he worked as a cleaner. In 1997, at age eighteen, he returned to Syria to stay with an aunt. Gaynor stated in court:

> At the airport, awaiting return to Australia, you were apprehended by security forces and told you had to undertake two years' national service with the Syrian army or pay $10,000. You did not have that money to pay and underwent two years in the Syrian army, a period you described to psychiatrist Lester Walton … as 'the worst thing in my life'. You did not simply serve national service with the Syrian army; the country was at war with Hezbollah and you were forced into hand-to-hand

combat where you saw a commanding officer killed
on being shot in the head, and other soldiers killed or
injured. You yourself suffered a gunshot wound in the
leg and later a stabbing injury to your left wrist.

After his discharge Barbour returned to Australia at
age twenty. Judge Gaynor's narrative of his downward
spiral went on: 'You continued to work as a cleaner
and car detailer and you returned to Syria in 1999 to
2000 to marry your wife, with whom you had been in
correspondence for some time, and she returned with
you to Australia.' The couple had two children. After
that, the Supreme Court was told, Barbour's life became
'blighted'—not because he had become a father but
because of his detrimental decisions. He obtained a
security licence (a good effort for an illiterate bloke),
and started using speed and its more potent form, ice,
around the age of twenty-five.

'He started gambling,' defence barrister Pearson
explained. 'He commenced spending more money than
he was earning.'

After working at a cousin's car yard, financial woes
led Barbour to commit an $8000 social security fraud in
2005—for which he was convicted and fined. And then he
stepped up to the big league. Having enlisted a security
guard to help as an inside man, Barbour—armed with
an imitation pistol—terrorised staff at the Olympic Hotel
pokies venue in Preston on the night of 11 June 2008.
Judge Gaynor summarised the hold-up.

During the course of the night, [your inside man]
contacted you and told you when the gaming machines
would be cleared ... Inside the car you put a blue
balaclava on your head and white latex gloves and

carried a bag with you when you left, as well as an imitation firearm. You placed a baseball cap on top of the balaclava and at 2.49 am [your inside man] rang you on your mobile phone, which police allege was a pre-arranged signal to indicate that he was keeping the side entrance doors open.

Barbour stormed the venue, pointing his gun at his accomplice's head as he marched him through the gaming venue. Judge Gaynor said:

You marched [your inside man] through the gaming venue behind the counter area to the cash office, pushing the firearm into the back of his head. As the two of you walked through the venue, [your inside man] was telling patrons to get down and you also told patrons and staff to get down.

Barbour yelled, 'Everyone get down on the fucking floor!' He kicked a male patron as he walked past and shouted: 'Don't move. This isn't a joke!' The female manager was counting cleared money in the cash office. Barbour forced his accomplice inside and thrust the bag at him. A female gaming attendant lying face down heard Barbour yell: 'Don't move or I'll shoot you!'

He had his accomplice fill the bag at gunpoint before forcing the manager to grab cash from the safe. He slapped his accomplice for an authentic touch, and struck the female manager to the head while yelling, 'Hurry up bitch!' Judge Gaynor commented:

She [the manager] told police the incident felt surreal and she felt like she could not breathe and was too scared to breathe while you were there. When you left she started to cry, began to panic and became extremely scared.

Barbour fled out the same entrance through which he had entered, dropping his cap and latex gloves in a nearby street. He drove home. When he got there he removed all of his clothes and placed them—along with the bag and firearm—into a barbecue and burned the lot. He then went inside and counted the money. He'd made a quick and violent earn of $93,000.

Detectives found his gloves and cap. Inquiries led investigators to him, and he provided a DNA swab. Forensic tests linked him to the discarded items. During a search of his home, detectives located an amount of methylamphetamine. He told police it was for his personal use only. Barbour made full admissions about the armed robbery, telling investigators he committed the hold-up because he wanted to do something for his kids. Barbour ended up pleading guilty to armed robbery, aggravated burglary and false imprisonment and drug possession. In September 2008, Gaynor sentenced him to five years' jail with a two-and-a-half-year minimum term. It was said that Barbour was a henpecked man when he planned the stick-up.

'You were ashamed of your inability to provide more for your family, such as being able to provide a home of your own—apart from rented premises,' Gaynor said at sentencing.

In about the eight months before this offending, relations with your wife soured dramatically. She believed that you were failing her as a provider and this belief, apparently, came from your [relatively affluent] sister who was constantly critical of you and who herself was ashamed of your inability to earn more money. Your wife, ultimately, believed, as I have said, you failed to provide for her adequately as a result of your sister's constant criticism of you. Your wife has no family in this country and was, no doubt, dependent on and influenced by her wealthier sister-in-law … You told Dr Walton that about six months before the offending you began coping with the domestic pressure by the use of methylamphetamine: that is, amphetamine in the form of ice, as well as occasional use of cannabis.

In a report, Walton wrote of the influence Barbour's wife and sister had on him.

There was an escalation in anxiety, in particular in the context of Mr Barbour being under pressure to provide materially for his family—that situation, seemingly, being fuelled by Barbour's sister's adverse influence upon his wife.

Walton also noted:

Despite him seemingly actively seeking work, Mr Barbour felt he was in a situation of not providing for his family according to his wife's expectations and thus he was tempted towards the ill-considered armed robbery. It is possible that his misjudgment in engaging in this foolhardy behaviour was contributed to by his taking of amphetamine, especially as he seemed to have reached a point of drug-induced psychositic symptoms at this time.

Gaynor described the hold-up as 'extraordinarily serious offending' that involved 'inflicting terror on a large number of people'. Continuing, she said that she accepted the commission of the crime was out of character.

> I accept this offending was motivated by feelings of inadequacy which, no doubt, lie in your family's treatment of you, exacerbated by your poor education limiting your capacity to obtain skilled and better paid employment. I accept that you have very good prospects of rehabilitation and that you are unlikely to offend again.

That opinion would be proved horribly wrong.

Barbour served some two years and eight months of his five-year jail term before he was released on parole in July 2010. After some work as a concreter, he quit. In her police statement, his cousin, Norma Doumith, says that he sat around at home growing bored and restless. To occupy him, Doumith set him up with a milk-bar business.

'However well intentioned that gesture was, it was to become an entirely ill-fated business,' barrister Pearson told the Supreme Court. 'He [Barbour] had no idea, it's clear, how to run the business. He was using ice and amphetamines at the time. He had started using steroids and he was going to the gym.'

Barbour also began dealing drugs on a small scale. His relationship with his wife was said to be deteriorating further. As his business floundered, his source of wholesale cigarettes dried up. Prosecutor Mark Rochford explained.

> The sale of cigarettes was part of this [milk-bar] business with the stock coming from a single premises in Coburg at wholesale prices. However, as time went by the milk bar started going into debt and was

running low on stock. Eventually, in October 2011, the supply was cut off with a debt of about $3000 owing.

Barbour was unable to pay any bills at all. Pearson described the situation: 'He locked himself in his bedroom [on one occasion]. He refused to come out ... even for family friends. It was when the prisoner was of that frame of mind that his path tragically crossed with Mr Nguyen's.'

A search for a new source of cigarettes led Barbour to Dzung Nguyen, and he started buying.

'[Apart from the post office] Mr Nguyen also operated a Tattslotto agency and a franchise selling wholesale cigarettes to various customers from that store,' Rochford told Justice Macauley. 'By 5 December of 2011 he [Barbour] had made a number of such purchases and spoke to Mr Nguyen and his wife about setting up an account.'

Nguyen organised the relevant paperwork but refused to strike a deal when Barbour said he wanted half the next consignment on credit. Witness Michelle Richard told police:

[Barbour] was a new customer. Dzung obtained the cigarettes for this man and brought them out the front. They then scanned in the cigarettes but the man wanted the cigarettes on credit and Dzung refused. There was no argument or yelling. The man just left.

The following day (6 December 2011) Barbour went to the post office and waited until closing time. He rang the rear doorbell and waved at Nguyen through the security camera. Nguyen let him in at 6.24 pm. CCTV footage from the office shows Nguyen gathering packets of cigarettes, scanning them and placing them into a crate on the floor. Barbour stands watching over him. At

6.44 pm, while Nguyen is leaning over the crate, Barbour pulls his wooden baton from his clothing and beats Nguyen several times. In explaining the murder before showing Macauley the footage, Rochford said: 'After an intense struggle the offender held [Mr Nguyen] in a headlock and then produced a knife and proceeded to stab him a number of times.'

Before the footage was played in court, a group of Nguyen's relatives, including most of his five sisters, left the court to avoid watching the murder. One of the grief-stricken sisters yelled abuse at Barbour and tried to jump into the dock. Barbour sat with head bowed as prison guards separated him from the howling mob. As the footage was played he continued to stare at the floor. A pathologist ascertained the cause of death to be 'stab wounds to the side of the neck causing injuries to major blood vessels'. Rochford said: 'The Crown case is this was a planned murder.' With a blood-stained Nguyen lying dead on the office floor, Barbour climbed up on a desk and cut wires leading to a DVD recorder and grabbed the machine. He then stole $12,298.58 from a safe and left Nguyen dead in the centre of the blood-spattered office.

Barbour may have ended an innocent man's life that night, but the ramifications were far greater. He destroyed other lives—the lives of relatives left to live with the pain and suffering. It was Nguyen's young niece Celine Cao who so eloquently explained that pain and suffering to Justice Macauley when reading a victim impact statement on behalf of several family members. On behalf of her mother, Linda, she read:

My brother was murdered on 6 December but his death still haunts us to this day seven months later. My dad suffers from diabetes and Dzung always visited him to take care of him and now because he's passed, my dad struggles to live his daily life, because he's lost his only son. We all know that he tried to hide his true feelings but it is obvious he is miserable … You can see the sadness in his eyes. My eldest sister cries every time someone mentions his name and whenever she comes across something that reminds her of him. When walking past his photo at home she starts to cry again … When it is raining she feels pain inside because he's at the cemetery by himself under the ground. Family gatherings affect her because the family will never be complete. She even feels guilty when having fun because she feels like she doesn't deserve the happiness while he's gone. She struggles to eat because every time she does she feels like she has everything next to his nothing.

On behalf of Nguyen's sister Vi, Celine read:

Her depression has worsened after his death. She has ongoing nightmares when she sees him in her sleep and frequently wakes up during the night to cry and pray for his return. The crying gives her constant migraines and results in swollen eyes making her wish she was blind … Vi always feels the need to accompany Dzung at the cemetery because she fears that he is lonely … Her brother's loss makes her feel empty inside and she feels no reason to continue living.

On behalf of his sister Hai, Celine read:

She suffers from insomnia and feels suicidal most days because of his absence. She misses her brother terribly and is traumatised by the event. She wishes to be with him all the time and for him to be alive and with us again. When she is sad she drives with no destination in mind and finds herself far away from home.

On behalf of his sister Lan, Celine read:

She finds herself sitting in her garden staring blankly into space. She loses track of time overwhelming herself with the memories she shared with her brother and his love for the outdoors. She locks away the photos of her brother because she is too afraid to look at them.

And then it was back to her mother on behalf of all five sisters.

Our hearts ache and have been aching for this awful past seven months. Any spare time is spent at the cemetery wishing for him to come back to us. Dzung was the only brother we had and was the eldest sibling in the family. He looked after us emotionally and financially and supported us when we were troubled. We are angry and frustrated at the fact that he is gone and will never come back. We can't let go. Dzung was a good person. He was loved by many and generous to all around him. He cared so much for his family and friends … We always ask God why him … Our one wish is justice for our brother Dzung … This is the pain we as sisters have suffered at the loss of our dear brother. I can't even begin to fathom the trauma endured by Dzung's two children losing their role model; their hero.

At the beginning of his submissions during the plea hearing, after the horrific CCTV footage was played in court, Pearson waded into the quagmire.

It's clear, Your Honour, and it's clear to everybody, that the death of Dzung Nguyen has significantly affected a large number of people. Whatever I am now about to say on behalf of the prisoner is entirely going to be cold comfort for those who are left behind to mourn his death. All the prisoner at the end of the day can do is to apologise for his behaviour and he does that through me. He knows, Your Honour, as he sits here today that it is entirely unlikely that that apology will ever be accepted. Your Honour has seen the recorded footage of the killing of Mr Nguyen in all of its abject horror. Your Honour knows therefore, as we all now do, how it was that this crime came to be committed. What remains for me to do at the end of the day is to seek to explain that which at the end of the day is entirely inexplicable.

Pearson proceeded to outline mitigating circumstances. Barbour's violent upbringing. His traumatic experiences fighting the Hezbollah. His depression and his drug use, including the use of steroids. His failed milk-bar business. Pressures on the home front. The fact that he was high on ice at the time. Barbour even claimed that he attacked Nguyen because he thought the post office man was looking for a weapon. Rochford was having none of that.

'That is disputed entirely, Your Honour, and is proved to be absolute rubbish,' Rochford told Macauley. 'Any suggestion that there's apprehension, tension, fear or concern that Mr Nguyen was going to get a weapon is just completely repudiated by viewing that video footage, in my submission.'

Pearson responded, 'That is a perception that is well and truly clouded by [Barbour's] use of drugs … He was heavily under the influence of ice—amphetamines—and steroids at the time.'

Psychologist Michael Bilyk would throw up another theory. Macauley would explain in his remarks:

Mr Bilyk raises the possibility of you [Barbour] having unresolved post-traumatic stress following your time in the Syrian army, without making such a diagnosis. But he says that whilst you reported that any such symptoms of such stress had subsided since being back in Australia, your experiences, including being the victim of family violence, led to the potential of you being particularly 'threat sensitive'.

He went on to add that your amphetamine and steroid abuse, in combination with stressors, was likely to have had an exacerbating effect on your behaviour … Although I do not accept the account that you were reacting to an immediate perception of threat when you commenced assaulting Mr Nguyen, I do accept that you were generally at a very low ebb with feelings of paranoia, anger and aggression exacerbated by the effect of drugs you were taking.

Barbour claimed that he carried the wooden baton on him 'due to concerns for his personal safety given involvement with substance trafficking'. He said he carried a box cutter—which he contended was the weapon he used to stab Nguyen—for use in the milk-bar business. (Macauley did not accept that a box cutter inflicted the stab wounds.)

Barbour had told Michael Bilyk of regret, shame and remorse. 'Consistent with an empathic response Mr Barbour was able to identity the impact of this offence on his victim and his victim's family,' Pearson said.

And then came a great understatement.

'Barbour contended that his victim would have been very scared and in pain. Mr Barbour commented that the victim's family would be deeply saddened and probably think of him as not a nice person.'

During the plea hearing, Pearson told Justice Macauley:

> Mr Barbour is a person who was clearly brought up in a violent home. He's clearly a man who was exposed to significant levels of violence in the army in Syria. And Mr Bilyk has something to say about people who are exposed to that level of violence—they are more likely to be people who react violently in turn … What I do say about the prisoner, beyond those factors to do with his psychological profile, is that his criminal record is not, in my respectful submission, overwhelmingly bad. He has that one matter involving a social security fraud in 2008 and then the significant matter concerning the armed robbery. He commenced criminal activity only relatively recently in his life … He has beyond that, Your Honour, a relatively good work ethic, notwithstanding his poor English language skills … Weighing everything in the balance it would be open to the court to conclude that he has some reasonably good prospects of ultimate rehabilitation and redemption.

Macauley interjected. He had specific sentencing considerations on his mind. 'Whilst dealing with sentencing objectives,' he began,

> it would seem to me that community protection looms reasonably prominently, does it not, in this case given that Mr Bilyk I think has with some balance concluded

that your client does have a susceptibility to stress. That stress arises, as it has, when he's under financial stress and other stresses. Financial stresses in his life may well be predictable given illiteracy and what does not appear to be any significant or obvious work skills and his tendency in those circumstances to descend to substance abuse and in those circumstances the threat that he represents to the community [is] violent re-offending, and violent re-offending of a fairly significant degree.

Pearson countered with:

Well, except to say this Your Honour. He was aged around thirty at the time that he committed his first offence involving violence which is the armed robbery offence. I can't sensibly say at the end of the day that the protection of the community is not a legitimate sentencing function in the circumstances of this case. But what I do say is that this is not a man who has page after page after page of entrenched violent offending from his teenage years right through to the commission of this offence. In other words, he is a person—however beastly his performance was on 6 December 2011—who has a capacity to behave himself and to not commit violent offences. And in my respectful submission at the end of the day the court would have some confidence that if he stays off drugs and that if he applies himself, that he has the capacity to live a productive meaningful life in circumstances where he would not further re-offend. So look, at the end of the day I would have to concede that community protection has a role to play but I don't necessarily concede that it has an overwhelming part to play in the circumstances in this case.

It also had to be remembered, at the end of the day, that Barbour had so cold-bloodedly murdered Dzung Nguyen. Amid the legal talk and defence submissions, that cold hard fact remained—a sobering truth not lost on the grieving family sitting to the left of the courtroom as Pearson batted on in an effort to gold-plate his client as best he could.

'He works as a cook down at Barwon [Prison],' he explained of Barbour.

> He indicates by way of instruction that he has stayed away from drugs—he has stayed away from drugs within the prison environment. He's put his name down for courses to do with anger management and violence and drug relapse prevention. He knows that he has a long stretch ahead of him … And he has resolved at least in his own mind that he will come out of jail, whenever he comes out of jail, a better man than when he went into jail.

When it came to the subject of the stolen money, again, Barbour said he was sorry—he had blown it on gambling and drugs.

Pearson asked for a sentence that would not 'crush all hope for the future'.

Rochford went in hard, branding the murder a planned killing. 'The Crown relies upon the waiting for everyone to leave,' Rochford said.

> Knowing that he had been refused credit for the cigarettes. [He] waits until all the cigarettes have

been scanned into the computer and placed into the cartons before he produces a weapon, commences his attack and then never ceases that attack—indeed produces another weapon which in my submission does not appear to be a box cutter. It appears to be some sort of knife that he folds out and folds back in again … [The] attack does not cease until Mr Nguyen is incapacitated and dying. And so he launches the attack and continues it for that whole period of time. He knew of the CCTV system and the removal of the DVD recorder can only be an effort to remove the evidence of what he's just done. Unfortunately for Mr Barbour it was being recorded on the computer hard drive, not on the DVD recorder … He then takes the cash from the safe, takes the DVD recorder and leaves.

Rochford said it was a simple case of Barbour covering his tracks. 'He knew that Mr Nguyen knew who he was and was able to work out who he was because he had purchased previously. He wanted to dispose of the witness who would be able to reveal who he was.'

A further insight into Barbour's true character was revealed when he had Pearson ask Macauley if he could avoid coming to court for his sentence and instead cop it away from the glare of Nguyen's relatives via a video link from Barwon Prison. 'He has a job at Barwon Prison,' Pearson said on instructions.

He has his routine at Barwon Prison and as I say at the end of the day it's a matter that the prisoner asked me to take up with Your Honour … I am not saying that it's an overwhelmingly big deal in the scheme of things but he says that he has his job, he has his routine and he has his placement at Barwon Prison and that his preference—for what it's worth—would be that the matter be dealt with by way of a video link to Barwon Prison.

Macauley dismissed the request. 'For my part I regard this as such a serious and solemn matter that it's desirable that it take place in the physical presence of the prisoner … with the judge speaking to the prisoner face to face,' the judge rightly said.

On 10 August 2012, Macauley sentenced Barbour to a maximum term of twenty-three years with a minimum of nineteen-and-a-half years—on top of which he had to serve twenty-two months he owed the Parole Board for the Olympic Hotel armed robbery.

'The absence of any criminal convictions before your late twenties suggests that you had managed to deal with certain disadvantages in your upbringing without resorting to offending,' Macauley told the doleful Barbour. 'Perhaps those disadvantages, namely your father's violence, your limited educational skills and your experience in the Syrian army left their mark upon you.'

Macauley spoke of the cold-blooded killing. 'Although somewhat clumsy and inept, your killing of Mr Nguyen was an act of savagery,' he said.

Over the several minutes during which you assaulted Mr Nguyen leading ultimately to his death, his experience of terror and physical pain does not bear imagination … The Crown contends that this was a planned killing. On your behalf, it was argued that it was not open to me to conclude, beyond reasonable doubt, that it was so. But I am satisfied, on that standard of proof, that you did attend the post office on the night of 6 December with the intention of stealing from Mr Nguyen and covering your tracks by killing him.

Macauley said he did not buy Barbour's explanation for carrying the wooden baton and the box cutter. 'You said you carried the truncheon because you were accustomed to having it with you when transacting drug dealing, for your personal safety,' Macauley said.

That explanation does not account for its presence on this occasion. Further, you claimed you took with you a box cutter because that is a tool of trade often used by you in your milk-bar business. But the injuries inflicted upon Mr Nguyen are not consistent with the use of a box cutter—some incisions being fifteen centimetres and twenty centimetres deep. The CCTV shows you using two hands to fold back the knife blade.

Macauley also shot down any suggestion that Barbour reacted out of fear. 'I reject as palpably false the characterisation of the assault as being provoked by a spontaneous perception of danger.'

The judge said he had come to the conclusion that the murder was, in fact, planned.

I come to that conclusion because you knew Mr Nguyen would not give you credit to enable you to get the quantity of cigarettes you wanted; you waited until Mr Nguyen was alone before entering the building; you were armed with weapons without any adequate explanation for carrying them except that you intended to use them on Mr Nguyen; you were clearly known by Mr Nguyen and could be identified by him if you left him alive; and the assault upon him, as seen, appeared to be initiated with deliberate calm.

Macauley also made comment about Barbour committing the murder while on parole.

> You were released on parole on 19 July 2010, having served two and a half years of your five-year sentence. Thus, you re-offended in this murder/theft within eighteen months. The fact that you resorted to the most violent of crimes, to obtain money, whilst on parole for armed robbery cannot be seen any other way than as an extremely concerning aggravating feature of your conduct … As may be expected, the impact of your crimes upon the family of Mr Nguyen has been, and will continue to be, absolutely devastating. Whilst it is bad enough that you have brought a violent and premature end to another person's life, you have also consigned another group of people—his family and friends—to an interminable period of grief and agony. Tragically, Mr Nguyen's children endured the horror of having to discover the bloodied body of their dead father … Relatively short moments of callous and violent behaviour on your part have not only ended one human life but have permanently injured the lives of many others.

In *In Cold Blood,* Capote wrote of the innocent Clutter family: 'The victims might as well have been killed by lightning, except for one thing: they had experienced prolonged terror, they had suffered.' The same could be said of Melbourne post-office manager Dzung Nguyen.

7

Lust's Fatal Bondage

'This marriage was sick in more ways than one.'

EILEEN CREAMER WAS A WOMAN TORN: TORN BETWEEN love and loathing. Her husband, David, liked having sex with other women, sometimes in front of her. He wanted Eileen to have sex with other men so he could watch. He really liked the idea of threesomes. David was a sex maniac who, according to Eileen, treated her like a 'dog'. But she couldn't help but love him. To try to salvage her marriage, Eileen enlisted the help of internet psychics to place spells on David's lovers, and his former wife. They were the actions of a desperate woman. It was alleged Eileen Creamer, a fifty-one-year-old woman 'of small stature', murdered David. It was a brutal killing. Blood was left smeared and spattered all around their Moe home—in the bedroom, bathroom, hallway, kitchen and out in the courtyard. David Creamer suffered numerous blunt-force injuries to his head and a stab wound to the upper abdomen, the knife ravaging his stomach and liver, causing massive internal bleeding. Was it a crime of jealousy, passion or defensive homicide? At Eileen Creamer's Supreme Court murder trial, defence counsel Jane Dixon, SC, said the killing was a case about 'human behaviour'.

'You need to get inside the skin of Mrs Creamer to understand her motivations and what would drive a person to physically attack her husband,' Dixon told the jury. 'You might need to know something of her prior background and the pressures affecting her in February of 2008.'

Born in Durban, South Africa, on 1 September 1957, Eileen spent her childhood growing up in a small town called Matatiele. Her father died when she was three, and the family moved in with relatives.

'My mother wasn't coping and she started drinking,' Eileen recounted in court. 'She couldn't take care of us.'

After primary school, Eileen was sent to boarding school in the nearby township of Flagstaff until her aunt intervened and brought her back to Durban. She completed high school in a place called Pietermaritzburg. It was there she met David Creamer. He was classed a 'coloured' boy, according to the racial classifications of the ruling apartheid regime. Eileen was classified as the same, as her dad was white and her mother black.

'We started dating from high school ... I always loved David from school and I think he felt the same way about me as well,' she said.

David, who spent two years in Bible school at Cape Town studying to become a minister, came from a strict Pentecostal background. He urged Eileen to go to church with him. She came from a Catholic upbringing. The religious differences caused tensions.

'I wasn't comfortable in his church,' Eileen told the jury during her Supreme Court murder trial.

Because of the religious backgrounds we were constantly getting into arguments. I was allowed to go dancing and

I started drinking then because I was working. David wasn't allowed to go dancing. All his family did was go to church. I did try and go to a couple of church services with him and youth groups with him, but it was just a totally different background to the Catholic religion.

Eileen was only nineteen when she tied the knot—not with David but a man named Aaron Butka. They had two children—son Elton and daughter Candice. It was alleged Butka drank a lot, and mistreated Eileen.

'We got divorced after that,' she said in court.

Eileen bought her own home and lived there with her children. In a bizarre move, she allowed Butka to move in 'for the kids' sake'. It wasn't long before David Creamer came back into her life. He reappeared through a surprise phone call during which he inquired how married life was going. She told him hers was over.

'He told me that his marriage was on the rocks as well and he wanted to meet up with me.'

David had married a woman named Lynn but separated in 1994. They had two sons, Dale and Lyle. Eileen met up with David in Pietermaritzburg only weeks after his phone call, and they resumed a relationship.

It was very passionate because David made it clear to me that his marriage was on the rocks and that he still loved me. And I still loved him from school days … It was good because he wasn't as religious as he was in his teenage years.

David admitted he loved the ladies, and admitted to an affair he had with a dance partner after choosing to be with Eileen. Eileen explained:

David was always a ladies' man. We spoke about it and he apologised and said it wouldn't happen again. And I believed him … He said to me that he would pick her up from her home and drop her off after dancing and one time she invited him in and things just got out of control … I did suspect that there were other women but I had no proof of it.

Once David's divorce was finalised, he and Eileen married and bought a house in Pietermaritzburg. David received mixed reviews from Eileen's children.

'David got on very well with Candice,' Eileen explained in court. 'Elton wouldn't give him the time of day. Elton never liked David from the word go.'

His former wife was also proving a thorn. It was a case of 'show me the money', apparently.

'Every anniversary of his divorce, he was dragged through the courts for more money,' Eileen told the Supreme Court. 'David just couldn't take it in the end.'

As a result he suggested they emigrate. New Zealand appealed as a destination and they sold up. David travelled there first to find a job and a rental property. Eileen and daughter Candice followed about eight months later. They all lived in a suburb called Tauranga. (Elton had decided to stay in South Africa with his biological father.) For work, Eileen did some fruit picking and worked as a hotel cleaner before gaining full-time employment in Auckland in credit management. That job saw her up at 4.30 am each Monday morning. To avoid the alarm clock she would stay in Auckland for the remaining working week and return home on Friday evenings. On the weekends she worked as a supermarket hand. Well settled, and believing rent money is dead money, the couple bought a home.

'We had a good marriage in New Zealand,' Eileen told the jury. 'We had a good life. We earned good money. Everything was fine. I loved my job. I had lots of friends.'

While a humble suburban home life suited Eileen, it left David restless and bored. As a consequence he started to stray. Again.

'He started going out often and I used to get left to clean up the house and do all the washing and ironing and all the other stuff—and I still worked over the weekends,' Eileen said in court.

And then I started suspecting that he was having affairs and I asked him about it and he didn't hide it. He was just amazed at all the white women that he could get in New Zealand because it wasn't something that he could get in South Africa. Because of the apartheid years in South Africa ... David wouldn't mix with white people [for some time] and when we got to New Zealand it was just a whole new world for him.

According to Eileen, David would become angry and accuse her of nagging him if she asked too many questions. He suggested she start communicating with people on the internet.

'He started going on the internet as well. He said to me it was fun and I had to have some fun in my life and experiment.'

Eileen became lonely at home on the weekends.

As I walked in the door [having arrived home from work on Fridays] David would leave, going dancing or going out to meet somebody. And in the end I just got really lonely so he set up a profile for me on the internet. And I started meeting people as well.

Eileen was drinking up to two casks of wine each weekend while David was out 'dancing'. It was during this period she started dating another man. That man cannot be named due to a court suppression order, so we shall call him Robert. He and Eileen met on a dating website in 2003. Her username was 'Can you spoil me'.

'We started talking over the internet and it was made very clear right from the beginning what Eileen wanted,' Robert told the Supreme Court. 'She was just after physical intimacy and nothing more.'

Robert knew Eileen was married. It didn't seem to bother him. To him, Eileen came across as a proud mother and a sharply dressed workaholic who 'always took pride in her appearance'. He told the murder trial:

> She just said that her husband was either away on business all the time or when he came home from business he basically used to go out dancing and she would be left at home by herself and that she just wanted some intimacy—and that's all it was.

Of Eileen's character, he said: 'She seemed conservative, yes.'

Robert lived some two hours away from Eileen but travelled a lot for business. He started making regular detours. Their first liaison was a dinner date. On their second meeting they had sex in a hotel room. David Creamer contacted Robert after that rendezvous. Theirs was certainly an odd conversation. Robert said in court:

> He just said that he was aware of us meeting and that he didn't want me to lead his wife up the garden path and that he was basically okay with me coming down and seeing her … I just said that, you know, 'If you

took care of your wife more you wouldn't be in this situation,' and he just acknowledged that. There was no angry tone in his voice. He sounded an absolute gentleman on the phone ... It was quite bizarre. I was shocked.

On another occasion Robert met David face to face. That happened after he picked Eileen up from work one lunch time and drove her to a marina at Mount Maunganui. David had tailed them and pulled up behind them. Robert described what happened to the court:

I basically got out of the car thinking, 'Oh, here we go, something's going to happen.' But he was very much a gentleman ... Very quiet spoken. Put his hand out to shake my hand. Basically he said, 'Hi, how are you? You guys have a lovely lunch.'

Robert said Eileen never spoke ill of David.

'Never mentioned to me in any form whatsoever that he was ever violent towards her,' he confirmed in the Supreme Court. 'In our times of intimacy I never saw any marks or bruises.'

Robert's work took him from New Zealand to Australia several times during his affair with Eileen. She went with him to Sydney on a couple of occasions. On one trip she took a naked photo of him as he lay on a bed unaware. Robert demanded she destroy it. She refused to do so. In court, Robert was asked if Eileen ever complained about her husband's 'sexual preferences'.

'Never,' Robert answered.

According to Eileen, it was obvious David Creamer was encouraging her to have affairs.

'To David it was like I had to prove to him that other men found me attractive for him to find me sexually attractive,' Eileen explained in court.

When I started seeing Robert, [David would] always want to find out what we talked about; what happened … David always wanted to know the sexual details … He presumed that there was sex and he always said to me that I must talk openly about it because it would make him horny.

David was constantly checking Eileen's website profile for new contacts. He was, meanwhile, very open about his own sexual conquests.

'He never hid anything from me,' Eileen told the jury.

David was quite open and frank and he would always want to show me the text messages that he was getting from these women. How they were chasing him. And he just felt that it was the best thing that could have happened to him. He had all these white women chasing after him wanting to have sex with him. And he thought I'd be interested in knowing all the 'ins and outs' but I would just brush it off.

David was apparently 'quite explicit' about the sex he was having with other women and what tricks they would perform and allow him to do in return.

'He always wanted me to be the same,' Eileen told the court. 'He said I was boring.'

To alleviate that boredom, David proposed some group sex. Eileen was not comfortable with the idea:

David kept on insisting that we meet other couples for group sex or threesomes and I would get angry with David and tell him that that wasn't what I wanted. And then he'd get angry with me—give me the silent treatment and he would just get really nasty with me.

David took his fantasy to 'sextraordinary' levels by taking Eileen to an Auckland swingers' bar where anything and everything was apparently permissible. David had sex with another woman in front of Eileen. She left the room and sat by the bar as he finished.

'He was angry because I didn't sit through it and watch, and he basically hauled me out of there,' Eileen said in evidence. 'He was really angry with me. He said that he wanted me to watch; that it wasn't that bad, so that I could do the same for him.'

To try to appease her husband, Eileen went with him to meet other men over drinks and dinners.

'I just preferred to keep it [an extra-marital affair] with [Robert],' she told the court. 'He was a good man. He treated me well. I didn't have to pretend I was something that I wasn't in front of [him]. He had a lot of respect for me.'

According to Eileen's evidence, David was 'happy' that she was seeing the other man but became annoyed when it appeared that she was sticking to just the one. 'He wanted me to meet up with other men and not just [Robert],' she said.

The problem was Eileen Creamer still loved her husband despite his proclivity for lady hopping. 'It wasn't always bad [with David],' she told the court. 'When he did treat me good it was special and I always believed that some day David would calm down and lead a normal married life.'

But it was like living with Doctor Jekyll and Mr Snide. 'One day he could be really nice. The next day he could be really nasty. And I just never knew what to expect from one day to the next. But I always believed that David would change.'

She told the jury that she carried a silent burden. 'There was no way I could tell my family what was going on and I never burdened my kids with stuff like that.'

Eileen started receiving queries from neighbours about all the different women David was seen to be bringing home. It was a close-knit suburb, after all. She explained them away by saying they were David's dancing partners. There was Gladys. And the woman we will call Melissa.

'A whole lot of women,' Eileen confirmed in court. 'He would always tell them that he was either separated or divorcing me, because he said that if he told them that he was married no-one would be interested in him.'

David continued to show Eileen emails and text messages sent from his lovers. He told her that mistress Melissa gave up her job and moved house to be closer to him. He spent weekends with Melissa, but she yearned for more.

In an effort to try to frighten Melissa away, Eileen embarked on a harassment campaign. It involved abusive phone calls, text messages and letters slipped in Melissa's letter box. One envelope contained a torn-up photo of Melissa.

I did that because David would come home complaining to me about [Melissa] with all the commitments that she wanted and I said to him, 'Well, why don't you tell her that you're married?' He would always have an excuse, so I just wanted [Melissa] to know that David was married and that I was still a wife to him.

A mechanical engineer, David began to chase work in Australia. There was good money to be made across the Tasman.

'He left New Zealand, as far as I know, to get away from [Melissa] because she wanted a commitment from him and he wasn't prepared to,' Eileen explained in court.

> He did a lot of [nine-to-five] work up in Auckland but when that dried up and jobs came to Australia, he took the jobs … He said it was great, he was getting good money and it was a lovely country to come to.

David left New Zealand for a permanent move to Australia—Melbourne to be exact—in April 2006. He found a place to live in trendy South Yarra: a cosmopolitan inner-city suburb known for its cafes and vibrant nightlife. It wasn't long before he struck up yet another affair. We shall call that woman Helen to protect her identity. Eileen remained in New Zealand. In mid 2006 she took work leave and travelled to Melbourne and stayed with David for a couple of weeks. She said they had a good time together, eating out at restaurants and riding the city's tram system. During her stay, Eileen said, David again tried to entice her into seedy sexual situations. Eileen explained in court:

> One day he said to me I should get dressed nicely, we were going out for the evening. We went to a bar across from Flinders Street station and when we got there we met another couple that David was corresponding with on the internet.

It soon became obvious to Eileen that David was trying to drum up some good old-fashioned group sex.

'David spoke about it. We left that evening and they wanted us to come over to their house the next weekend, but we couldn't because I was leaving back for New Zealand,' Eileen said.

David returned to New Zealand for a visit in September 2006. 'There was nothing wrong with that visit,' Eileen said in court. 'David was still in my bed.'

According to Eileen, David phoned her often from Melbourne saying he was lonely and that he had no-one to talk to. She said he begged her to pack up and come to live in Melbourne with him as soon as possible.

'So that we could start a new life,' she said. 'I wasn't too sure because I knew I was doing well in New Zealand and I was just sick and tired of David's games ... I didn't want to leave New Zealand.'

Eileen told the jury she received a letter from David's lawyer regarding their marriage. It contained a threat of divorce.

> It shocked me because I didn't know there was any divorce or separation pending. But I knew that when I got that letter that it was David's way of saying to me it's either you pick up your bags and come to Australia or I'm going to leave you ... I realised that I still wanted the marriage to David.

Barrister Jane Dixon would ask Eileen of her suspicions about further affairs.

DIXON: At the time that you were taking steps to arrange to come to Australia, did you know that he was in a relationship with [a woman named Helen]?

EILEEN: No. I did suspect though because some days I would get hold of him and some days his phone wouldn't be available.

In March 2007, David paid Eileen a surprise visit in New Zealand. According to her evidence, he became angry upon discovering that she had changed the house locks. She told the jury that after breaking his way inside he forced himself upon her. Eileen told the jury that the sex was painful.

'Every time David forced himself to have sex with me and I would complain, he said I was his wife and he could do whatever he wanted to do with me. So I just didn't go to the police station.'

Despite the rough sex, Eileen had made up her mind. She was going to make the move to Melbourne for the sake of their marriage.

'He was hot and cold all the time … and I still loved him no matter what,' she said in court. 'I thought I would give this another go because he also said that coming to Australia, a town where nobody knew us … it was giving us a chance at our marriage.'

David Creamer was either very, very smooth or Eileen Creamer was very, very gullible. After handing in her resignation she informed David of her decision. He told her, via email, that he had changed his mind and did not want her in Melbourne. She informed him that it was too late—she had already resigned.

Eileen arrived in Melbourne in May 2007 for a preliminary visit. She stayed with relatives in the south-eastern suburb of Noble Park. She quickly found a job working in retail.

At that stage, David had moved from inner Melbourne due to work changes and was boarding with a lady in the semi-rural town of Traralgon. David told Eileen that she could not stay there with him. Instead, he asked Eileen to move into a house with him. For Eileen, that meant a lot of train travel to and from work. She accepted the deal nevertheless. At some point David had given her his old mobile telephone—as he had purchased a new one. The phone held many secrets.

'David hadn't deleted the messages on the phone,' Eileen said in court. 'They were from [Helen], probably from [Melissa] and there were a few other names I didn't know. Deanna. Julie.' Eileen didn't ask about the romantic messages, at first. 'I knew it would start an argument so I just read them.'

One, dated 18 October 2006, read:

Hi David, I am happy today despite no message from you. Ha ha. Never mind, I am fully aware you may not have an opportunity for a chat. (I do hope you have at least had a romantic thought about us.) Are we going to explore the possibility of a real connection? Do you feel inspired? I do. [Helen]. XXX

Another, dated 21 October, stated: 'Want to exhaust you. Take care. XXX Dede.'

According to Eileen: 'He always said it was the women who were chasing him; they couldn't get enough of him … He wasn't the one chasing them.'

Eileen did finally ask about the messages one night when David stayed at Noble Park. 'That's when he told me about [Helen] and the other woman that he was seeing.'

It seemed [Helen] was a serious flame.

'David would leave [Helen's] house after a weekend and come back to Noble Park and want to have sex with me,' Eileen told the jury. 'David would always send me a message when he left [Helen]'s house to tell me to open the door and make sure that I had no panties on because he needed a fuck.'

Despite this, according to Eileen, 'David promised me that he was going to break off with [Helen] when she went [on a planned trip] to Germany,' and that he would stop 'all his fooling around' and give the marriage 'a go'.

They should have gone their separate ways.

Eileen returned to New Zealand and packed up her belongings. David also returned to New Zealand for a work commitment, and the two spent a night together at a motel. They had sex, Eileen said. They then flew to Melbourne and started afresh in a new home in Traralgon, in Victoria's south-east. Or at least that's what Eileen thought.

In July 2007, a war of words exploded between Eileen and Helen via email. Helen responded to one particular message. 'Eileen, do not forward me any further e-mails or set foot on my property again. David does not love you. Nor does he wish to have any kind of future with you.'

Eileen responded with:

Are you trying to threaten me? Don't go there. You don't know me. David is my husband and you're a slut sleeping with him. He brought me to your house, you little whore, take a long look in the mirror. Who are you trying to destroy? My family. But wait and see. He's using you and you can't see it. Ask him about the other females he's screwing. Did he tell you?

David showed me where you're staying. Remember,
I'm living with him and, yes, we have made love since
then no matter what he's telling you, stupid. He has
a future with me, not with you in it. Find your own.
Don't threaten me. Eileen.

Eileen said that while Helen was on her holiday in
Germany, she and David had 'the best five or six weeks
that we had ever had in Melbourne'.

'We did everything together,' Eileen told the jury.
'Even David commented and said that he was just so much
more relaxed and it was definitely over between him and
[Helen].'

But when Helen returned, David collected her from
the airport. Eileen gave his reasoning in court: 'He said
he felt bad to leave her stranded there because her plane
was arriving at an unearthly hour.'

Eileen ended up driving David halfway to Melbourne
Airport. She spent the night at her relative's house in
Noble Park and let David go on to the airport on his own.
He turned his phone off and went AWOL.

'David said to me that he was finishing off with
[Helen], collecting all his stuff and I must wait for him,'
Eileen recounted in court. 'I waited in Noble Park and I
waited, and I never heard anything.'

Eileen called David's phone. It went to his voicemail.
She looked up Helen's number in the phone book and
tried that too. In the end she caught a train and knocked
on Helen's door. David answered. Eileen told the court,
'David just said to me that he wasn't coming home with
me that [Saturday] night and I didn't say anything further.
I just turned and walked away.'

With tail between her legs Eileen rode a train all the way
home to Traralgon on her own. It was a long and lonely trip.

It was around this time that she turned to the internet for help. US-based psychics, she figured, would prove valuable allies.

'I was just so tired of not knowing what was going on,' she said. 'Every time I spoke to David he gave me a different story.'

By late 2007 Eileen felt trapped and isolated in Traralgon. She had no real friends or close family.

'I was on my own. I was left alone on weekends.'

As a reminder for Eileen, David took a photo of his penis with her phone.

He said that I should keep the picture so that I would always remember it … I had to have pictures of him on my phone and I wasn't allowed to delete them … As much as he said that I wasn't fit or I was lazy or despicable to sleep with, he came to my bed when he had nobody else.

And he still harboured the group sex dream. Eileen said she remained not interested.

I made him know that I wasn't comfortable with it. I kept on telling him that. But he would get angry with me and say that I never ever wanted to make him happy. That's what he wanted. He wanted to bring men over for me to have sex with while he watched. And I said to him I wasn't going to do that.

David also had a porn fixation. 'He loved watching blue movies,' Eileen told the jury.

He had lots of pornographic magazines ... He used to say to me that I should watch more blue movies to get me in the mood and I would be more fun. And the things David wanted me to do I just wouldn't do to him—with him or anybody else. And that always ended up in arguments. And he started getting on to the swingers sites, contacting men to come over. And then he wanted us to go to the parties as well.

David became abusive when Eileen—who was drinking heavily—refused to play the sex games.

'I was alone at home. I had nothing to do,' she said. 'I would clean up the house and yes, I started drinking ... David used to get angry and compare me to his mother.'

Amid her time of turmoil, Eileen searched through personal ads in the local newspaper in the hope of finding a secret male companion. 'I was looking for somebody that I could go somewhere with over weekends ... and just be friends with,' she explained in court.

I was so lonely at home. I had nobody. I was isolated. I had no transport. I just had nobody that I could talk to ... David always made out that I wasn't attractive anymore. He basically made me feel like I had passed my use-by date.

Eileen met up with a couple of blokes and had a coffee or a wine with them. She had several men listed as women in her phone to hide their existence. Some of the blokes only knew her as Louise.

'I think I met [a Mr Hooper] twice but he was too old and nothing happened,' she said.

In September 2007 she found 'John'. John scored the code name 'Claire' on Eileen's phone. Like Robert, he cannot be named.

'[John] and I decided that we were going to see each other,' Eileen admitted in court. 'I didn't even tell David that I was seeing [John] because David was always away. He had no idea that I was seeing anybody.'

The relationship between Eileen and David remained a tortured and dysfunctional one. Eileen said she was growing scared.

> I was petrified because David ... would bring people to the house that we didn't even know and I was always scared of what would happen with these people when he wasn't there. I got to the stage in Traralgon where I bought a chain and a padlock for the gate. When David would go I would go outside and padlock the gate closed ... I had no control over the situation. The more I told David how I felt it didn't seem to bother him.

David kept pushing for group sex. At one point in October 2007, he contacted a hotmail group called Party Insatiable in his effort to broker what Jane Dixon described as a 'gang bang'. This is part of an email he received from Party Insatiable.

> The best thing is to have a look at our website which will give you a clear picture of what our parties are about/total hardcore gangbangs for women who enjoy the attentions of multiple men in a total group scenario (one open play room). On the party page the scrolling text at the top of the page links to party reviews which give a vivid description of what goes on at Insatiable.

The planned orgy party was cancelled due to a lack of willing women.

Eileen said she was relieved. 'If I ever stood up to David and said no, there were always consequences,' she said in court.

> David never ever stopped at the couples thing. The threesomes thing: it seemed like that's all that he wanted from me. He couldn't take me out to a normal place … He would get angry with me. He wouldn't talk to me for days. Some days he would just pretend that I wasn't even there …

Eileen's anti-Helen campaign continued. Around October 2007 she sent a used condom to Helen's workplace with the message: 'Just to let you know how good last night was with David. Sorry you're not women [sic] enough for him. Ha ha ha ha.'

Eileen also speared off an email to David. It read in part:

> I just want to ask you to please share accommodation with me for the next nine months. I will stay out of your way. You won't even know that I'm around David. Following the next nine months I will leave you to your happiness, David, as I've tried to make conversation with you and you can barely open your mouth to me. So, yes, I think I've tried my best and you're just not interested. As I said, David, I didn't come to Australia for a job—I had that in New Zealand. I came here to try and salvage what was left of or marriage.
>
> I want to thank you for the years that you and I have had together. I just want you to know that you've been a great husband and friend to me and

I'll always treasure the memories—yes, the good and the bad or hard times that we went through because we both certainly did have some trying times, especially after your divorce but somehow we managed to survive those and we came out whole. Guess that's because we both wanted to. And now I'm trying my level best to make us come out whole again but I'm not winning because I'm trying all on my own. I don't have you trying with me. Love always, Eileen.

But still she stayed. Homicide detective Allan Birch later asked Eileen why.

'I loved David from when we were at school,' she told Birch during a record of interview. 'I just don't know why he was never happy. He was happy with me at the beginning but in the end it was all just sex. We were good together before he got on to this internet.'

BIRCH: Why didn't you leave David?
EILEEN: Where was I going to go? At least I had my own home with David.
BIRCH: Do you think he treated you appallingly?
EILEEN: He treated me like a dog … I loved David. He had no idea how much I loved him.
BIRCH: Did he show you the same love in the end?
EILEEN: No.
BIRCH: Did he show it to other ladies?
EILEEN: Yeah.

To help turn the tide and defeat her competition, Eileen went back to the internet mystics. She contacted a woman calling herself 'Psychic Ma' who cast a spell on Helen. It seemed to work. David began to talk about moving with Eileen to the nearby township of Moe. Then, in December 2007, Eileen and David took a trip back to their homeland together. Eileen's son was getting married, and David wanted to see his former wife and his two sons. Jane Dixon examined Eileen about the trip.

> **DIXON**: And at that stage did you believe that he was nursing fond feelings or romantic feelings for his ex-wife Lynn?
>
> **EILEEN**: No … David said that he would have to do whatever he could to see his kids with Lynn, and I just said to him, 'Well, do what you have to do. You have to see your boys.'
>
> **DIXON**: What about Helen? Did you understand that his relationship with her was still continuing when he was planning to come to South Africa with you and planning to move into the unit at Moe with you?
>
> **EILEEN**: As far as I knew David was over with [Helen].
>
> **DIXON**: So what were you hoping for at that time?
>
> **EILEEN**: I was hoping that David would finally calm down and just stay at home and we would have a normal relationship.

According to Eileen, she and David enjoyed each other's company at her son's wedding and shared the same bed that evening. The following day David met up with his former wife.

Eileen unsuccessfully tried to contact David over the next few days. 'I had no idea where he was.'

Due to work commitments, Eileen had to return home. She collected David from Melbourne Airport upon his return from South Africa on 10 January. He spoke fondly of the time he'd spent with his sons and ex-wife. He also spoke about money problems. During the trip he'd maxed out his $10,000 credit card. Eileen sent a new message to another internet psychic. This request concerned David's ex-wife, whom he now seemed to be yearning for. Eileen's message to the psychic read: 'Hi, having problems with my husband at the moment. He wants to go back to his first wife and I love him too much to let him go. Please can you help me keep him. What is your cost?'

In late January 2008 Eileen caught David posting a lewd photo of her on a sex website. The photo only showed her torso and legs. Her face was cut off the picture.

'David was back into the group sex thing and the threesomes,' Eileen told the jury. She demanded he remove the image.

'We got into an argument but eventually he huffed and puffed and said, "Okay, I'll take the photo off."'

> **DIXON**: Did you believe that he had removed
> everything or what was your state of mind about what
> David was doing and what he had in mind for you?
> **EILEEN**: I knew that David still had profiles on
> the internet. I knew he had an active one, and
> to get into the couples' thing and threesomes
> you have to have both parties having a profile.
> I didn't put any profile of myself on the internet
> but I did suspect that David had put one up of
> me with him.

On 2 February Eileen contacted 'Psychic Ma' again.

Hi Ma, thanks so much for your help. Last time it worked wonders but now I need your help again for

another spell. Over Christmas my husband and I went
to South Africa and he met with his ex-wife whom
he had not seen or spoken to in thirteen years and
now that we are back in Australia he has changed. He
ignores me and is always on the computer talking to
her. And now everything she says to him is like gospel.
What happened? And he hardly talks to me now. I
know she's done something—to have him change the
way he has. Please, please can you reverse this? Please
Ma, help me again. Love and regards, Eileen.

Eileen was confused. 'I didn't know who he wanted to be
with,' she said in court.

I was good enough for David to have sex with when
there was nobody else around and I was also scared
about the internet dating thing because I knew he was
back on that internet dating stuff with the threesomes
and group sex.

Phone records showed that David was contacting his
former wife Lynn twice a day via text messages, and was
continually calling and emailing her.

Prosecutor Tom Gyorffy told the jury that Eileen had
ample motive for murder.

By February 2008, Eileen Creamer knew the relationship
[with David] was over. She was not going to keep David
Creamer from his first wife and children. She wasn't
prepared to accept that. The Crown says that's the
motive for her to kill him.

On the night before Eileen killed her husband at their
Moe home, she spent the night at the Quest apartments

in Melbourne with her gentleman friend John. She did not arrive back in Moe on the train until the Saturday afternoon. David demanded to know where she had been.

'I was hoping that he wouldn't be home that weekend,' she said.

While downing a glass of wine she told him she'd spent the night with girls from work. David didn't believe her. 'I could see it was getting out of hand,' Eileen said in evidence.

> I asked David if I could use the car because I needed to go and get some stuff in town. I needed to go to the butcher, and get my scripts [filled at the chemist shop] and David told me I should walk. So I just took my wallet and I walked out of the house.

She claimed in court that when she got home David was standing outside the back door talking to two strange men. She claimed she could not hear what they were discussing. After they left, according to Eileen, David became all friendly towards her.

> I asked him why and he said to me because he had a surprise for me for the evening. I asked him who the two men were and he just said that I mustn't worry— he had a nice surprise for me for that night. And I said to him if he thinks I was going to have sex with those two men I wasn't going to do it ... David poured me another drink of wine because he said he needed to put me into the mood.

Eileen said David took the wine away when she told him there would be no gang-banging involving her. She said he called her a drunken whore, a bitch and a cunt.

> I argued with him because I thought I'm not going to have sex with these men. And he carried on swearing. I don't know how long he swore at me because then he started pinching me as well, and he smacked me across the face … David always pinched me. He'd give me a few smacks in the face as well but he always pinched me. He pinched me under my arms. I always had blue arms—blue marks under my arms and in between my legs and my thighs.

Eileen told the jury that David's tirade eventually tapered off and she fell asleep on the couch. She said she awoke with David standing over her while brandishing an African tribal club referred to as a knobkerrie.

'He hit me on my vagina,' she told the jury. 'I fell off the couch and asked him what he thought he was doing by hitting me. I went into the kitchen and he carried on abusing me and swearing at me. And hitting me.'

Eileen said she took refuge in her bedroom, and David stormed from the house with a bottle of wine under his arm. Eileen said she didn't see him until the next morning— Sunday, 3 February 2008—when the atmosphere in the house was 'really tense'. The jury was told David smothered her head with semen-stained bedsheets and demanded that she smell them. He made wild accusations about Eileen and read aloud saucy text messages from his lovers.

> He kept on asking me who had a bigger penis … He just wouldn't stop … calling me all the names under the sun. I went outside to sit on the garden furniture. I tried reading a book. He grabbed the book out of my

hands. Every time I went inside he was behind me. It just carried on all morning. All afternoon.

According to Eileen, she resorted to doing some cleaning and was wiping David's ensuite shower when he called her a 'half-caste white bastard'. The jury heard that was the final straw.

'I don't know what happened,' Eileen said in evidence. 'I snapped. I thought he was coming towards me and I had nowhere to go because I was stuck in the shower in the bathroom.'

She said she managed to grab the knobkerrie in David's room and began to hit him.

I lost all my control. David screamed at me and asked me what the fuck I was doing lifting my hands to him. And I just carried on hitting him … I tried running out the back door. He followed me and we rolled around in the back. And then we went back inside. I tried to run out the front door. David got to the door first and he slammed the door shut.

Eileen claimed that David then came at her with a knife.

He got on top of me on the bed. He smacked me up. And then he tried to put his penis in my mouth. And when I wouldn't open my mouth he said to me he was going to piss on me and when he was finished pissing on me he was going to finish me off once and for all.

At that stage, Eileen said, the knife was on the bedside table.

'I couldn't get David off me. Then I heard him saying that I'd knocked him in the balls. He lifted his weight off me. And I think that's when I grabbed the knife and I must have stabbed him.'

Outside, Eileen threw the blade and the knobkerrie into a clutch of trees next to a nearby school oval. Upon her return home much later, she said, the home was in darkness. 'David's door was closed. I thought he was sleeping. I showered and I was just so tired. I went and I got into bed.'

Eileen told the jury that she awoke on the Monday morning and went to David's room to ask him to drive her to the station. 'I didn't think David was dead,' she said in evidence.

She found him lying at the foot of his bed. 'I tried waking him up. He wouldn't wake up. I tried washing his face. I smacked him a little bit. David wouldn't wake up. I didn't know David was dead until that morning when I opened the door.'

Eileen ran to a neighbouring home and hammered on the door. It was about 5 am on Monday, 4 February.

'This woman was saying that she thinks somebody has broken in and she can't wake her husband up and to call for the police,' neighbour Mary Parnaby recalled in the Supreme Court.'

Of playing dumb and pretending to know nothing of the bloody killing, Eileen admitted in court: 'I was scared. I panicked. I didn't know what to do. And I was ashamed of what was going on in the house. I didn't want anybody to know.'

Police units arrived at the bloodbath.

'I could see clearly down the corridor and there was blood basically all over the corridor floor and all over the side of the walls,' Detective Senior Constable Stephen Cook told the trial.

I noticed that he [the victim] had extensive trauma to his head. There appeared to be a puncture wound to his abdomen and also what appeared to be a bite mark and bruising to his right side. The room was literally covered in blood. There was blood all over the carpet, the floors, over the bed, over the walls. The ensuite area was covered in blood also … In the kitchen living area, there was a heap of blood throughout there as well.

After she was arrested, Eileen denied killing her husband. 'The alarm went off and I got up and I saw all the blood in the passage and that's when I ran outside and went to the neighbour,' she told Detective Sergeant Birch.

Homicide detectives gathered forensic evidence and statements. They charged Eileen with murder.

During the trial, Dixon asked Eileen what she intended to do when she hit David with the knobkerrie.

'I didn't intend to hurt David,' Eileen replied. 'I don't know what happened. I can't explain it. But I just wasn't going to get another hiding. David kept on threatening me. I snapped. I just lost control.'

Defence witness clinical psychologist Jeffrey Cummins told the jury he believed Eileen was living in an 'abusive relationship'.

'She said her husband actively encouraged her to date other men and repeatedly requested she bring other men home so he could witness her having sexual intercourse with other males,' Cummins said.

DIXON: In terms of the issue of Mr Creamer
wanting her to participate in the swingers' scene or
some sort of group sex episode, how significant did

you consider that aspect of the dynamics of their relationship?

CUMMINS: On the basis of what Ms Creamer said at interview I regarded that as being of crucial significance. She said she found those issues abhorrent … She provided a history of being verbally abused and intimidated by her husband. She also provided a history which indicated she perceived her husband as being more interpersonally powerful than herself.

Prosecutor Gyorffy told the jury that in order to establish murder, the prosecution had to establish four elements beyond reasonable doubt. Those elements were that Eileen caused David Creamer's death; that her actions were conscious, voluntary and deliberate; that she either intended to kill or cause really serious injury; and that she killed him without lawful justification or excuse. He made mention of the nature of the attack.

'The Crown relies on the sheer ferocity of this attack which extends from one end of the house to the other,' Gyorffy said. 'There was no domestic violence in the relationship. That's what she told the police.'

Jane Dixon told the jury that David Creamer viewed his wife Eileen as a 'diminished' commodity.

In order to stay interested in her, she really had to be prepared to go along with some of the kinkier ways of having sex. For example, having sex with other men is what he wanted her to do for his titillation … Apparently her value was in the lower parts of her body.

This marriage was sick in more ways than one … [and] bound to end in wrack and ruin. Eileen Creamer was really living on the edge … The defence say family violence or domestic violence—it's not just about battering people. It can be about sexual abuse, psychological or emotional abuse or other things.

During his preliminary directions, Justice Paul Coghlan told the jury that they would have to determine whether Eileen 'did not believe that it was necessary to act in the way that she did to defend herself against the threat of death or really serious injury which she thought she faced at the time'.

'You will have to consider the circumstances as she perceived them to be at the time she killed her husband,' Coghlan said in part.

> The question here is what Eileen Creamer believed was necessary in the circumstances ... If you decided she was not guilty of murder, because she was acting in self-defence, you must consider whether she is guilty of defensive homicide and I will explain that offence to you. The law is that people who kill in the belief that what they're doing is necessary to defend themselves from death or really serious injury do not commit murder even if their belief is unreasonable. However, if they do not have reasonable grounds for believing that what they are doing is necessary in self-defence, they are guilty of the offence which is known as defensive homicide.

The legal definition of defensive homicide is an oddly complicated one. It is amazing that juries consisting of laymen and women can get their heads around its complexities. Nevertheless, the jury in the Eileen Creamer case acquitted her of murder, instead finding her guilty of defensive homicide. Eileen Creamer became the first

Victorian woman to be found guilty of that offence, which was introduced in 2005 to treat female victims of domestic violence with more compassion. Ironically, up until the 2011 verdict, only men charged over killing women had benefited from defensive homicide laws. In sentencing Eileen to a maximum eleven years' jail with a seven-year minimum, Coghlan said the events leading to David Creamer's death turned in part on the nature of the couple's dysfunctional relationship.

'I am satisfied that you regarded your position as extremely unsatisfactory and the future of your relationship with David Creamer as bleak, and you resented strongly any attempt to engage you in group sex,' Coghlan said.

The injuries described by [pathologist] Professor Cordner demonstrate that David Creamer was struck a number of blows to the head in what can only be described as a very severe beating, demonstrating that you were out of control. I doubt you actually remember all of the details of what occurred.

In the absence of any finding as to domestic violence, it was inevitable that you be convicted of murder. I will sentence you on the basis that you had been overwhelmed by the whole of the circumstances as they surrounded you and, in particular, by your concern that you were being forced into a sexual scenario which you did not want … You are now fifty-three years of age. You have no prior convictions and your prospects of rehabilitation are good. You are unlikely to re-offend, particularly in this way.

Eileen unsuccessfully appealed against the severity of her sentence.

No comment: Matt Johnson says very little to police after the jail killing.

Murder weapon: The bike seat stem that killed Carl Williams.

The Grim Reaper: Johnson fixes the camera with a cold stare as he is lead into court.

'Nothing will ever bring Sue back': Lorna Brazendale told daughter Susanne Wild that she was praying for her.

Backyard grave: Susanne lies wrapped in plastic next to the hole Sherna dug for her.

The final straw: An upset puppy named Hubble sparked Sherna's brutal actions.

Hard times: A dejected Anthony Sherna tells detectives about life with his wife.

SUN 10/02/08 06:22:09 X 053

SUN 10/02/08 06:33:36 X 041

SUN 10/02/08 07:39:11 X 034

Out of luck: Aaron Rolls is taken into police custody on the Gold Coast.

Inset: Patrizia Rolls says it's a miracle she is still breathing.

The mistress: Mirvat 'Mel' Sleiman suggested a fatal Gold Coast skinny dip.

Too young to die: Murder victim Yazmina Acar is carried in her tiny coffin.

Inset: Yazmina's mum, Rachelle D'Argent, holds on tight to the last memories, above, and Ramazan Acar tries to hide his face outside the Victorian Supreme Court, left.

Life without parole: John Leslie Coombes is led from the Victorian Supreme Court.

Inset: Dismemberment victim Raechel Betts in happier times, above, and an early mugshot of triple killer Coombes, below.

Butterflies and tomatoes: Killer dad Arthur Freeman raises his cuffed hands in a form of ineffectual protest.

Inset: Floral tributes to Darcey Freeman lie in the shadow of the Westgate Bridge.

In cold blood: Riad Barbour looked into his victim's eyes as he murdered him.

Where's the cash? Barbour in action during a pokies venue hold-up.

'The non-parole period of seven years was, if anything, significantly lower than what might have been expected given the head sentence of eleven years,' Justice Mark Weinberg said in an August 2012 Court of Appeal judgement. 'There is nothing to indicate that his Honour failed to give adequate weight to all of the mitigating factors that were present. There is no justification, in my opinion, for interfering with this sentence.'

8
The Stepfather

*'I just wanted him to go away. He'd threatened
to kill me so many times and I just thought
it would all stop if he wasn't there.'*

LIKE A SCENE FROM THE COP TELEVISION DRAMA
Blue Heelers, it was just past 6 pm and the country police
station was quiet—apart from the intermittent cop
chatter on the in-station police radio. But in an interview
room in the criminal investigation unit, a sinister and
violent story was unfolding: a story of sexual domination
and a liberating close-range killing. It would prove to be
material too graphic and perverse for television viewing.
Homicide detectives from the big smoke had arrived in
town—situated a few hours' drive from Melbourne—
in response to a report that a man's torso had been
uncovered in a shallow back-garden grave. The victim's
head, arms and legs had been removed in crude fashion.
The Homicide men had arrested their suspect, who now
lay wrapped in a blanket in an interview room. That
suspect was a teenage girl: a local, aged eighteen. (For
legal reasons preventing the identification of sexual
assault victims we shall call her Vanessa. That is not her

real first name.) Detectives Adam Forehan and Barry Gray had made initial inquiries. It appeared Vanessa's stepfather (whom we shall call Matthew) may have been sexually abusing her. Suspicion among family and friends had been rife for some time. Forehan and Gray had one question on their mind if, in fact, this slight eighteen-year-old girl had killed and dismembered her stepfather: what could have driven her to such drastic lengths? Forehan talked with Vanessa as she lay wrapped in the blanket in the interview room, the record of interview having not yet begun. The girl sounded broken inside.

'Can I talk?' she asked. 'I don't want to go to jail.'

'I can't control that,' Forehan replied.

'I need to tell you what happened.'

'What do you want to tell me?'

'I took him to … a camping spot.'

'Is he buried?'

'No, just [dumped] in the bush. [And] in the toilets.'

'What sort of toilets are they?' Forehan inquired.

'Just holes in the ground.'

'Okay. We need to go and get him now. Do you want to see someone?'

'I want Mum.'

Forehan maintained a sympathetic approach. 'I give you my word that we will do our best to help you. You must be going through hell.'

Vanessa nodded. 'His head … it's in the bush not far away.'

Matthew had been sitting in a chair in his shed stuffing his deflating manhood back into his pants when Vanessa opened up the back of his head with his own double-barrel shotgun. Only minutes before he had forced her to perform oral sex on him, a regular occurrence. A giant of a man in his mid-thirties, Matthew had been a local in the same Victorian country town all his life. To his family and friends the qualified mechanic was a knockabout big man; he liked motorbikes and water skiing and enjoyed beers with his mates.

'He had no enemies and was liked by everyone he met,' his brother said in a police statement.

But a pernicious demon lurked within Matthew, a demon he regularly revealed to Vanessa. Matthew had met Vanessa's mother during the mid-1990s and they became de facto partners. Vanessa was about six years old at the time. Matthew sired a couple of boys with Vanessa's mum over the following years. According to Matthew's sister, Vanessa took a shine to her stepfather during her childhood.

'She used to gravitate to [Matthew],' the sister said in her police statement. 'Like you would expect any young child to gravitate to their own parent, [Vanessa] used to bond really well with [Matthew]. She was always happy to see him and excited to have him around.'

But Vanessa's mother painted a darker picture of Matthew—despite their relationship having started out as what would have been deemed normal for an average blue-collar family. '[Matthew] and I became good friends and began a relationship together,' Vanessa's mother said in a police statement.

[Matthew] decided we should buy a house. At this time I had already given birth to my eldest boy. He was about two and a half years old when we moved. [Matthew's] and my relationship was really good and we got along really well. We often had friends and family around for barbecues and dinner.

But after the birth of their second son, things began to change. 'He became a control freak,' Vanessa's mum continued in her statement.

> He didn't like me going out of the house or speaking to other people and believed I should always be at his beck and call. I suppose I got used to his ways ... He had a lot of obsessive and compulsive disorders.

Vanessa's mother said that by the time her third son was born, Matthew had refocused his attentions onto a maturing Vanessa. She was now the sweet apple of his eye. 'He sort of let go of me and started to control her,' Vanessa's mother told police.

> He all of a sudden would not let her go out of the house. [Vanessa] was about fourteen to fifteen years old and was starting to mature into a young woman ... Shortly after I noticed the change in [Matthew] he then moved out of our bedroom and stayed in [Vanessa's] room. She slept in the bedroom with her brothers ... I knew our relationship was over but for the sake of the kids we remained friends.

Matthew's brother told police that he thought it strange that, as a teenager, Vanessa spent so much time with Matthew.

'I always thought it was a bit strange where I would go on motorbike rides with my wife and he would always bring [Vanessa],' Matthew's brother told police. 'Everyone commented on the fact that [Matthew] was always with [Vanessa]. Wherever [Matthew] went [Vanessa] would always be there. This included camping, fishing, skiing and motorbike riding.'

It was a situation not missed by Matthew's own mother.

[Matthew] was very controlling of [Vanessa] in
relation to boys, when she went out at night and going
to birthdays. I don't think she went to any parties.
When I asked her about knocking around with her
school friends, she would put them down saying all
they thought about was drinking. I don't know if that's
what she really thought, or not.

Vanessa's mother told police that while she grew
suspicious of Matthew, she had no proof that he was
sexually abusing Vanessa. Vanessa had never complained,
although her brothers provided their mum with some
disturbing information.

'The boys told me that [Matthew] and [Vanessa] were
always in the bedroom while I was at work,' Vanessa's
mum said in one police statement.

In another she added: 'There were other things like
[Matthew] not letting [Vanessa] have a shower at home
unless he was home as well. She wasn't allowed to go to
any parties or see anyone outside of school. [Matthew]
was very controlling.'

She often asked her daughter if Matthew had 'ever done
anything to her'. Vanessa denied that he had. Vanessa's
mum accused Matthew 'that there was something going
on'—an accusation he never really answered.

'It just didn't add up why he was so controlling of her,'
Vanessa's mum stated.

She wasn't allowed to have a life unless he was beside
her. I was very worried that I might have been wrong
[about suspecting that he was sexually abusing her]
and I didn't want to tear the family apart … I never

saw anything that 100 per cent confirmed that there was an inappropriate relationship going on between them and this is why I could never be satisfied that there was something going on.

According to Vanessa, Matthew's sexual domination of her began when she was about fourteen. The sordid history was all to come out during the record of interview with detectives Forehan and Gray.

> **FOREHAN**: Did it start with touching you?
> **VANESSA**: Yes.
> **FOREHAN**: Can you tell me where [Matthew] would touch you?
> **VANESSA**: Anywhere.
> **FOREHAN**: Would that include—are you comfortable if I use the term 'vagina'?
> **VANESSA**: Yes.
> **FOREHAN**: Did he touch you on your vagina?
> **VANESSA**: Yes.
> **FOREHAN**: Whereabouts did these things take place?
> **VANESSA**: In my room.

Vanessa said that the touching included digital penetration, which in turn led to oral sex and sexual intercourse after she turned fifteen. Matthew would regularly photograph and film the sex acts.

> **FOREHAN**: Did he have you do anything else to him?
> **VANESSA**: Yes.
> **FOREHAN**: What other things did [Matthew] ask you to do?
> **VANESSA**: Lots of stuff.

That 'stuff' included him penetrating her with her mother's sex toys, she said.

> **FOREHAN**: Did he use or penetrate you with items?
> **VANESSA**: Yes.
> **FOREHAN**: What sort of items? Did he use sex toys?
> **VANESSA**: Yes, my mum's.
> **FOREHAN**: Okay. When did he start using your mum's vibrator on you?
> **VANESSA**: When I was still fourteen, I think.
> **FOREHAN**: How often would he do this to you?
> **VANESSA**: Every night when I was little. Twice now, recently.

'Emma' (not her real name) first met Vanessa in Grade 4 at primary school. Within a year they were best friends and inseparable. They were the innocent times.

'In primary school [Vanessa] would ride her bike to my house every morning and then we would walk to school and we would then hang out after school; usually at the pool every night in summer,' Emma recalled in a police statement.

But stepfather Matthew's influence soon became apparent.

'Probably in about Year 7,' Emma told police,

> [Matthew] began to not let [Vanessa] ride her bike to my place and she couldn't come to my house as often as she used to. I had to visit her at her house all the time. She was not allowed to wear the right school uniform. [Matthew] would make her wear the boy's pants to school … At school [Vanessa] was always really happy but when I would visit her at her home she was always upset … When I stayed at her house, she and

I were never allowed to be alone. [Matthew] would always have to be around us and with us whatever we were doing. If we wanted to play Playstation in her room by ourselves Matthew would always just come in and lie on the bed and watch us.

Vanessa told Emma that she hated Matthew.

'[Vanessa] told me that [Matthew] used to check all the messages on her mobile phone,' Emma said.

Another school friend, 'Natalie' (not her real name), told police about a camping trip she and some friends went on with Vanessa, Matthew and his young boys during the 2005 Easter break in Year 10. Natalie said 'a lot of things went on' between Vanessa and Matthew.

[Matthew] was very involved in everything that we did. He was hanging around us all the time. I remember when we were swimming he made inappropriate comments about [Vanessa] being cold and making inappropriate reference to 'headlights' in reference to [Vanessa's] breasts. I thought it was extremely awkward and inappropriate for him to be commenting this way about any girl that age, especially his own stepdaughter.

Another teenage girl who went on that camping trip, whom we shall call Olivia, told police she thought Matthew was 'a bit off'. She, too, was disturbed by things that happened on the camping trip.

'We had two tents,' Olivia said in her tendered statement.

The boys and [Matthew] slept in one tent and the girls all slept in the other. At night [Matthew] put the boys to bed and then came into our tent and wanted to sit with us and find out every detail of what [Vanessa] had done at school.

Olivia also made mention of the creepy comments Matthew made. '[Vanessa] got out of the river and [Matthew] was commenting on her breasts.'

There was strange behaviour noticed at home as well. Emma recounted:

Another thing that I remember from Year 9 or 10 was that whenever I stayed at [Vanessa's] house, [Matthew] would always come and get her just before we were going to bed. He would tell [Vanessa], 'Come with me', and tell me, 'Stay there'. [Vanessa] would be with him for five to ten minutes and then come back into the room … I just thought she was getting into trouble again.

During the Christmas holidays after the Year 10 year, according to Emma, Matthew made Vanessa ring her and tell her that they weren't allowed to be friends anymore.

I used to say to [Vanessa] why don't you just come and stay with me. My mum used to say to me that she wanted to just go and get [Vanessa] from her house and bring her home to our place. I would tell this to [Vanessa] and she would just say, 'No, because he will just come and get me.'

Friends noticed Vanessa drop away from them in Years 11 and 12.

'During school we would always invite her to our birthdays and she seemed not to care anymore,' Emma stated.

She would say, 'No, I'm not even going to bother because I won't be allowed.' It was like she was always with us at school and then telling us she didn't want to hang out with us after school. It was just really weird. When she turned eighteen, [Matthew] would take her out clubbing every Saturday night with all of his friends. My friends have told me that if they saw [Vanessa] out, she would come over and say hello and then just as quickly say, 'Ah well, I gotta go' and she would go and stand back with [Matthew] and his friends.

It appeared that Vanessa had become Matthew's possession. Natalie described Vanessa's relationship with her stepfather as 'very awkward'.

'It is probably an understatement to say that [Matthew] was very controlling of [Vanessa] and everything she did,' Natalie said in her police statement. 'He was controlling of where she went, what she wore, who she saw and everything in general about her life. He wouldn't let her see any boys.'

Olivia told police of her school memories:

[Vanessa] was not allowed to wear skirts. She wasn't allowed to go to our Deb ball or any school formals. In 2007 she wasn't allowed to go to our swimming sports or athletic sports. She wasn't allowed to wear costumes. In the end she wasn't allowed to be in school productions. She told us that [Matthew] would get angry with her and it was too much of a hassle to try and be involved in these things as [Matthew] wouldn't let her be involved. She wasn't allowed to go to sleepovers or come out to movies or anything like that with her friends.

According to Natalie, Vanessa was 'generally bright and bubbly' at school and never hinted that she was being sexually abused.

Her friends, including myself, would often ask her if there was something wrong, or what was wrong. She would just say something along the lines of there was nothing wrong and that she was fine. [But] I know there were a number of people who knew [Vanessa], including myself, that thought there was something wrong with the way [Matthew] was treating her. I always suspected that he might have been sexually involved with her.

Emma's mother, who admitted to being scared of Matthew, also told police about strange behaviour that raised suspicions about sexual misconduct. Here's what she said:

I was present when [Vanessa] took phone calls from [Matthew]. I did notice that [Vanessa] always said, 'I love you' to him at the end of every conversation. Simply from the tone of her voice and the nature of the conversation I felt that she was being forced to say this to him. The impression that I got from these conversations was if she didn't do it she would be in such shit. At the time I remember thinking, 'God, how over the top is that?' I always had an uneasy feeling about [Matthew] and his behaviour towards [Vanessa]. My impression was that [Matthew] saw [Vanessa] as his and his only … My concerns about [Vanessa] got to a point where I told my daughter that I just wanted to go and get [Vanessa], take her from her home, get her out and hide her somewhere.

Like Emma and Natalie, Olivia also feared that something was happening to their schoolmate behind closed doors.

'In the last year of school, [Vanessa] started to withdraw a bit,' Olivia stated.

We were pressing her a bit more to find out what was going on between her and [Matthew]. We knew that something wasn't right between her and [Matthew]. We suspected that there might have been a sexual relationship and we asked [Vanessa] if there was something wrong. We asked her to tell us if there was anything wrong. We were hoping to get some information from her which we could have taken to someone else to get help for her. [Vanessa] never stated why she was having problems with [Matthew] or what the problems were about. She only ever said that he was very strict and when we asked about her and [Matthew] she would often just reply by saying, 'He's an arsehole' and not talking about it anymore.

A male school friend recalled that Vanessa would sometimes open up to him.

She would talk about [Matthew] being violent towards her mum and to herself. At times I saw bruises on [Vanessa's] arms. A couple of times I asked her about these bruises and she would tell me that she had fallen over. The first couple of times I believed her but when she was constantly 'falling over' I began to think otherwise about her bruising.

On the days that we were able to walk to school together I would often ask her how her night was. Often she seemed withdrawn and without emotion. I just knew something wasn't right and that [Vanessa] had had a bad night at home. A couple of times I thought there could have been a rape, or something like that, but I was frightened of asking her in case my concern was interpreted the wrong way. I know that a lot of her closer friends have all had the same assumptions. A lot of my friendship group assumed that something like that had happened between [Matthew] and her ... I know that [Vanessa] was always fearful of [Matthew] and when we spoke of her getting away she would always respond in a negative way. She would say that it would never happen and that [Matthew] would know where to look for her.

Despite people having their suspicions, no adult—including any of Vanessa's relatives—reported anything to the authorities. They believed they needed proof, and were also fearful of Matthew. Emma, Natalie and Olivia—with Natalie as their 'spokesperson'—tried to take action. They went to a school counsellor. Natalie said the trio believed that Matthew was hurting or sexually abusing Vanessa. In a coronial finding handed down in September 2012, State Coroner Jennifer Coate said: 'According to [Natalie], the school counsellor told them there was nothing she could do about it unless [Vanessa] came to her directly. [Natalie] stated that after this meeting she did not know what else to do.'

(While the three girls gave evidence at the inquest about the meeting, the school counsellor said she did not recall the discussion with the trio.)

A concerned mother told a second teacher of her lingering suspicions about Matthew and Vanessa. That teacher told police:

We talked about the school formal and whether or not [Matthew] was going to let [Vanessa] go. The mother told me that [Matthew] had been shopping with [Vanessa] and bought a dress for her and that seemed a bit odd for a stepfather to take his stepdaughter dress shopping. The mother said to me that she thought [Matthew] was 'doing' [Vanessa]. I asked her why she thought that and she told me that the girls had voiced concerns to her ... We also discussed the fact that there was no proof that there was some type of sexual relationship between [Matthew] and [Vanessa].

That teacher spoke to Olivia, who told her she did not know anything. The teacher also talked to Vanessa's grandmother, whom she knew. '[Vanessa's grandmother] told me that she had concerns of her own,' the teacher says in her statement.

Judge Coate said later, in her finding:

[Vanessa's] grandmother told the teacher that she had raised concerns with [Vanessa's] mother and as a result, [Vanessa's] mother stopped talking to her and severed the relationship between [Vanessa] and her grandmother. The teacher stated that she had only observed [Matthew] and [Vanessa] together on one occasion. She had been out shopping and saw [Vanessa] walking hand in hand with an older man. She had not known it was [Matthew] at the time. She stated however that they were walking like the way a couple would walk together rather than a teenage stepdaughter and stepfather.

In a separate statement, the teacher said that she had concluded that what she had heard about Vanessa and her stepfather was 'only gossip'. She did not refer the matter or raise it with the school hierarchy.

Vanessa finally snapped on the night of 13 March 2008. She told detectives Forehan and Gray that her stepfather first had sex with her in her bedroom that evening.

FOREHAN: How did that make you feel—at that time on March 13?

VANESSA: Like shit.

FOREHAN: Yeah. Did it make you feel angry?

VANESSA: Yes.

FOREHAN: How would [Matthew] start the sexual intercourse or how would you know that something was going to happen?

VANESSA: He'd tell me, 'Go down to the bedroom.'

FOREHAN: Were you frightened?

VANESSA: Yes.

FOREHAN: What would [Matthew] do if you said no?

VANESSA: He threatened to kill me or he'd strangle me or throw me against the wall.

FOREHAN: Did he throw you against the wall?

VANESSA: Not then, no.

FOREHAN: When was the last time he was violent towards you?

VANESSA: Only a couple of days before. He said he was going to stab me.

FOREHAN: Why did he say that?

VANESSA: Because I didn't want to have sex with him.

FOREHAN: And did you end up having sex with him?

VANESSA: Yes.

FOREHAN: And did you do that out of fear?

VANESSA: Yes.

FOREHAN: I suspect I know the answer to this question but I need to ask it. Would it be fair to say that at no time did you enjoy what was happening to you?

VANESSA: No.

FOREHAN: Did you at any stage consent to what [Matthew] was doing to you?

VANESSA: No.

FOREHAN: Would it be fair to say that you engaged in sex with [Matthew] simply out of fear?

VANESSA: Yes.

About an hour after the sex, Vanessa said, her stepfather ordered her outside into the shed, which contained all his 'toys', including a pool table and motorbikes.

FOREHAN: Did you know what was going to happen?

VANESSA: I had a fair idea.

Vanessa said she was told to perform oral sex in the shed.

'I had a sore throat and I said I really didn't want to, please,' she told the men from Homicide.

And he opened up the gun safe and got his shotgun out and he put a bullet in it and he pointed it at me and he said, 'Do you want to re-think that?' and I said, 'Yes.' And he said, 'So, will you suck me off now?' and I said, 'Yes.' And then he sat the gun on the couch just behind where he was sitting and I did it [performed oral sex] and the gun was just sitting there and I thought I'll never have to do it again if he wasn't there. So I shot him in the back of the head … I just wanted it to just all stop. Go away.

After cutting up Matthew's body she dumped the arms, legs and head at the camping ground. Sent text messages from his phone. Created a false story about how he had taken off with another woman. Even took money from his bank account to make it appear that he was still alive. It wasn't until 4 April that Matthew's brother went to police and filed a missing person's report. Police spoke to Vanessa four days later. She denied knowing where her stepdad was. Little did police know that he was lying dumped in three or four different places. The next day, on 9 April, Matthew's torso was found buried in Vanessa's family's back garden. It was the night of 10 April when Vanessa sat wrapped in the blanket at the country police station as the two Homicide detectives began to question her.

'Would you like to wrap yourself up in the blanket?' Forehan asked Vanessa before the record of interview began. 'You just look a bit cold.'

Vanessa had drawn a rough diagram as a guide to where she had dumped her stepfather's body parts. 'That's a river,' she explained to Forehan. 'These are two camping grounds, two toilets, whereabouts the grass starts and where [Matthew's] head is.'

Forehan stopped her there. 'Okay. Did you put his head there?'

Vanessa nodded. 'Mm'm.'

'When did you do that?'

'I don't know. I don't remember …'

'Okay. Did you do it at night time or day time?'

'Night.'

Vanessa explained how she had driven her stepfather's 4WD to the chosen dumping ground after ramming the vehicle into the letterbox in a panic as she left her driveway.

'Did you take anything else out to that location?' Forehan quizzed.

'Mm'm.'

'What did you take?'

'His arms and legs.'

'All right. Whereabouts in the car did you put his head, his arms and his legs?

'In the back seat.'

'And were they wrapped in anything?'

'Garbage bags.'

'What sort of garbage bags?'

'White ones.'

'And where did you get those garbage bags from?'

'The kitchen.'

'Okay. I understand this must be difficult for you, but we have to ask you to speak to us about how [your stepfather] died ... Did you kill him?'

'Yes.'

Vanessa began to cry.

'Do you remember how you did it?'

More crying. No reply.

'Where did you do it?'

'In the shed,' she said through her tears.

Vanessa said she had been alone. Forehan told her to take a deep breath. Offered her some tissues.

'In my opinion,' he said, 'it's a very drastic step to take so I think you must've had good reason in your mind for killing him.'

Vanessa broke down again.

'Can you try and explain to me why?' Forehan continued.

'I can't say it.'

'Okay. Is it because you don't want to or because it's just a difficult thing for you to talk about?'

'It's difficult for me to talk about.'

'Okay. Would you like me to maybe help you start?'

'Yeah.'

'I suspect from what I have gathered during this investigation that [your stepfather] was a controlling person. Is that right?'

'Yes.'

'That you have lived with him for a long time and he is your stepdad but you call him 'Dad', is that right?'

'No. I call him [Matthew].'

'You call him [Matthew]. Yes, that's right. You do too. How long have you known him for?'

'About twelve years, I think.'

'Okay. So you're now eighteen?'

'Yes.'

'So when you were six, [Matthew] and your mum were together, is that right?'

'I think so.'

'Okay, as a young girl, I suspect he may have done something to you that has caused you considerable pain in your young life. Is that true?'

'Yes.'

'Can you tell me what [Matthew] was doing to you?'

Vanessa broke down again.

'From my point of view as the investigator here, [Vanessa], it's really important that we understand why this has occurred.'

'Mm'm.'

'Can you try and tell me what it was that [Matthew] was doing to you? Was he behaving inappropriately towards you?'

'Yes.'

'Was that behaviour sexual?'

'Yes.'

'Can you tell me the nature of that behaviour?'

Silent tears. A sniffle.

'Would you be happy if I asked you questions more specific and you said yes or no to those questions?'

'Mm'm.'

'Can you tell me at what age [Matthew] started to abuse you?'

And so Vanessa's sorry tale began; the history of Matthew's sexual abuse and his death threats and violent intimidation. She spoke of the sex assaults on 13 March and how she shot her stepdad from behind.

> FOREHAN: Was he talking [when you shot him]?
>
> VANESSA: No. He was doing his pants up.
>
> FOREHAN: What was going through your mind— why did you pull that trigger?
>
> VANESSA: I just wanted him to go away. He'd threatened to kill me so many times and I just thought it would all stop if he wasn't there.

Vanessa said she was ill after she blew a hole in Matthew's head. 'I threw up. I just couldn't even comprehend what had happened.'

With her mother at work on night shift and her brothers tucked up asleep in bed, Vanessa, wearing pyjamas—'a white singlet and pink shorts with monkeys on them'—went inside and sat on the couch and thought for a bit. She then headed back out and into the shed. She had decided on what had to be done. The body was heavy; Matthew's head a mess. The shed was painted in blood and brain matter.

'I went out there and couldn't move him or anything, so I cut him up,' she said.

FOREHAN: Can you tell me how you cut him?

VANESSA: With a saw … The hand saw.

FOREHAN: Where did you cut him first?

VANESSA: The arm.

FOREHAN: Did you cut both arms completely off?

VANESSA: Mm'm.

FOREHAN: What else did you cut on him?

VANESSA: His legs.

FOREHAN: Where did you cut those legs?

VANESSA: I can't remember if it was below or above his knee.

FOREHAN: And where else did you cut him?

VANESSA: On his head … His neck.

FOREHAN: And what were you thinking when you did this? What was going through your mind?

VANESSA: I don't know. I was just crying … I just wanted him to be gone. I just wanted it all to go away. It's like a bad dream. I was waiting to wake up.

FOREHAN: How long do you think it took you to cut his arms, legs and head off?

VANESSA: Maybe an hour.

Vanessa took some garbage bags from the pantry and filled them with body parts. She placed them in the back seat of her stepfather's car and began to drive 'out the bush somewhere'. After driving aimlessly for a while, she chose the camp site as a dumping spot.

VANESSA: I thought I could just maybe chuck them on the side of the road and some animal would eat them. But I couldn't stop.

FOREHAN: Why couldn't you stop?

VANESSA: Because someone would see me.

She arrived at the camping ground.

I was going to go on the sand bar and fill the bags with sand and then tie them and chuck them in the river so that they'd stay down … But there were people camping there. So I went up to the toilets and I chucked the bags in there … I didn't know how deep they [the toilet holes] were … I didn't know if the bags would all go in one [of the holes].

Forehan asked what she did with her stepfather's head.

'Walked into the bush a bit,' she said, 'and chucked it out near a log.'

FOREHAN: Why did you do that?

VANESSA: I don't know. Just to get rid of it.

FOREHAN: Why didn't you put it in the drop toilet?

VANESSA: I don't know.

She returned home. It was nearing 5 am and the clean-up job was not yet finished: the 4WD's interior was marked with blood, and Matthew's hacked torso still lay in the shed. Vanessa started with the vehicle.

I went inside and got a face washer and wiped up—there was some blood on the car and then I realised … I seen the big dent where I hit the letterbox … and I rubbed that so it didn't look as noticeable. And then checked the back seat, which had blood on it. So I wiped that.

Forehan asked Vanessa what she did with her stepfather's torso.

'Nothing. I couldn't go back out to the shed.'

FOREHAN: Was there lots of blood in the shed?
VANESSA: Mm'm.
FOREHAN: How much do you think?
VANESSA: Heaps … All over the floor. In front of the pool table … and the couch.

Exhausted, Vanessa locked up the shed and washed herself of the blood. She pretended to be asleep on the couch when her mum arrived home from work at about 7 am. When Forehan asked what she was thinking at that point in time, Vanessa replied: 'It was just like I didn't exist.'

It wasn't until Monday, 17 March—four days after she'd shot and dismembered her stepfather—that Vanessa turned her mind to removing his torso from the shed. She started by digging a hole in the garden. Her young brothers interrupted and asked what she was doing. She told them she was weeding.

'They wanted to help, so we ended up digging a hole,' Vanessa told detectives Forehan and Gray. 'We said we were digging a hole to China. I said I'd cover it up later on. That night I put the rest of [my stepfather] in there.'

FOREHAN: How did you get him out there?
VANESSA: I dragged him on a sheet … There was cardboard and stuff on the ground that had been soaking up the blood, so I chucked that in there too and burned it.
FOREHAN: How did you start the fire?
VANESSA: A lighter.
FOREHAN: Did you use accelerant?

VANESSA: Yes.

FOREHAN: What did you use?

VANESSA: Petrol … Then I covered the hole over.

Using the garden hose, Vanessa washed the blood from the shed. The following night she returned and wiped down with methylated spirits the furniture and other items, including a motorbike and a punching bag. She was also sending SMS messages from Matthew's phone to her mum.

'I sent ones to Mum to make her think that he'd left … I [also] wrote back to a few messages from people so that they didn't wonder why he wasn't writing back.'

She also sent a message to a new boyfriend, a young man Matthew had ironically said was a 'cockhead' who 'treated women like shit'.

FOREHAN: Why didn't [Matthew] want you to be with [your boyfriend]?

VANESSA: Because I was his.

Vanessa started going out with the guy, whom we shall call Lachlan, only days after she shot Matthew dead.

'This was her first boyfriend that I am aware of,' her mum said in a statement.

Lachlan had been Vanessa's chosen one for some time, apparently, but Matthew had forbidden Vanessa from going out with him.

'The boys said [Matthew] was going to kill [Lachlan] if he went near [Vanessa],' Vanessa's mum stated.

I spoke with [Matthew] and [Vanessa and Lachlan] and told him that if [Vanessa] wanted to go out with [Lachlan], she was eighteen and he shouldn't be trying to stop her. [Matthew] said that [Lachlan] wasn't good enough for her. As far as I knew, [Lachlan] was a good kid … After [Matthew] went missing I noticed a few changes in [Vanessa]. Initially she did seem quite ill. I thought she must have had gastro or something. After a while she got better. We went out for dinner and she wore a skirt, which she had never been allowed to do in the past. She got a mobile phone and started to get back into contact with all of her [previous] friends from school.

Vanessa withdrew $500 using her stepfather's ATM card (she knew his PIN) and left cash in her family's letterbox, before sending a text message to her mum purporting to be from Matthew.

'Mum was complaining,' Vanessa told Forehan and Gray. 'She was upset. She didn't know how she was going to feed the boys. She had no money.'

Vanessa also tried to send a text message from her stepfather's phone to his boss, saying he wouldn't 'be able to come in for a couple of days'. She sent another message to her mum purporting to be from Matthew, saying he and another woman wanted to start a new life in Tasmania.

He always talked about going to Tasmania, so I thought that would sound right … And mum was really upset by the whole thing so I thought maybe if I said that he was with someone else she wouldn't be as upset—she'd be angry at him instead.

The message did anger Vanessa's mother. Her neighbour told police: 'She got upset and angry and after receiving this message put an end to the thought of reporting him missing since he was supposed to have run off with another woman.' Vanessa's mum fired off a return text: 'Now I can tell the boys the truth. Does she have name or do I tell your kids you left them for a slut.'

On behalf of Matthew, Vanessa replied: 'Her name is Sarah but tell them what you want.'

Vanessa's subterfuge only lasted so long. The discovery of Matthew's hacked headless torso in the garden bed was a dead giveaway that he wasn't the one sending the phone messages.

> **FOREHAN**: When the police became involved in the investigation, what was going through your mind at that stage?
>
> **VANESSA**: That my life was over.

Friends did not believe that Vanessa would have been capable of carrying out such a grisly killing, despite their fears about what was more than likely happening to her at home.

'She is not the type of person to be violent at all and I have seen her put up with an extreme amount of pressure,' Olivia told police. 'For her to be responsible for someone's death, particularly [Matthew's] death, would have taken something catastrophic.'

During a search of the shed, police found a contraceptive pill prescription in Matthew's gun safe. Vanessa told detectives she would purchase the pills or her stepfather would do it for her so she wouldn't fall pregnant.

'I either had to take them or have a baby because he wasn't gunna wear protection,' she said.

> **GRAY**: What do you think would have happened if you got pregnant?
>
> **VANESSA**: I probably would have killed myself.

Gray asked Vanessa if she had a school counsellor.

'I couldn't do anything 'cos [Matthew] would kill me,' she explained.

GRAY: I appreciate where you're coming from … Why didn't you report it to the police?

VANESSA: 'Cos I didn't want anyone to know … because I hated it and if anyone else knew then I had to accept that it was real.

GRAY: You said that [Matthew] had threatened to kill you so many times … was it becoming a more frequent thing?

VANESSA: No, it wasn't becoming more frequent because I didn't argue with him as much. I just did what he said.

GRAY: And what kind of threats had he been making to you previous to that night where he produced a shotgun?

VANESSA: He'd always say that if I ever told anyone or if I ever left or anything, he'd find me and kill me. He'd always say that he'd shoot me. He said he'd stab me. He's got a knife out a couple of times. Yeah. Stuff like that … He's hit me a few times and thrown me up against walls.

Gray asked Vanessa if she'd thought the abuse was going to continue well into the future.

'I'm not really sure,' she replied:

but he said that for my sixteenth birthday, my present from him was going to be that he would stop. And then on my sixteenth birthday he had his so-called 'last one' and then the next day he said, 'Nuh, I can't stop.' And so then I knew that, yeah, it wasn't going to ever stop then.

Matthew had taken a large number of sexually explicit photos of Vanessa and made video recordings of them having sex.

'He used them to blackmail me to do stuff 'cos I didn't want anyone to see them,' Vanessa explained.

According to Gray's statement, detectives seized a computer hard drive, DVD discs, camera memory cards and USB memory sticks from the family home. Gray said in his statement:

> At the Computer Crime Squad I was present when the items were examined and I examined the computer hard drive and found it to contain a large number of images including pornographic images of unknown adult females and pornographic images of the accused and deceased engaged in sexual activity.

He continued, 'The sexual activity involved oral sex being performed on the accused [Vanessa] by the deceased [Matthew], oral sex being performed on [Matthew] by [Vanessa], and vaginal sex on [Vanessa] by [Matthew] with his penis and fingers.'

Of the images and homemade sex movies Gray said: 'All images and movies were of a type that identifies that both parties were aware that the images were being taken. In many of the images, [Vanessa] does not appear to be happy being photographed.'

In total, there were more than 7800 pornographic images found on memory sticks and cards.

'These images include images of [Vanessa] being tied to a chair by the arms and legs with cable ties and towels,' Gray said in his statement. 'Force is being used to hold [Vanessa] in place.'

Vanessa was charged with murder. After a preliminary hearing in the Magistrates' Court she was committed to stand trial. During a directions hearing in the Supreme Court on 10 March 2009, Justice Philip Cummins asked the prosecution to reconsider its position due to the evidence about prolonged sexual abuse and violent threats. On 27 March, the Director of the Office of Public Prosecutions, Jeremy Rapke, filed a notice with the court stating that the prosecution was being discontinued. The charge against Vanessa was being dropped. Rapke told Cummins:

> I have reached the conclusion that there is no reasonable prospect that a jury would convict [Vanessa] of any offence arising from the tragic events that led to her shooting dead [Matthew] on 13 March 2008 and interfering with his body. I stress, Your Honour, this decision has been made solely on the basis of a careful consideration of the strength of the evidence in this case and the likely impact on the jury's consideration of that evidence under the new statutory provisions relating to self-defence and family violence.
>
> I recognise that the physical or sexual or psychological abuse to which [Vanessa] was subjected since the age of fourteen and the circumstances that confronted her immediately before she shot the deceased were such as to make it extremely unlikely that a jury would convict her of any offence arising from the death.

In late 2011, Judge Coate held a four-day inquest into Matthew's death. The inquest focused on issues such as the mandatory reporting of child sex abuse and the training provided to teachers with respect to their statutory obligations, and also community awareness about such sex abuse. Coate said in her finding:

> Those issues arose in light of evidence that a number of members of the adult community around [Vanessa] held concerns about the nature of the relationship between her and [Matthew], and based on evidence that two teachers at [Vanessa's] school appeared to have information about the abusive relationship but had not acted upon it.

She noted, 'No question has been raised as to the veracity of [Vanessa's] account of what happened.'

Coate also said:

> One of the important findings to come out of this investigation is the need to be constantly vigilant and challenge our assumptions about whether or not abuse is occurring and a child is at risk. By its very nature, childhood sexual abuse is an insidious crime. Those who perpetrate it typically go to great lengths to avoid detection and ensure that the victims do not reveal what is happening to them.

Vanessa's mother still stands by her daughter, who will no doubt carry mental scars for the rest of her life. The fact that Vanessa, as an eighteen-year-old, blasted a man in the head with a shotgun and then forced herself to hack his limbs and head from his body for the purposes of disposal shows her level of despair and desperation.

'I am upset that [Matthew] will never be held accountable for what I believe he has done to my daughter,' Vanessa's mum said in one of her police statements.

It is extremely upsetting to me and my family what
has happened to [Matthew] and [Vanessa] but I am
finding it hard to see [Matthew] as the victim in all of
this. He took [Vanessa's] teenage years away from her
and only God knows what else he has put her through.
I can accept what my daughter has done and I will
always be there to support her in any way that I can.

9

A Tale of Passion

'I swallowed so much blood that to this day
I can still taste Mark's blood in my mouth.'

JEALOUSY IS A POISON THAT CAN MAKE MEN, AND WOMEN, do crazy things. It can whisper and entice, needling and pinching at common sense and hollowing the stomach. It can cause its victims to gnash their teeth and begrudge all possibilities. And rue what might have been. Love-struck Leon Joseph Oscar Borthwick fell victim to jealousy's curse and killed another young man as a consequence. Borthwick's vision had been clouded to the extent that he glared upon young university student Mark Zimmer as a rival: a love rival who, he believed, had stolen his girl. Seventeen-year-old Nicola Martin—Borthwick's former flame of two years— was at the apex of a teenage love triangle. Borthwick, aged eighteen at the time, and Mark, aged nineteen, represented the remaining two angles. This case might have read like a bad teen romance novel brimming with immature angst had it not ended with the death of an innocent young man on a vehicle's bullbar in a suburban street. It is not a cautionary tale. It is not a melodramatic *Twilight*-style saga. It is a real-life tragedy for all involved.

One of three siblings, Mark Zimmer lived with his parents, Christian and Ruth, in the middle-class Melbourne suburb of Endeavour Hills. He had an older protective sister, Kornelia, and a baby brother named Zachary. Mark had grown up in the southern beachside suburb of Carrum and completed his education at Mazenod College in Mulgrave. The family had moved to Endeavour Hills in 1999. They were a typical loving family. At the time of his death, Mark was studying an IT and business course at Swinburne University. He was 'outgoing and very popular amongst his friends', according to the police summary.

Leon Borthwick had grown up in Hyderabad, India. He and his family—dad Reginald, mum Lana and older brother Shawn—moved to Australia in 2000. In around 2003 the family moved from Hampton Park to Narre Warren in the south-east suburban corridor. Borthwick had completed Year 12 in 2007 and was employed in casual jobs. It had been in September 2006 when Borthwick had hooked up with high-school girl Nicola. The two met through a friend of Nicola's. They stayed together as boyfriend and girlfriend until about September of 2008.

'We split up after I started to get fed up with his laziness,' Nicola said in a police statement tendered in Melbourne Magistrates' Court. 'I was also losing my friends because of him. He appeared to have an anger problem … When I say angry I mean he was protective of whom I associated with or even spoke to.'

It was around this time that Nicola met Mark Zimmer through mutual friends, including Mark's best mate Sean Heneric. There were a large group of teens at the same house that night.

'The night I met Mark, Leon was with me,' Nicola told police. 'On the night we all met Mark, Leon almost straight away took a dislike to him.'

Comments made about Borthwick's mum's silver and blue Tarago van only enflamed the animosity.

'Mark and Sean made comments about the car he was driving,' Nicola said in her statement. 'Mark and Sean told Leon to go and collect [one of his friends] Jeremy in "the van of courage". Leon did not say much, but I knew comments like this were upsetting him.'

Borthwick demanded Nicola leave with him. She refused.

'When she refused he became angry,' according to the police summary, 'and threw a bottle on to the road and drove off at fast speed. [Those who witnessed that] were all surprised and scared by his actions.'

Sean Heneric recalled the incident in his police statement.

He was drinking alcohol. He had the bottle. Nicola had wanted to go and pick someone up. Leon got angry and threw the bottle along the road, just missing a car. He drove off and took off really hard. We knew then he was weird.

After Nicola broke up with Borthwick, she started calling Mark on his mobile phone, and at home.

'We started talking to each other nearly every night,' Nicola said in her statement. 'We talked mainly on our house phones … We were just friends and were never boyfriend and girlfriend.'

Heneric told the Supreme Court that he was of the belief that the two were 'friends with benefits'.

'It means that people are friends but when they see each other they have sex, like, there's no feelings in it— they are just there to have fun,' he explained during

Borthwick's murder trial in the Victorian Supreme Court.

Whatever the relationship, Mark appeared to be playing the confidant.

'Nicola had indicated to me that Leon was becoming too possessive and that she felt comfortable talking to Mark about her problems,' friend Chernish Thomas says in her police statement.

Borthwick got wind of the burgeoning friendship between Mark and Nicola.

'Even though I had broken up with Leon he did not like me talking to Mark,' Nicola told police.

> He told me to stop talking to Mark as he did not like him … Once Leon found out I had been talking to Mark he seemed to show up more often and [appear] at houses of friends of mine. I felt at times Leon was checking up on me, even though we had split up.

Borthwick, meanwhile, was telling his mates that he and Nicola were still an item. In the Supreme Court, Nicola said later that when she and Mark started talking on the phone, she and Borthwick were 'kind of off/on at that point'. She later told prosecutor Michele Williams, SC, that she and Borthwick had remained friends.

> **WILLIAMS**: You'd meet up with him and so on?
> **NICOLA**: Yeah, we were still friends.

Over the following months before the fatal night of 15 November 2008, Borthwick regularly threatened Mark.

'If you still see Nicola, I am going to tie you to a tree and hit you like a piñata,' he yelled down the phone on one occasion, while Sean Heneric listened in.

'Leon was angry,' Heneric said in his police statement.

> Mark could put up with them [the phone calls] and hang up. Mark would try and reason with him. He would say he wasn't seeing Nicola and Leon should move on. Mark would always be calm. He just tried to get it across to Leon that he and Nicola weren't going out.

Borthwick also threatened Heneric over the phone, blaming him for introducing Nicola to Mark.

'He would make phone calls to my mobile phone,' Heneric told police.

> They would be at night. He would say things like: 'You're going to regret introducing Mark to Nicola.' I felt he was trying to find someone to blame for him and Nicola breaking up and he was trying to put the blame on me … He would ring a couple of times and then it would die down, then he would ring again.

Heneric said Borthwick 'was always angry' when he called, with some calls lasting up to between thirty and forty minutes. Heneric tried to play the peace maker.

'He wanted to know what was going on and whether he should confront them,' Heneric told police

> I was telling him that they weren't going out and he shouldn't worry. Leon would say that he and Nicola were still going out and he thought they were cheating on him. You could not reason with him. You would end up with threats. All through these calls he would still be making threats against Mark and I … The constant threats to Mark was that Leon knew where he lived and was going to get him, beat him up.

On at least two occasions Leon was heard to say that he was going to kill Mark. He said he would stab him and that he had a gun in his house and would go and shoot him.

'Leon was saying that Nicola was an angel or something along those lines,' Heneric said later in court. 'He blamed Mark for their break-up.'

In late September or early October 2008, Mark and Heneric went to Chernish Thomas's house to see Nicola to discuss the Borthwick situation—and possibly resolve it.

'Mark was at breaking point,' Heneric said in his tendered statement.

Not long after they arrived, Borthwick turned up with friends. Borthwick confronted Mark and demanded to know if anything sexual had happened between him and Nicola. He asked 'how far' the two had gone. Mark assured Borthwick that the relationship was purely platonic. A hug was as far as it had gone, Mark said. Borthwick stood face to face with Mark. Chernish Thomas told the Supreme Court that Borthwick became 'more and more upset'.

'First he got really red because he was about to cry— he had tears in his eyes,' Chernish said. 'He was stuttering and then he just kept getting louder to try and get his point across.'

'If I cut your balls out maybe you will tell me the truth,' Borthwick reportedly said.

From his bag Borthwick pulled a knife and held it to Mark's crotch. It appeared to be a silly boy's game— until it became apparent that Borthwick was not fooling around.

'I'll cut your dick off,' he was said to have threatened. 'Please don't lie.'

'Mark had one of his hands on Leon's hand or wrist and Leon had his left hand on top grabbing Mark's wrist,' Heneric told police. 'Mark was pushing the knife away.'

One of the young men present, Jeremy Dardenne, pulled Borthwick back. Some of the girls were crying.

'Mark and I had had enough and left,' Heneric stated. 'In the car as we drove away Mark was freaked out by what happened.'

In court, Heneric added: 'He was honestly, like, really scared.'

It wasn't the first time Borthwick had produced a knife, according to some of the group. On two previous occasions he had pulled a blade and threatened young men he believed were looking Nicola up and down, according to the police summary.

Mark went on to tell his dad about the close encounter.

'Mark told me that he was threatened with a knife at a party and that someone was giving him a hard time,' Mark's father, Christian Zimmer, said during Borthwick's trial.

I tried to get some details out of Mark—as much as you can from a nineteen-year-old teenager who didn't want to elaborate too much on it. I said, 'Tell me more,' and he said, 'Well, there's this crazy guy. He's trying to get at me because I'm friends with his ex-girlfriend. I was at the party and he came at me with a knife.'

At that point I said, 'Mark, you need to go to the police … He's broken the law. He's done something wrong.'

Prosecutor Williams asked Christian some questions on that topic.

WILLIAMS: Did he tell you the name of the person?
CHRISTIAN: He just told me that this guy was called Leon.

WILLIAMS: And so far as the topic of an ex-girlfriend is concerned, did you know who your son was talking about?

CHRISTIAN: I knew that he mentioned in that conversation the name Nicola.

WILLIAMS: Did you at that stage have any knowledge of whether your son was seeing or having any contact with Nicola?

CHRISTIAN: I was aware that he saw her on and off, as they were friends, and that there was phone conversation on a regular basis.

WILLIAMS: And when you say phone conversation on a regular basis, how did you know that?

CHRISTIAN: My phone bills were very high during that period and I had a word with Mark about it.

(Mark and his buddy Sean Heneric did in fact go to a local police station on 10 November to report the knife threat. 'He wanted to get a restraining order or an intervention order against Leon Borthwick,' Heneric said in court.)

Under cross-examination by defence barrister Carmen Randazzo, SC, Christian Zimmer said that he believed Nicola was staying over some nights.

'Mark did mention it,' Christian said:

and I was going to have a more serious conversation with him [about that] but we never had that chance … We were seeing more of her and I was a bit upset that Mark didn't introduce her at that point … They didn't come out and say, 'We're a couple.'

Christian told the jury that he was 'very forceful' in trying to get his son—who was growing ever concerned about home security—to alert the authorities about Leon

Borthwick. Christian described the issue in court as a 'teenage love problem'.

'[Mark] just kept on saying, "This is my problem and we've got mutual friends … and they're assisting me with trying to calm down the situation,"' Christian said in court.

Mark had also mentioned the threatening phone calls in passing, Christian said.

> Mark was behaving odd. He wasn't his normal self … He told me on one occasion that [Borthwick] had called him and threatened to kill him, and he also mentioned the fact that he was continuously threatened and then [Borthwick] would say, 'I'll cut your tongue out' and then he would bring up, 'I'll kill you.'
>
> I think there was maybe a one- to two-week period where nothing occurred after the knife incident and it looked like Mark was saying that his mutual friends [had] managed to calm the situation down, and then I think it must have started up again and got worse because that's when Mark started to tell us about these phone calls … Mark was saying 'I've got everything under control' because he didn't want to concern us … I said, 'Look, you know you have to do something [by going to the police], this could get out of hand.' But he was adamant that this was his problem and he wanted to deal with it.

A couple of weeks before Mark's death, Borthwick rang Heneric and told him that he was at a local McDonald's store in Endeavour Hills with about six mates.

'He demanded I give him Mark's address and said if I didn't he would come to my house and make me come out,' Heneric said in his statement. 'He said he would drag me out of the house, strip me naked and tie me to the back of a car and drive my body around.'

According to Haldane Bensley, who worked at the McDonald's store, Borthwick turned up on another occasion asking for Mark's address. 'I told him Mark was a friend and I wasn't giving him the address,' Haldane told police.

He told me he wasn't scared of Mark and he'd already held a knife to his balls and he'd kill him for his girlfriend. I asked him, 'Isn't she your ex? Why do you care?' Leon said they were still together. I went back in and called Mark to tell him. It was about 2.20 in the morning … Mark said, 'Yeah, he speaks a lot of shit.' Mark told me that Leon had split up with his girlfriend but he wasn't over her … Mark told me [he and Nicola] were close but they weren't seeing each other. They were getting closer and Mark liked her. Mark told me how Leon had been calling his house over the last couple of weeks, like calling him in the middle of the night and hanging up, and another time held a knife to his balls.

On 13 November, Borthwick confronted Mark at a park near the Zimmers' home. Mark told his dad about it. 'He looked very distressed,' Christian told the jury.

The only detail he said was that Leon was out in the park with his mates [and that] he was being threatened again. Then he mentioned the fact that maybe it's not worth it all and he should just forget this Nicola and I then said to him, 'Maybe it might be better if you just forget her.' Then he said, 'But I really like her' and I said to him, which was probably my mistake, 'Don't let

anyone tell you that you are not allowed to see her.'
I shouldn't have told him that. I should have said he
should have forgot her.

Leon Borthwick was a vindictive young man with
jealousy stoking his immature ego. He was not willing to
let Nicola go. The two were still hanging out as friends
and, along with a large group of pals, they spent the
afternoon of Saturday, 15 November milling and chilling
at the Fountain Gate Shopping Centre. In the words of
one of the group, Ed Gutteres, they were all there 'to kill
off some time'. Late in the afternoon Gutteres invited
everyone back to his parents' house.

'We were just hanging out there like a normal day—
playing basketball, Playstation, watching DVDs, listening
to music,' one of the group, Jermaine Berenger, explained
in court.

That evening at about 9.30, Borthwick dropped
Nicola off at her aunt's house for a fiftieth birthday
party, stopping at her house along the way. They had a
discussion.

WILLIAMS: You had an argument, was it?

NICOLA: No, not an argument. Just, like, if we were
going to get back together or not.

WILLIAMS: Tell us what was said.

NICOLA: He just asked me pretty much if we were
going to get back together or not, or if we were just
going to stay friends.

WILLIAMS: And what did you say?

NICOLA: I just explained to him I didn't want to be
in a relationship any more and that, yeah, just stay
friends—at least for then anyway.

WILLIAMS: And how did he react to that?

NICOLA: Well, he kind of just went along with what
I said, I guess … He kind of just stayed quiet.

Borthwick then drove back to Gutteres's house with
mate Phillip Pellegrin in tow.

'He was crying and he told me that his girlfriend,
Nicola, couldn't tell him she loved him whilst looking
into his eyes,' Pellegrin told police. 'He was questioning
whether or not Nicola loved him anymore.'

Back at Ed Gutteres's place, Borthwick could not hide
his inner pain. He was still crying.

Jermaine Berenger said in court: 'He was crying. We
pretty much knew at once it had something to do with
Nicola.'

That night Borthwick told one of the group: 'I can tell
my girlfriend doesn't love me as much anymore because
Mark has come in the middle of everything.'

Borthwick asked Gutteres if he could use the home
phone. He called Mark Zimmer's mobile number. Mark
and Sean Heneric were together at the Zimmers' home
eating pizza and KFC while watching a *Stargate* episode
when the call came through.

'Mark came up with an idea he wanted to watch the
whole series of this show,' Heneric recalled in court,
with half a smile in the only light-hearted moment of
the trial.

Because I wasn't a big fan of *Stargate*, and he wanted
me to get into it, he wanted me to start from season
one, episode one—my God—and work our way down
through all of the twelve series.

Mark put Borthick's call on loud speaker. Borthwick
asked Mark if he'd spoken to Nicola recently.

'Leon was saying that he'd had enough of this shit and it was going to finish tonight,' Heneric told police. 'I heard Leon say to Mark that he was going to be at his house at 12 [midnight] and then the call ended.'

Those at Ed Gutteres's house also caught the conversation at Borthwick's end. There was talk of fighting 'one on one'. Berenger heard Borthwick say that he used to be a lover, not a fighter, until Mark took his dignity away. It might have been laughable banter between two young rams were the consequences not to turn so horribly ugly in the hours that were to follow. Back at the Zimmer home, Mark went into his mum and dad's bedroom.

'He was very distressed and he said he just got a call from this Leon and he was coming to get him tonight,' Christian said in the Supreme Court. 'My wife said, "What do you mean by that?" and he said, "He's going to come and kill me tonight" … I told Mark to ring the police.'

Mark did make a call to the local cop shop but did not fully explain the situation, or leave any details. The policewoman taking the call reportedly replied: 'There's nothing we can really do right now. It's only when he comes to your house, call 000.'

'Mark said thanks and hung up,' Heneric said in his statement.

Christian Zimmer told the court what happened next:

After probably about ten minutes I went back into the study and said, 'Have you rung the police yet?' and Mark said yes he had. I looked at Sean and I said, 'Sean, did he ring the police? And Sean said, 'Yeah, he rang the police,' and I said, 'So what did they say? When are they coming?' and Mark said, 'They're not coming,' and I said I couldn't believe that they're not coming. I said, 'What did they say?' and he said, 'They told me to dial 000 when this person arrives.' At that point Mark decided to try to get help from his friends.

Mark began to drum up reinforcements over the phone. Heneric told police: 'Mark asked everyone to come to his house to help make sure nothing happened.' Christian told the jury:

Mark's friends were out the front in the reserve, playing cricket. He felt that they had no weapons so they should arm themselves and he went to the kitchen and said, 'Maybe I should get some knives,' and I said, 'Mark, you're not getting any knives. You are not going out of this house with a knife.'

He said, 'Dad, they're going to come with weapons. I need something. We need something,' and I said, 'Mark, people just get killed with knives. Please don't take a knife.'

He went out to the shed and I had some spanners and I said, 'Look, if you want you can take some of these.' Mark grabbed some of the spanners and took them to his friends … Probably about half a dozen.'

(A neighbour would find spanners and a broken cricket bat left behind in his garden the following morning.)

Mark returned the call from Borthwick. Attack, apparently, seemed the best form of defence.

'I heard Mark say to Leon that if he didn't come to his house then he was going to go to Leon's,' Heneric stated. 'Leon was asking Mark who was going to be at his house. In the end Mark just hung up.'

At Borthwick's end, Pellegrin heard Mark say that 'there was about fifty guys there to get Leon and that Mark was going to crowbar Leon in the face and if he wasn't there at twelve that he was going to go to Leon's house.'

The two young warriors then immediately rang Nicola. Borthwick got through first.

'After the [fiftieth birthday] speeches at around 11 pm I received a call from Leon and he told me this would be the last time I would speak to him,' Nicola said in her statement.

I asked him what he was talking about and he said, 'It was set.' When I questioned him further he said, 'Me and Mark are punching on tonight.' He told me that this was to occur at Mark's house. While I was talking to Leon I received another call at the same time. This call was from Mark, so I placed Leon on hold and spoke to Mark. Mark said, 'Leon is coming to my house tonight and I am waiting for him and I have over thirty guys here waiting for him also.' Mark did not say what they were going to do when Leon arrived at his house. While I was talking to Mark, Leon hung up and Mark told me that everyone has had enough of being threatened by Leon.

In court, Nicola added: 'Mark was angry and frustrated and he didn't want to deal with Leon any more and he was just fed up with everything so he wanted everything to stop … He just wanted to sort everything out.'

Borthwick got back in touch with Nicola.

'I told him that Mark had a whole lot of people with him and he probably shouldn't go to Mark's house 'cos, you know, he could have got hurt,' Nicola said in evidence. 'I was just warning him that Mark was ready if he did come.'

Borthwick reached out to his older brother Shawn, who was at a mate's place in nearby Hampton Park having a drink and a feed after work. Borthwick rang him.

'Leon told me that someone was after him; some boys wanted to bash him,' Shawn said in his police statement. 'I didn't pay much attention to what he was going on about and told him to come over.'

Borthwick scored a lift back home where he grabbed the keys to his mum's Tarago. He drove the van, with Jermaine Berenger and Phillip Pellegrin on board, to go meet up with his brother. Upon his arrival, he and Shawn had a conversation.

'It was Leon filling his brother in on what was going on and then it was just his brother cracking it back pretty much saying, "Why are you fighting over a girl? That's stupid,"' Berenger said in court.

By midnight there was a group of up to eight young men assembled at the Zimmer home.

'These friends were all aware of the on-going threats [Borthwick] had been making towards [Mark],' the police summary stated.

But Borthwick never showed, and at 12.05 am Mark decided it was time to travel to Borthwick's house. Borthwick was informed that Mark and his crew were coming to him to 'resolve the situation'.

According to the police summary: 'His friends agreed.' One of those friends, Noel Amarasinghe, put it eloquently enough when he told police: 'We all decided to go to Leon's place to sit down and talk to tell him to lay off—that Nicola doesn't like him and to stop being jealous.'

'It sounded to me that these guys wanted to get into a fight,' Shawn Borthwick said in his police statement.

Leon and his friends told me that the guy wanted to fight Leon and was going to get him with a crowbar. They told him that they were going to come to our house with thirty people. I told Leon to leave it for now, just wait. The guys were being stupid. I told Leon not to worry about it. That they weren't going to come to our house.

Christian Zimmer was fighting against the tide trying to dissuade the young men—some of whom, according to differing versions, had armed themselves with spanners, lengths of steel pipe, a cricket bat handle and a windscreen wiper—from heading over to Borthwick's house.

'Mark came in—it would have been around midnight,' Christian recalled in court:

and said to me that, 'It looks like they're not coming. We have decided we're going to go down to his house.'

I said to him, 'No, you're not going down to his house.'

He said, 'Dad, I am,' and I said, 'No Mark, you're not going. I don't want you to turn into what this person is,' and he said, 'Dad, I can't live like this anymore. He's been threatening me and intimidating and harassing me for so long. I just need to do something. I've done everything you've asked. I've gone to the police. They're not doing anything. I've rung them tonight. They're not coming. My friends think they can sort this out. My friends know Leon. Maybe we can go down there and sort this out. I just cannot live like this anymore.'

By that stage tears were welling in Mark's eyes. Christian continued:

I said, 'Mark, let me come with you,' and Mark said, 'No, this is my problem Dad. I don't want you there,' and I said, 'Let me, at least, you know, come with you, we need to sort it out,' and he didn't want to have me there. He walked off, and then about five minutes later he came back and said, 'Dad, can you take some of my friends because we can only fit, I think, four people in my car. Can you take some more, and I'll have more people there to help me in case things get out of hand.' I decided I would help him.

Mark drove a couple of his friends. Christian Zimmer drove the others. They drove past the Borthwick house, turned at the next intersection and parked. Jeremy and Michael Dardenne (who had been in Borthwick's company earlier that evening) had earlier picked up Jeremy's girlfriend, Jessica Cardamone. They drove past Borthwick's home. They saw Mark and his group, and had a short chat, before parking opposite the house. A message was then relayed back to Borthwick: Mark Zimmer and his crew had arrived.

'Leon told me that he was pretty sure that they had weapons,' Shawn Borthwick said in his statement.

Leon and I said that we would go and have a look to see what was happening. We needed to sort it out. I was concerned. I thought that these guys must be serious. I was concerned for my parents and my house.

Shawn and three of his mates left in his vehicle. Borthwick, with Berenger and Pellegrin still on board, were to follow.

'He was pretty angry at the time that they had the nerve to go to the front of his house,' Berenger said in court. 'And then along those lines he goes, "If I see them I'm going to run them over with the van." Me and

Phillip both reacted. Said, "No, don't be so stupid" sort of thing.'

It was a two-minute drive from Shawn's mate's house to the Borthwick home. Christian Zimmer, already parked down the road near the house, watched Mark and his mates march on.

'All the boys got out of the cars and started to cross the road,' Christian recalled in court.

> I called back to Mark. I asked him to come to the car. Mark walked back to the car and I said, 'Mark, please don't do anything silly. If anything gets out of hand, I'm here. Just come here. Run back here … Make sure that no-one does anything silly.'
>
> He said, 'Don't worry Dad, everything will be fine. I will be back in ten minutes.'

That was the last time Christian Zimmer saw his son alive.

Prosecutor Williams questioned Christian about the presence of weapons.

> **WILLIAMS**: Did you see whether he or anybody else took anything with them?
> **CHRISTIAN**: [One of the boys] was carrying my squeegee and I thought what is he going to do with that? I usually clean my windows [with it].
> **WILLIAMS**: What about anyone else?
> **CHRISTIAN**: No, I didn't see.
> **WILLIAMS**: What about your son? Did you see him with anything?
> **CHRISTIAN**: I didn't see him with anything … I am not saying he didn't have anything. I didn't see him with anything.

Christian continued:

I was sitting in the car thinking, 'Should I follow them?'
Then I knew Mark would be upset with me. I was also
concerned that it might aggravate the situation. I was
hoping that, you know, these kids could sort it out
together.

Most who were there said they were not expecting any
real trouble. Joshua Madeira told police:

Prior to the accident I was not aware of what Mark's
plans were and I did not expect there to be any
trouble. I never saw anyone I was with take any
weapons with them, or Mark carrying any weapons. I
did not take any weapon with me.

Mark, Sean Heneric and mate Troy Polifrone had
crossed the road to stand by the car containing the two
Dardenne boys and Jessica Cardamone. Mark stood near
the driver's door talking to the occupants.

'I don't know whether it was to me or Jess but he
did say that he wasn't there to fight, he just wanted
to sort things out,' Jeremy Dardenne said in court.
'He was holding, I guess, like a metal cylinder-looking
thing.'

Heneric and Polifrone were standing on the roadway
next to Mark.

'They were all standing just within or on the white
parking lane line,' according to the police summary.

Shawn Borthwick said in court: 'It seemed like there
was a lot of people.'

As Shawn was driving along his street, his brother
flashed his lights at him.

'He just flashed the lights for him to slow down and then sped up to try to catch up to him,' Berenger recalled in court. '[Leon] was driving pretty steady, close to the speed limit.'

Leon Borthwick drove over to the incorrect side of the road, overtaking Shawn and swerving in towards where Mark, Heneric and Polifrone were standing. According to passenger Pellegrin, '[Leon] unexpectedly swerved the van towards them. He was on the wrong side of the road ... As he did this, Jermaine and I started screaming at Leon to stop.'

Heneric and Polifrone saw the Tarago coming and stepped in closer to the parked car next to which they were standing.

'I heard a loud rattling sound of a car and I looked to the right and I saw a blue Tarago van coming towards us on the wrong side of the road with its high beams on,' Heneric recalled in his statement. 'I had to move in close to Jeremy's car to avoid getting hit.'

In court he tried to describe the feeling of the van brushing past him.

I don't know how to describe it—when you feel like it's very close; going fast like the wind ... It definitely didn't brake ... I sort of froze ... I heard the bang and I looked to the left ... I wondered where Mark went.

Leon Borthwick hit Mark with the front right side of the van. Mark had turned to run but was too late to avoid the fatal impact. Here's what the witnesses said.

Passenger Jermaine Berenger: 'I just looked over to the windshield and just saw someone on it.'

Jessica Cardamone:

The last thing I know was that we were just talking and out of nowhere I just heard this 'bang' and I thought our car might have got hit. Sean screamed out 'Mark!' It was really quick but I saw Mark go through the air and his shoes came flying off. He was hit and landed so many metres away.

Christian Zimmer told the jury of his memory of the sickening impact. 'I heard one almighty bang. It actually sounded like a gunshot went off. I was just taken aback.'

Mark ended up lying in a nearby driveway. Leon Borthwick continued to drive, leaving the carnage behind. 'Oh my God,' he said to his two passengers. 'I can't believe I just did that.' He and Shawn pulled up down the street. The siblings got out of their vehicles and spoke. Shawn was unaware that his brother had just hit someone—or that anyone had been hit for that matter.

'He seemed normal,' Shawn said in his statement. 'I told Leon to stay there, and told him that I would go and see these guys and see what the problem was. I didn't want Leon to get hurt.'

Leon Borthwick then hid in a backyard. Berenger told the jury: 'I just remember Leon crying, being like, you know, "I have screwed up my life. I will never get to be with Nicola now." I remember him saying, "I'm going to jail."'

Back at the scene, Mark's friends had crowded around him in a panic.

'His eyes were half closed and blood was everywhere,' Jessica Cardamone told police. 'I was not sure if I should check his pulse or not, and some nurses came out from a neighbouring house.'

Josh Madeira recalled: 'I had a ringing in my ears and felt so sick that I had to go and sit in the gutter … I was in my own world of shock.'

Sean Heneric told police: 'I was screaming out that Mark needed help.'

Christian Zimmer drove to the scene.

'I noticed that there was a gathering of people on the left-hand side of the road,' he told the jury. 'It looked like a commotion.'

He got out of his car to find his son lying in a pool of blood. He rushed to him and tried to resuscitate him, but Mark's mouth was full of blood. Shawn Borthwick and his mates had reached the group, and saw the dead boy.

'I couldn't look at him for too long,' Shawn told police. 'I was in shock, I seen blood everywhere. He was pretty messed up.'

Shawn walked back to the Tarago and found his frightened brother, who by that stage had returned to the van. Not knowing what had happened, he told Leon and his two friends to split.

'I did not tell him about the guy I saw lying on the ground because what I saw was bad,' Shawn said in his statement. 'I was shocked. I didn't want him to know … I did not see Leon hit anybody in his car and I did not hear the sound of a car hitting anything.'

Borthwick drove towards Pellegrin's home. Pellegrin later told police: 'Leon thought he had killed the guy. He kept saying how he wanted to see his girlfriend Nicola. He was saying things about how he could avoid getting in trouble.'

Berenger told the jury: '[Leon] was saying, "Should I burn the van or drive it off a cliff or something so that there wouldn't be any evidence?"' Borthwick also talked about trying to fix the windscreen.

'There was a bit of a pause, like a silent moment, like we were just all in shock,' Berenger said in evidence. 'He was just like, "I need to see Nicola."'

At the scene, paramedics had arrived but could not bring Mark back.

'They determined that—because there were no signs of life, he was unresponsive, had massive head injuries, blunt trauma and massive external blood loss—[Mark's] injuries were incompatible with life and no further resuscitation attempts were made,' the police summary said.

News began to spread. Ed Guterres was on the internet around 1 am in his parents' study.

I got a call from Michael [Dardenne] and he told me that Leon killed Mark. I thought he was joking at first and then he started crying and I realised he was serious. He told me there was blood everywhere and the ambulance had arrived … [Another friend] came on-line and asked me what happened to Mark. I told him Leon hit him with the car and killed him.

Having hidden the damaged Tarago in a sidestreet, Borthwick borrowed Phillip Pellegrin's father's car and drove to Nicola Martin's home like a moth to his former flame. He paid her a visit under the cover of darkness. It was about 2.30 am.

'I had what I thought was a dream,' Nicola said in her statement.

In that dream I heard knocking on my bedroom window and when I looked out Leon was standing there. Leon has actually done this in the past. He told me that someone died and he hesitated and then he said 'Mark'.

She told Leon to go home. Unsuccessfully she tried to ring Mark Zimmer. On the way back, Borthwick stopped off for a quick feed of McDonald's then fell asleep at Pellegrin's house. Detectives arrested him later that morning.

The Major Collision Investigation Unit worked the scene. The police summary said:

> A survey of the crime scene was conducted and a scale plan produced. At the scene it was noted that there were no visible tyre scuff or skid marks on the road surface leading up to and past the scene. On the driver's side of Dardenne's vehicle were visible scuff marks. On the road surface to the rear of the vehicle and to the north of the parking lane, were shoe scuff marks. This area was identified as the point of impact ... The examination of this crime scene concluded that the deceased was hit whilst standing on the north-west bound lane, just over the parking lane line. He was struck by a vehicle traveling in a south-east direction which would have been travelling totally on the incorrect side of the road. The force of the impact pushed the deceased backwards where he landed on the grassed nature strip, rolled for a short distance before coming to rest in the driveway.
>
> A collision reconstruction was conducted after a further examination of the vehicle. The reconstruction concluded the vehicle was traveling between 35 kilometres per hour and 56 kilometres per hour, but likely to be about 45 kilometres per hour at the time it collided with the deceased. There is no evidence of emergency braking or evasive steering having been applied by the accused.
>
> The accused admitted he did not brake before the collision or stop at the scene immediately after

the collision and render assistance in any way. The accused stated the collision was an accident and he did not intend to kill the deceased.

At the start of Borthwick's murder trial, prosecutor Michele Williams told the jury it was the Crown case that Borthwick 'deliberately drove' his mum's Tarago van at Mark Zimmer.

'Mark Zimmer was, if you like, his love rival,' Williams said in her opening address.

> So we say he [Borthwick] had a motive. He had a motive to wish [Mark] harm … There was, if you like, a background of jealousy, anger, possessiveness and obsessiveness demonstrated by the accused man towards Mark Zimmer … Before the killing [Borthwick] confronted Mark Zimmer in a park near Mark Zimmer's house and on the night, the actual night, at 9.10 pm, the accused man rang Mark Zimmer threatening yet again to kill him, which is what we say he ultimately did. We will be saying that on the night in question he was angry and he was prepared to act out his jealousy—and he did.

Williams stressed to the jury that Borthwick was not speeding at the time. 'This is not a case where we say he drove at 100 miles an hour at him. We are not saying that at all.'

Williams also made mention of what Borthwick had told police after he had been picked up.

> He tells, we say, lies to the police—minimises what he did, the way he acted and what he saw. He says, 'I was not going that fast. I had bald tyres. He popped out of

nowhere.' By the way, the van was looked at afterwards; examined mechanically. [It was] roadworthy. [There was] nothing wrong with the vehicle he was driving.

She harked back to the 9.10 pm death-threat call Borthwick made to Mark only hours before his death.

It indicates that the accused man is having a go at Mark Zimmer for still seeing or even daring to talk to Nicola. We say that is very strong evidence as to what was going on in [Borthwick's] state of mind when he drove that car down the road and, we say, drove straight into Mark Zimmer. In other words, he carried out the threat. He intended to kill him and did, or at the very least when he drove that car—no brakes, no swerving—intended to cause really serious injury.

Defence barrister Randazzo focused her opening on the question of Borthwick's intent.

Mister Foreman, ladies and gentlemen of the jury, have you ever heard the expression 'to keep an open mind?' It is an expression that I use every time I stand up to first address a jury … What you are going to hear [in this case] is Leon Borthwick's record of interview in which he tells police time and time again that this was an accident. If the Crown cannot negate accident then, as tragic as the events of that night are, it is your duty to return a verdict of not guilty.

We dispute emphatically that it was a deliberate act … Whether Leon Borthwick is a jealous man, whether he is a possessive man, whether he liked or disliked the deceased Mark Zimmer is ultimately not going to be an issue for you because your task is to say, 'Well, on the evidence that we hear are we satisfied beyond reasonable doubt that he intended to kill or cause really serious injury?' That's it. Not even something less than really serious injury. If you come to the conclusion, 'Well, he was going there to confront him and harm him,' that doesn't satisfy that requisite element of the offence.

In her closing, Williams left the jury with this observation: 'Three people were on the road and Leon Borthwick just happened to get the one person he'd been threatening to kill. I've got to say, he's either pretty lucky or pretty unlucky.'

After a six-week trial, the jury acquitted Borthwick of murder and found him guilty of manslaughter. It was a verdict that crushed the Zimmer family. At Borthwick's pre-sentence hearing, a haunted Christian Zimmer read out his victim impact statement.

'My son died in my arms and he was only nineteen,' the sobbing father read aloud.

I attended the crime scene within minutes to find my son Mark lying on a driveway covered in blood … That image will stay in my mind until the day I die. I desperately tried so hard to save my child's life by giving him mouth to mouth, but so much blood was coming from his mouth and nose that it was difficult for me to get air into his lungs. I swallowed so much blood that to this day I can still taste Mark's blood in my mouth.

The despairing father said a part of him died with his son that night.

Ruth Zimmer said the death of her elder son had left an empty space in her heart.

> Mark's room is still untouched and looks as if he has just left it, with his socks still on the floor where he dropped them, the book he read still open on his bedside table and his clothes still in his wardrobe.

The shattered mother told Justice Katharine Williams, 'I just can't make myself change anything.'

Ruth said Mark's death had devastated his sister, and had also had a detrimental effect on young brother Zachary.

'Sadly, Zachary feels at home at the cemetery because we spend so much time there,' she said.

Justice Williams sentenced Borthwick three days before Christmas in 2010. She handed him seven-and-a-half years' jail with a minimum of five.

'Mark Zimmer was a treasured son, brother and family member,' Justice Williams said when sentencing Borthwick.

> Immediately before hitting him, you did not swerve away or try to stop by jamming on your brakes. I am nevertheless not satisfied beyond reasonable doubt that you deliberately drove into him because everything happened very fast, you were driving too fast and too close to those by the parked car and Mark Zimmer had stepped back onto the roadway.
>
> The prosecution argues that you have shown no remorse for your crime, pointing to your failure to go back to help Mark Zimmer, your flight and talk about destroying the van. As for fleeing, I agree with

your submission that your failure to go back to Mark
Zimmer and hiding is understandable given your
probable reception by those at the scene.

[Melbourne Remand Centre chaplain] Father Joe
Caddy did not say that you had specifically expressed
remorse to him, but he thinks you have developed
a deep sense of remorse in custody—to the extent
that you had asked him to pray for Mark Zimmer in
November when the dead are remembered. You told
Father Caddy that you pray daily for Mark Zimmer
and his family ... I consider that you have only
demonstrated very limited remorse for your actions.

You went to an area where you knew young men
were gathered and you saw those on the road. Yet,
despite the screamed protests of your passengers, you
took no evasive action before tragically taking a young
man's life. Even if events occurred too fast for you to
stop when Mark Zimmer moved on to the road, his
death occurred because of the extremely dangerous
way in which you were driving.

It was to prove a hollow Christmas, not only for the
Zimmer family but all the young people involved. As one
of Mark's friends, Mikhail Quinless, told police: 'I thought
Leon was obsessed with Nicola. I told Mark once, when he
was talking about Nicola, he should stay away from her. I
never thought it would end the way it did though.'

Borthwick unsuccessfully appealed against the length
of his sentence. Some were surprised he even tried.

10
Murder Call

'The method by which the two of you intended to dispose of Patrizia Rolls is spine chilling and horrifying.'

IF THE LIFE OF PATRIZIA ROLLS HAD FOLLOWED A MORE sinister script, her naked body may well have washed up on a Gold Coast beach. If it had gone that way—the way Aaron Mickael Bruce Rolls and his lover Mirvat 'Mel' Sleiman had wanted it to go—then the Italian-born beauty's death would have proved premature and ghastly with her husband holding her head under the tide as she thrashed helplessly against his intent. Aaron Rolls, a Gold Coast security-company man, had hatched the plot to kill his loving wife of more than seventeen years after having several extramarital affairs. His eventual mistress Sleiman, a one-time sex escort, had actually suggested that he murder Patrizia during a romantic skinny dip. Patrizia Rolls might well have died in the surf had it not been for a complete coincidence. Divine intervention. A lucky fluke in the form of a randomly tapped public phone box in the suburb of Arundel on the Gold Coast. Of all the street-side public telephones that Aaron Rolls chose

to use to discuss the murder plot with his lover, he picked
the one being bugged by Victoria Police as part of a high-
priority investigation: an investigation that had nothing
to do with the kill plan that it unwittingly uncovered. It
was truly a one-in-a-million chance that alerted Victorian
detectives to an imminent murder.

'That particular phone box was the subject of a
legal telephone intercept, so that calls made from that
telephone box would be monitored and recorded by the
police,' Crown prosecutor Paul D'Arcy would say in the
Victorian Supreme Court.

> I might say, the warrant was obtained for an
> investigation completely separate from this case—had
> absolutely nothing to do with this case. Victoria Police
> was, in fact, monitoring the use of that telephone for
> their investigation purposes and that's really what
> started this investigation off: what they hear on a
> particular telephone call on 16 January of 2008.

Patrizia was born in Sulmoma, Italy, and arrived in
Australia aged eleven with her mother. She grew up in
Blackwater in central Queensland. In 2008, at the time
of the plot to murder her, she was majoring in marketing
while completing a Bachelor of Business degree at Griffith
University's Gold Coast campus. She had previously
worked at the Marriott Hotel in Surfers Paradise as the
spa and health club manager. Patrizia was an intelligent
and attractive woman who simply fell for the wrong kind
of bloke. She had met Aaron Rolls in February 1990 at the
age of seventeen while working at a pizza shop. He was
drunk when he entered the store and the manager called
police. It so happened that Patrizia and Rolls worked out
at the same gym, and a friend of hers was dating Rolls's

brother. They recognised each other and he asked her out. The two started dating. Four months later Patrizia was living with Rolls at his Blackwater home. At that stage, he was working as a coalminer and security guard.

Born in 1968, Aaron Rolls was the eldest of three boys. He had led an itinerant childhood due to his father's work commitments and left school at age fifteen. He had been married once before. In late 1991 he and Patrizia holidayed in Italy where, amid romantic surrounds, he asked her to marry him. They remained engaged for seven years, during which time Rolls was retrenched as a mining union delegate.

'He had a lot of trouble finding work in other mines,' Patrizia said in a police statement. 'As a result, we had to leave Aaron's mum's house and we moved in with my mum, who was also still living in Blackwater. I kept working as a full-time dental assistant. Up until this stage, I was of the belief that we were in a happy relationship.' In September 1998, Patrizia and Rolls finally married. With her mother in tow the newlyweds went to live in Italy where they resided with Patrizia's grandfather. After six months Aaron returned to Australia to find work (where he would pick up a job as a mine contractor back in Blackwater). Patrizia remained overseas and scored work on a cruise ship in Panama, but returned to Queensland eight weeks after her husband had flown home.

'When I returned I found Aaron cold towards me,' she told police. 'He had moved into my mum's house and didn't want me in there. I had to live with a friend for about two weeks.'

The day after Patrizia and Aaron got back together, a woman named Michelle appeared on the doorstep claiming to be in a relationship with Aaron.

'I later confronted Aaron about who he wanted to be with and he responded by picking up a knife and trying to stab himself in the chest,' Patrizia said in one of her statements. 'I then called the police. Following that incident, Aaron came to my friend's house begging me to take him back. We then moved back in together.'

By the end of 1999, their marriage seemed on track again. Over the next eighteen months Patrizia worked as a fitness instructor. Due to a mining dispute, Rolls was sacked as a mine contractor.

'There were a number of court processes which resulted in Aaron being paid out $40,000,' Patrizia told police.

In 2001, Rolls and Patrizia decided to make a move to start afresh on the Gold Coast: the glimmering stretch where dreams seem about to come true. Patrizia applied for and won the health and spa manager's job at the Marriott. Rolls, a big enough bloke who had worked nightclub security, picked up full-time work with a security company.

The couple lived in a nice little unit. In 2006, Aaron Rolls moved to a new job with Bodyguards International and worked at Horizon Shores Marina.

'It was around this time that our relationship soured again,' Patrizia told police.

While checking his mobile phone one night in November she found several provocative messages. 'I found a number of forwarded text messages with messages like "I want to lick you all over,"' she told police. A corresponding number was listed under the name of 'Don'.

'Later I had to check the phone again and saw that he had received a picture message,' Patrizia explained.

The message referred him to a Vodafone website and provided a password … I checked the website and saw that it was a picture of a girl ... a blonde girl. I confronted Aaron and he denied involvement with other people. He said that it must have been a joke or someone playing tricks. I became angry over the situation and tried to put it behind me.

In April 2007, the pair started their own company. It was called Aus Marine Security Pty Ltd. Aaron Rolls was the director and Patrizia Rolls the beneficiary. The company, which had up to twenty-five subcontractors, held a contract with Horizon Shores Marina to safeguard luxury boats worth millions. Away from work, old problems seemed to raise their ugly head once more. Patrizia told police: 'In July 2007 I saw another text on his phone saying words like "It's my birthday tomorrow. Hubby will be away in the afternoon."'

Once again, Aaron explained his way out of the jam. 'He said that she'd been ringing because she was having problems with her relationship,' Patrizia told police.

She would later say in the Supreme Court: 'He said that he was not attracted to me physically. He was constantly putting me down, including the way that I looked.'

Aaron Rolls met Mirvat Sleiman through a businessman mate of his named Matt, who had known the sexy temptress for a couple of months.

'I first met Mirvat at Sanctuary Cove Boat Show after I paid for an escort for one of my workers who had worked long hours at the show for me,' Matt said in his police statement.

I initially contacted Mirvat through an advertisement under the name Electric Blue in the newspaper. This occurred on the last night of the boat show which was May 2007. Mirvat wasn't the escort, however she chaperoned the escort and I started talking with her. I found Mirvat as very convincing and manipulative. She told me how hard a life she'd had. She said that she had a sixteen-year-old son to her husband in Lebanon, who she had never seen.

Sleiman was born in 1977 in Tripoli, Lebanon. Her family immigrated to Australia when she was seven. She left school after Year 9 and travelled back to Lebanon where her father had arranged for her to be married to an older man, who turned violent and abusive.

'The marriage was not a good marriage to say the least,' her barrister, Wayne Toohey, said in court.

Justice Stephen Kaye would note much later when sentencing Sleiman: 'Not only was your husband abusive towards you, but you also were pressured by his large and religiously observant family.'

After giving birth at age sixteen, Sleiman returned to Australia with her young son in 1994.

'On your return,' Kaye said, 'your own family disowned you and you had to make a living … Your lifestyle collapsed. You took to using party drugs such as ecstasy and Mogadon. In order to support yourself and your son, you began to work in the sex industry.'

According to Toohey: 'She worked for various escort services and in various brothels.'

Her son went back to Lebanon and stayed there with his father. After a return to Lebanon, where she worked as a bartender and in nightclubs, Sleiman came back to Australia at age twenty-three and attempted to straighten out her life. She kicked the drugs and booze and took up taekwondo (in which she would gain a second Dan qualification). But she continued as a sex worker. After a client was acquitted of falsely imprisoning her and threatening her with a knife, she relocated to the Gold Coast—where she continued as an escort before starting her own escort business.

'She had a number of girls working for her and with her while she was there and towards the end of 2005 the business was, I am instructed, fairly successful,' Toohey told the Supreme Court. 'She would have, in the good periods, anywhere from one to two to eighteen girls working for her and with her at a time. She would advertise in the Yellow Pages, various brochures, magazines and commercial radio.'

After their initial meeting in May 2007, Aaron Rolls's mate Matt stayed in contact with Sleiman.

'I arranged for a mechanic to fix her car,' Matt said in his police statement. 'I also lent her several thousand dollars for some advertisements for her business. She never paid me back.'

Matt told police why he introduced Rolls to Sleiman. The Supreme Court was told it was 'love at first sight' for the Lebanese beauty.

'I introduced them on the grounds that Aaron could potentially do security for her and her escort workers,' Matt stated.

Over the next few weeks, Aaron told me that he had been to see her at her address to further discuss business. It was also around this time I organised an opening party [at the marina] for my business. I arranged for Mirvat's Electric Blue business to supply promotion girls for the event. The girls wore promotional outfits and served drinks and food throughout the night.

Shane Hay, general manager of the Meridian Marinas Horizon Shores company, remembered the night. He told police:

> In early June 2007 we had a party in one of the business offices. I believe eighty people would have attended. Whilst at the party I noticed three girls that I hadn't seen before. One of the girls [whom he would later identify as Sleiman] approached me and asked me for money for the two other girls to strip. I told her I was the general manager and it was very inappropriate for me to fund such activities. She told me that I should put money in and I told her to go away. I then rang [my wife] Karen and asked her to pick me up.

Sleiman grabbed the phone and spoke to Karen Hay. Karen told police: 'When I said that she should go and harass one of the other men at the party she said something like, "It's not like I want to suck his cock."'

Shane Hay explained what happened next:

> I told her to go and she became violent. She told me that she was Lebanese and that she would get her friends to come up to the marina and destroy the place. She told me that she had connections with people who arranged the Cronulla riots. She was excessively violent to the point where she threw punches at me. I stood back and told her she was acting like a bloke and that I would have to hit her if she continued. Aaron, who was working [security] that night, pulled up and I told him to remove the girl. I told him that either the police would be called to do it or he could handle the situation.

Rolls drove Sleiman from the marina. Justice Kaye noted: 'At first, you [Rolls and Sleiman] formed a friendship which reasonably quickly developed into a sexual relationship. I accept that ... you, Mirvat Sleiman, held deep and sincere feelings for Aaron Rolls.'

While being questioned by Wayne Toohey at trial, Aaron Rolls tried to explain his attraction to the foul-mouthed yet saucy Sleiman.

> **TOOHEY**: She would get her temper up and ...
> although you didn't like to see her perhaps upset,
> from time to time it used to amuse you, didn't it?
> That she was so fiery and she could swear so much.
> **AARON ROLLS**: She had different personalities, yes.
> **TOOHEY**: Was that one of the attractions that you
> had with Mel—that she was a fiery personality and
> perhaps the making up would be pretty good?
> **AARON ROLLS**: Some of it, yes.

In evidence in the Supreme Court, Sleiman's former neighbour, Roman Alexander, said Sleiman did not like the fact that Aaron Rolls was married.

'All she said, if I can recall, is that there was no love in the marriage and Aaron didn't love his wife—but because of the business he had to stay married,' Alexander said. 'She just said that the security business he had was in their names and it would have been big trouble to get divorced.'

According to Patrizia Rolls, Aaron started showing signs of depression.

'When I asked him what was going on he said he was having nightmares and was basically stressed,' she told police in one of her statements. 'He said he had demons in his head and he couldn't get them out.' In another statement she added: 'In September I remember asking him, "Aaron, are you in love with me?" He replied, "I don't know." We had an argument and he left the house overnight. I don't know where he stayed.'

In court, Aaron Rolls admitted he was 'confused to how I felt about both women'.

'I was trying to repair my marriage at that time ... I'd been having an affair [with Sleiman] at the same time.'

Patrizia went and saw a solicitor and moved in with her cousin in the suburb of Bundall. On an occasion while visiting her dog at home, she found another woman's underwear in the laundry basket and a used condom in the bin. In her husband's gym bag she uncovered twenty business cards. 'The business cards had the name "Electric Blue Nights" on them,' she said in one of her statements. 'There was also a phone number, however no names. The cards offered ten per cent off escort services. I left the underwear, condom and cards spread out over the bed.'

Patrizia sought advice from a family lawyer in Bundall in the belief her marriage was over. 'That night ... Aaron came to see me and wanted to talk to me. I was too upset.'

Aaron Rolls contacted a relative and said he was planning on 'going to see' his dead father. He also said he had a gun. Patrizia finally agreed to meet him and discuss their relationship. Again, she asked him if he loved her. Again, he said he did not know.

'I told him that I couldn't be with someone that didn't love me and it was best if we finish it,' Patrizia said in one of her statements.

About a week later (possibly early October), I spoke to Aaron about sorting out our financial assets and separation options. I told him that I'd seen a solicitor and he should also. The following morning after that conversation, Aaron rang up crying. He told me that he did have affairs with women … I still had hope that we could fix the relationship and went to see him.

Patrizia arrived at her home to find her husband there with a mate of his named Cameron Pill.

He told me in front of Cameron that he had gone out the previous night to drink. He told Cameron and I that he had taken some drugs. He said that he had been to Shooters [nightclub]. He said that he nearly also hit someone really bad. He then said, 'Have a look at this' and opened his shirt. I saw a love heart with the name 'Mirvat' tattooed across his chest.

In court, Aaron Rolls would try to explain how and why he got the tattoo.

That night I went out and drank a lot and got plastered … The night was a blur … After I'd seen the lawyer and that, I guess I thought the marriage was over and I wished to be with Mel. Just drunken stupidness, and I ended up with the tattoo.

After revealing the ink work, according to Patrizia, Aaron admitted to several affairs.
'He told me about a normal girl from the gym,' she told detectives.

He said the text message lady, who was married. He also said that he'd met a girl named Mel who was his last fling. He said that she managed Electric Blue Nights and had a lot of problems and issues, which was

too much for him to cope with. He said that he didn't
want anything to do with her anymore. He also told me
that he had started taking drugs recently. I asked him
what kind of drugs, because I was aware that he always
used steroids. He told me that he would use anything
he could get his hands on—he said cocaine, ice and
others which I can't remember. I asked him where he
got them and he replied: 'We're on the Gold Coast.
You can get them anywhere.' I never confronted him
about the underwear and the condom.

Patrizia said her husband blamed *her* for his
infidelity—saying she worked long hours at the Marriott
and was 'never there for him'. She told the police, 'He
also commented on my weight, saying that he had issues
with my weight.'

For her own reasons Patrizia decided to give him
another chance. 'He acknowledged that he needed some
help and needed to see a psychologist,' she said in one of
her statements. 'I moved back into the house the next day.'

Aaron Rolls told the court that he had convinced
Sleiman to go back to Melbourne.

I believed while I was having any sort of contact—
sexual contact—with her, I couldn't give my marriage
a chance … I had suggested she go there but if things
didn't work out in my marriage that I would still
maybe take up with her.

In court, Patrizia tried to explain her benevolent and
forgiving nature.

I believe that, even though he did all those cheating
and wrong things, I'm Catholic and I believe that

everyone can—should be given a second chance. I mean everyone makes mistakes … I became very confused and I didn't want to leave him because I thought if he was so depressed should I leave my husband? At times he would go on the floor in foetal positions and start crying, and I fell for that. What am I supposed to do? I felt like, should I leave my husband when he's in this state?

I just could not walk away from him because I didn't think it was right—especially after being with someone for eighteen years. He was like my friend.

But nothing seemed to change. Aaron Rolls apparently only attended one session with a psychologist.

'He still refused to have sex with me,' Patrizia stated.

He was down in the dumps and not happy. He was always tired. He was still working a lot of night shifts. Small things were getting blown out of proportion. Around mid October we had another fight over him not wanting to make another appointment with the psychologist. He said that I wasn't giving him enough time to make an appointment and he didn't have enough time. I argued that he always had time to go to the gym.

Aaron Rolls's cousin Debbie-Lee Wall remembered the up-and-down relationship. 'They were good as a couple,' she told detectives.

They were both into fitness and health. They always wanted to succeed and better themselves … Just before the Indy weekend in October 2007, Trisha had come over and she was very upset and crying. She told me that Aaron told her that she was fat and that he did not find her attractive. Trisha also told me that he was not at all affectionate towards her anymore and that he did not want to have sex with her. Trisha was very upset.

Wall spoke to her cousin over the phone on one occasion. That's when he mentioned he had a gun.

He told me that he could not fight with Patrizia anymore. He told me that he could have any woman on the Gold Coast he wanted and he told me that they hand him business cards all the time … The whole conversation scared me. He sounded angry and upset.

At that time Mel Sleiman was suffering emotional and psychological problems in Melbourne. Justice Kaye delivered up the narrative in his sentencing remarks.

You [Aaron Rolls] telephoned her and told her that your relationship with her was over. As a result you, Sleiman, became particularly distressed and made an attempt on your own life … I interpolate that in the meantime, in November, the relationship between you, Aaron Rolls, and your wife Patrizia remained fraught.

It was during November 2007 when Aaron Rolls told Patrizia that he was going on an overnight fishing trip (he stayed at a hotel instead). Not a renowned drinker, and still full of suspicion, Patrizia drowned herself in rum and swallowed a bucketload of Panadeine Forte. She woke up in the Gold Coast Hospital. Rolls never went to visit her while she spent three days recovering. It was then, Patrizia said, that she decided to split up with him for good. To finally go her separate way. After her release from hospital she moved back in with her cousin in Bundall. Later, with Debbie-Lee Wall at her side, she went to talk to Rolls.

'Aaron turned into a different person,' Wall told detectives.

> He snapped and threw a three-seater couch up into the air. He was pacing angrily around the room back and forth. At that stage Trish went into the kitchen and Aaron walked back past me, turned around, pointed at Trish with his right hand, walked past me and punched the wall with his left hand. Aaron then turned around. I was scared at that stage. He had hatred for Trish. Aaron banged his head down on the kitchen counter and said, 'Right, that's it, it's over and you're not going to see one bit of your mother's money.' I immediately grabbed Trish and we got out of the house.

In mid November, Aaron's mother called Patrizia and said her son was sick. She asked Patrizia if she could visit him.

'He was lying in bed with his hands shaking and a tea towel on his head,' Patrizia said in court.

In one of her statements she said:

> He told me that he was confused but although he had feelings for this girl Mel, his feelings for me were stronger. He said that Mel had a lot of issues and bad friends and that our marriage was more important. I told him that I would stay in the house as a friend for the moment and that we should see how things went.

Arrangements were made for appointments with a psychologist. According to Justice Kaye: 'After a short time, you, Rolls, continued to be in telephone contact with Mirvat Sleiman. The two of you resumed your relationship—at least on the telephone.'

Poor Patrizia had no idea.

'Although there was still no sexual contact [between Aaron and I] he seemed to be a lot happier and more content,' she told police. 'There was an argument on or about 1 January 2008 when I was upset over not even getting a New Year's kiss.'

A couple of weeks later, Patrizia reminded her husband that she had 'needs'. 'I wanted to resolve any of his unresolved issues so we could move forward and perhaps renew our sexual relationship, or even affection,' Patrizia said. 'He didn't want to talk about it.'

According to Patrizia, Aaron later pulled her near him on the couch. Things were about to get rough. 'He then pulled my head by a handful of hair and pulled my head into his groin,' she told police.

He said, 'Is this what you want?' I said, 'No. It's not.' He then let go and he walked into the kitchen. I started crying and he walked back towards me. He then grabbed me by the throat and said, 'Why did you have to do this to me? Why can't you just let it be— the way it was going?' He squeezed hard around my throat … He also hit me with an open hand on the forehead. Since that incident I thought maybe I was going overboard and I shouldn't push it.

In early January, Aaron asked Patrizia if she wanted to go hiking. 'The comment came from nowhere,' Patrizia told police.

'I found the conversation odd,' she said. 'Firstly, we hadn't been hiking and he was complaining about how busy he was with work. I also found it odd because it had been constantly raining.' In another statement she added: 'The Gold Coast was having the worst weather I think I've ever seen.'

While giving evidence during his own trial, Aaron Rolls said, 'I wasn't planning to kill Patrizia at all. I had plans to go on a hiking trip for her birthday.'

According to Justice Kaye, Rolls and Sleiman had previously spoken about Aaron's ideas to kill Patrizia before their damning murder plot conversation on 16 January 2008.

'In my view,' Kaye said in his eventual sentencing remarks, 'the evidence makes it clear … that in the period shortly before the conversation of 16 January the two of you had already discussed the idea of you, Rolls, ridding yourself of your wife by murdering her.'

The call that brought Aaron Rolls and his lover unstuck was made at 8.45 pm on 16 January, Rolls using a Gold Coast public telephone box to call Sleiman on her mobile phone in Melbourne. Here's what Victorian detectives heard through the phone line they had tapped as part of a top-secret investigation totally unrelated to the Gold Coast kill plot.

SLEIMAN: Yeah baby.

ROLLS: Hey bud, how are you?

SLEIMAN: Good. How are you?

ROLLS: Good.

SLEIMAN: That's good.

ROLLS: What's gunna happen is …

SLEIMAN: Yup?

ROLLS: I either gotta go for a beach walk …

SLEIMAN: Mmm …

ROLLS: Right?

SLEIMAN: Mmm …

ROLLS: She's gunna have an accident there …

SLEIMAN: Mmm …

ROLLS: I've gotta make sure that it's done properly.

SLEIMAN: Yep.

ROLLS: Then I've gotta leave the car there. Then I gotta go home, so I'm gunna have to walk all the way from Surfers to home.

SLEIMAN: Leave the car there?

ROLLS: Her car.

SLEIMAN: Okay.

ROLLS: So that she's …

SLEIMAN: Oh yeah …

ROLLS: Right?

SLEIMAN: Yep. Yep.

ROLLS: Then I've gotta get home. I can't take taxis. Buses. Anything that I can be recognised on or maybe put on camera.

SLEIMAN: Mmm.

ROLLS: Then go home. Then I'll have to report that she's gone missin'.

SLEIMAN: Ah huh.

ROLLS: All right?

SLEIMAN: Ah huh.

ROLLS: The other one is … is that I go for this hike thing up in the mountains and there's an accident.

SLEIMAN: What, like falling over?

ROLLS: Ah huh.

SLEIMAN: Okay.

ROLLS: But it's gotta look like … the beach one's the only real safe one …

SLEIMAN: Yeah, but …

ROLLS: Because …

SLEIMAN: Yeah, but how you gunna get her in there?

ROLLS: She wants to go for a walk on the beach.

SLEIMAN: Yeah.

ROLLS: So she's gunna go to the beach with me.

SLEIMAN: Mmm …

ROLLS: I just gotta make sure it's the right time, and that, to do it …

SLEIMAN: Mmm …

ROLLS: But it's the best way …

SLEIMAN: Yeah …

ROLLS: 'Cos there's not prints.

SLEIMAN: Yeah, that's why …

ROLLS: No foot … there's no anything. It's in the water—accidental drowning.

SLEIMAN: Mmm …

ROLLS: All right?

SLEIMAN: Yeah. Yeah. Yep, yep. Yep, yep.

ROLLS: So … I gotta leave it 'til after Tuesday, right? Because of … 'cos the weekend. Just can't do it on the weekend.

SLEIMAN: Ah huh.

ROLLS: 'Cos of what I'm doin' … with work.

SLEIMAN: Ah huh.

ROLLS: And then I got the other thing on, on Tuesday. But straight after that I'm gunna … play it. So I'm gunna try doin' it by the end of the week.

SLEIMAN: But how the hell are ya gunna get back home, with like …

ROLLS: I'm gunna walk.

SLEIMAN: All the way?

ROLLS: Yes.

SLEIMAN: Fuck, it's a long way.

ROLLS: I did it the other day to time it and to do it.

SLEIMAN: Did ya?

ROLLS: Yeah. Took me an hour and something.

SLEIMAN: Okay.

ROLLS: So that way the car's left there. The whole lot. Toss the phone …

SLEIMAN: Okay.

ROLLS: Toss the keys.

SLEIMAN: Her car?

ROLLS: Yeah.

SLEIMAN: Ah huh.

ROLLS: Then report her missin' and everything like that.

SLEIMAN: But then you gunna be wet, aren't you?

ROLLS: I'm gunna go home. I got it all worked out, what to do. The clothes and boots and stuff like that. They're … gunna be dumped and I'll have other stuff waiting.

A little later the pair expressed concern about talking of such grave plans on a landline. Their concerns had proved a tad too late. Rolls said: 'I don't like … sayin' too much on these, because … you never know if somebody's listenin'.' But despite their concerns the killer of a conversation continued.

SLEIMAN: Yeah, the beach one seems to be … kind of more …

ROLLS: It's the best one … okay?

SLEIMAN: Yeah, cool.

And later still:

ROLLS: And then what'll happen is that I, you know, the grievin' and all that sort of shit.

SLEIMAN: Mmm …

ROLLS: And go through all the process with the law and stuff like that.

SLEIMAN: Ah huh.

ROLLS: And then we'll be right.

SLEIMAN: Yeah, yeah, you just gotta … like a nice, um, romantic walk or some shit.

ROLLS: Mmm …

SLEIMAN: Skinny dipping.

ROLLS: Yeah … that's the easiest and best way.

SLEIMAN: Yeah …

ROLLS: Just like, I physically gotta do it.

SLEIMAN: Mmm. Yep.

ROLLS: Which is the hard bit.

SLEIMAN: Mmm.

ROLLS: But it'll be right, okay?

SLEIMAN: Yeah. You gunna be all right doin' it?

ROLLS: Well I got no fuckin' choice, have I?

SLEIMAN: All right … Okay honey.

ROLLS: Now, are you cool with that?

SLEIMAN: Yeah. Absolutely. Absolutely. You know … absolutely.

ROLLS: All right then.

Talk later turned to the Gold Coast's unseasonal weather and how that could determine the timing of the murder. It had been a wet, tropical summer. Rolls's work roster—and the inconvenience the death of his wife might cause his schedule—also proved a pressing issue.

SLEIMAN: Mmm, yeah, but if the weather goes fuckin' good any day, like before that, then just fuckin' do it.

ROLLS: Yeah, but I can't 'cos then I gotta have time off from work to grieve and do all the stuff with it.

SLEIMAN: Mmm.

ROLLS: Everybody's gunna think, 'Oh, he's not even takin' time off work.'

Talk turned to plans to relocate after the grave soil had settled.

ROLLS: Then once, er, all the … dies down and that, then I'll just pack up, er, you know—the week after, or whatever, and then say, 'Oh, I gotta get out of here and bolt.' I'll go to Sydney … you can come up there.

SLEIMAN: Ah huh.

ROLLS: All right? And then a coupla weeks after that then you can just leave down there and come up.

SLEIMAN: Yeah. Yeah. For sure.

ROLLS: You know and if anyone starts a query, I'll just say you come up to help me and everything.

SLEIMAN: Yeah.

ROLLS: Okay?

SLEIMAN: Mmm.

ROLLS: You cool with that?

SLEIMAN: Yeah, of course I am.

ROLLS: Yep.

SLEIMAN: Of course I am.

And later:

SLEIMAN: I just want it to get over and done with fuckin' … just be able to relax and just say, 'Yep, cool.' Ya know?

ROLLS: Yep, well it will … I've been waitin' to get it over and done with too, but I gotta … be careful, so …

SLEIMAN: Mm, mm …

ROLLS: That's what I said to ya. I'm not gunna rush …

SLEIMAN: Yep, yep. Of course.

ROLLS: 'Cos I'm gunna get looked at straight away.

There was further discussion about covering up the crime.

SLEIMAN: It'll be good if, um, there'll be alcohol in her system.

ROLLS: Yeah, well I'm workin' on that … Thinkin' about how to do that.

SLEIMAN: Because that way is better.

ROLLS: Yeah, well … that's what I'm … I'm thinkin' of that. All right, I got two dollars left [on phone credit], so this might cut out bub.

SLEIMAN: Okay. Do you want me to call you on your phone? The other phone?

ROLLS: Er, how much credit have you got?

SLEIMAN: I've got credit babe.

ROLLS: You sure?

SLEIMAN: Yep, I've got credit …

ROLLS: All right.

SLEIMAN: All right, cool. We'll just change our conversation then.

ROLLS: Okay then. Bye. Bye.

Talk about being shit out of luck. By that stage it was too late for Rolls and Sleiman to change anything. Thanks to an absolute fluke, police knew exactly what they were planning. While giving evidence during his own trial, Rolls denied the existence of a kill plot.

'I never had any intention of hurting Patrizia,' he claimed.

I never agreed with Mel to kill my wife. I just simply talked to her. I was telling her a story … I was telling Mel a story to keep her off my back … It was just talk.

Justice Kaye had his own thoughts about the call:

What is particularly chilling about that conversation is the matter-of-fact-manner in which the two of you calmly discussed the details of the plan formulated by you, Rolls, to dispose of your wife by murdering her. I listened carefully to the recording of that conversation, as no doubt did the jury. Not once could I detect any hesitation, or note of regret, by either of you as to the evil plan that you were then discussing. Not once was there evident, to the slightest degree, any recognition or feeling by either of you of the enormity of what the two of you were undertaking. In your case Rolls, it is particularly disturbing that there was not the faintest indication that you, then, were feeling any regret or pang of conscience about betraying your wife: by planning to cold bloodedly murder the woman who had been loyal to you for almost two decades.

On the morning of 19 January while talking with his wife, Aaron Rolls brought up the topic of the beach. It came out of the blue. To Patrizia it sounded odd. Out of context.
'Have you gone to have a look at the beach?' he asked her. 'I wonder what the beach looks like. It's been on the news that it's eroded.'
Patrizia said she had not.

'The conversation was left at that,' she told police. 'I found it very unusual as we'd never discussed the beach.'

That afternoon, the couple visited a Bunnings store. On the way home, Rolls suggested they drive through Surfers Paradise. According to Patrizia he said: 'We'll go for a drive to the beach and we'll see what the sand is like.'

They drove past Southport Surf Lifesaving Club, but didn't stop.

'It's not too bad, you can still walk on it,' Rolls is said to have suggested of the beach. 'I thought it would be worse.' According to Patrizia: 'I couldn't understand his interest in the beach but didn't say anything.'

While cross-examining Patrizia in court, Aaron Rolls's defence counsel Sean Cash suggested his client's fascination with the beach was genuine.

CASH: What he was inviting you to have a look at was really something quite extraordinary that was apparently unfolding at the time; extraordinary erosion on the beach. Is that right?

PATRIZIA ROLLS: I couldn't really notice that much erosion that was extraordinary. It was just normal erosion … Apparently the erosion was really bad in Burleigh but not Surfers.

In court, Aaron Rolls said in his defence: 'At that time there had been a cyclone and a lot of erosion—debris through the marinas and things like that—and I just wanted to have a look at Main Beach.'

After driving past the beach, but not parking and taking a walk, the couple went out to dinner at an Italian restaurant with friends.

'We went to Cantina Napoli and had a really nice night,' Patrizia recalled in her statement.

Aaron Rolls faked his way through the dinner, putting on a show for those present. He talked about future business ventures and possible trips to Italy and Egypt. Justice Kaye would say:

Such was the extent of your evil plan that you were even able to deceive two of your closest and most loyal friends of your feelings towards your wife, when the four of you met for dinner. Clearly you successfully deceived your trusting wife as to your murderous intentions towards her.

At home that night, Rolls showed affection. 'Aaron put his head on my chest and his arm around me and slept there like that until the morning,' Patrizia recalled in one of her statements.

We wouldn't have slept touching one another for fifteen years. Aaron got out of bed before me that morning because he had to go to work and I opened my eyes at one point and saw Aaron standing in the doorway staring at me. He stared at me for a long time until I asked what he was doing. He said that he was just watching me and didn't realise that my eyes were open. I thought it was a bit strange at the time but in hindsight found it really disturbing.

Detectives, meanwhile, had managed to identify the players involved in the kill plot. They located Patrizia and removed her from harm's way. Aaron Rolls noticed her missing. Feigning concern, he made some calls to friends asking if anyone knew where his wife might have been. He twice called Sleiman. One conversation went in part:

ROLLS: Yeah, so any luck she's driven away and more likely done it for herself.
SLEIMAN: That'll be great.
ROLLS: Ha.
SLEIMAN: Be perfect.
ROLLS: That'd be too easy, that.

Kaye said of this call: 'In the first call, at about 8am, you Rolls and you Sleiman speculated that Patrizia might have saved you the effort of drowning her by killing herself. You both, somehow, found that that prospect caused you great mirth.'

Patrizia made statements to her saviour detectives. 'Our assets are around one million dollars,' she told them on 20 January at the Gold Coast CIB. 'However, we have liabilities such as mortgages et cetera of around $600,000. There is also about $100,000 in our savings accounts. Life insurance policies were taken out under my name and Aaron's name.'

Rolls and Sleiman were arrested and charged with conspiracy to murder.

In his closing address to the jury during the duo's joint trial, Aaron Rolls's barrister, Sean Cash, said:

What a decent person she [Patrizia] is. And what a rotten scoundrel he [Rolls] was to her. And he ought to be ashamed of it, ladies and gentlemen. But he's not on trial for being a scoundrel. He's not on trial for infidelity. If he was, you would convict him straight away ... The central, most pivotal question is this: you have to ask yourself—can you conclude without reasonable doubt that on or about 16 January 2008 Mr Rolls genuinely intended to follow through to kill his own wife?

The extraordinary pressure that was being exerted he felt in this case was a set of circumstances where he saw two females, quite extraordinarily, trying to kill themselves over him. He must have hidden talents. Goodness knows what they are. But two women in the space of about two months tried to kill themselves in circumstances associated with him … That's the reason why he made the stupid decision to say what he said in the telephone conversation on 16 January 2008.

At the start of his closing, Wayne Toohey, for Sleiman, told the jury a fascinating analogy.

Mr Foreman, ladies and gentlemen of the jury. It is 1942 in a small house in North Carlton. Young Jack is fifteen years of age, soon to be sixteen. And he's full of dash. Full of the desire to save the world. He's one of fourteen children. His mother and father love him. And all of the children dearly. His older brother Jim, the eldest in the family—ten years older than Jack—has gone off to war. Jim is going to save the world too. When Jim went off to war his mother and father are distraught. They hate war. They hate the idea of any of their children going to war. Young Jack is still at school. And for week after week and month after month he drives them mad. He drives his parents mad: 'I'm going to war. I'm joining up. I'm going to go and help Jim. I'm not going to let the Japanese take Australia.' His mother and father are horrified. 'No way Jack, are you going to war son. Bad enough your brother has gone. We hate war and we are not letting you go so get it out of your mind.'

On and on goes young Jack to the point where he's becoming almost a nuisance; a pest to his family and then one night young Jack comes home and he's in a uniform. He's in an army uniform. He's joined up. His mother is horrified. His father is beside himself with rage. 'What have you done?' 'Oh Mum, Dad, I've joined up.' 'We never signed anything. We have told you you are not going to war.' 'Don't worry about it. I got some papers here and I got some papers there. I'm in. You can't do anything about it. I'm in.' They are horrified. 'And furthermore, Mum and Dad, I'm leaving for camp tomorrow morning.' During the course of the night his father takes him aside and says to him, 'You've let your mum down. She didn't want you to go. I didn't want you to go. Under no circumstances did we want you to go, but look what you've done. When you get over there son, be careful. When you get over there if you are shipped out of Australia—you go to fight the Japanese up in Borneo, up in the Pacific—be careful. There is jungle warfare going on up there. We read about it in the papers Jack. You watch yourself. And if you see any of those Japanese, make sure you shoot them Jack, before they shoot you. Make sure you wear your tin helmet Jack. Make sure you've got ammunition in your rifle Jack. Make sure you come back to us Jack.' And off he goes to save the world. Fortunately he comes back years later after he goes to Borneo: sees fighting.

That mother and father of young Jack in that house in North Carlton never agreed for him to go to war. They were not part of young Jack's desire—plan—to go to war. But young Jack's father told him once it was a fait accompli and young Jack wasn't going to be talked out of it and in fact was not talked out of it— comes home in a uniform—his father gave him some advice. The father was never part of any agreement for Jack to go to war. Never. And yet, when the young man came home in a uniform, his father gave him plenty of advice; part of which was 'Make sure you shoot the Japanese before they shoot you son. Don't ask questions.' Here we have a scenario where someone comes up with a plan. And what happens, that person—Mr Rolls—wants it to be clear to Ms Sleiman that he's hellbent on this plan. She has never agreed to it at all. She's never agreed to enter it at all. But he's hellbent on it, and after a while she offers a couple of suggestions. Exactly the same scenario, but it does not make her part of the agreement. She never agreed for Aaron Rolls to do anything to his wife, just as young Jack's mother and father never agreed for him to go to war or to join up even though the father gave him some advice.

She [Sleiman] may have done a number of things that you don't like, not the least of which is having an affair with a married man … She might have said things [about Patrizia Rolls] like 'fucking moll' or 'fucking slut'—awful things to say about another human being; particularly someone who is as well presented and as fine a person as Patrizia Rolls. But that doesn't make her guilty of a crime.

In May 2009, the jury found Aaron Rolls and Mirvat 'Mel' Sleiman guilty of conspiracy to murder. Justice Kaye sentenced Rolls, aged forty-one, to eleven years' jail with an eight-year minimum. Sleiman, aged thirty-one, copped nine years with a minimum of six.

'The method by which the two of you intended to dispose of Patrizia Rolls is spine chilling and horrifying,' Kaye said when sentencing the pair.

Your role, Aaron Rolls, could only be described as utterly despicable … A husband's duty is to love, protect and care for his wife. Your treacherous plan involved the very opposite of that. Your wife, Patrizia, gave you no cause for your vile plan. She was at all times a good, loving and loyal wife to you.

Rolls had no previous convictions.

'I accept that, apart from your involvement in this crime, you are a man of otherwise good character who had, hitherto, earned a high reputation among those who knew you both professionally and personally.'

Sleiman had no prior convictions either.

'You, Mirvat Sleiman, were not only an intentional but indeed a willing participant in the murderous plan,' Kaye told her.

You had difficulty coping with the prospect of losing Rolls and that heightened your anxiety to take steps to secure your future with him … I accept [Mr Toohey's] submission that it was Rolls, and not you, who instigated the idea of murdering Patrizia Rolls.

Kaye told them both:

The callousness of the two of you, as evidenced by the phone call of 16 January and two conversations you had on 21 January, reflects just how heartless you each were in your sinister plan.

The fact that Patrizia Rolls was saved from the evil plan which the two of you had hatched was to some extent a matter of good fortune. Her rescue was also due to the effort, skill and commitment of the Victorian and Queensland [police] investigators in this case. They are to be commended … The object of the conspiracy was thwarted by the timely intervention of the police.

Aaron Rolls and Mel Sleiman sought leave to appeal against their convictions and sentences. Three Court of Appeal judges refused.

'Some conspiracies to commit murder are particularly heinous: mafia conspiracies to murder the mafia's honest pursuers are an example,' Justice David Harper stated in the judgment.

Others encompass a much lower order of criminality: a plan to kill an evil oppressor would be such. This conspiracy falls between the two. It clearly lacks the gravity of the worst cases; yet I agree with the sentencing judge's description of it as 'vile' and 'evil'. It was motivated by pure selfishness. And even though she herself owed Patrizia Rolls little more than the respect which every human owes to every other, Sleiman must have appreciated that its proposed victim deserved from her husband affectionate protection rather than the extreme opposite. This consideration links her level of criminality with this, though hers remains at a lower level.

Outside court after the appeal was refused, Patrizia Rolls thanked the Victorian detectives—Nathan Favre, Stuart Bailey and Philip Gynther—who had reacted to the 16 January phone call and made the mercy dash to Queensland to save her, with the help of Gold Coast detectives.

'I really feel like justice has prevailed. I'm blessed to be alive,' a buoyant Patrizia said.

New crime fiction from Paul Anderson

The Armed Robbery Squad has long been considered the state's most formidable group of detectives. But there's a change coming. Force command and a new police watchdog want the squad gone. And there's a new threat on the streets—a bandit with a passion for demeaning victims ... and shooting detectives.

Crime journalist Ian Malone has assigned himself the task of finding out whether the men from Armed Robbery have been demonised or are deserving of their fearsome reputation.

As Malone builds a unique bond with streetwise detective Shane Kelso and the rest of The Robbers, he enters a dark and seedy world where right can be wrong but wrong might also be right. A world where cops and bandits fight a ruthless war, everyone has their own agenda, and the most dangerous enemies could just be the bureaucrats and political powerbrokers.